Relational Freedom

Relational Freedom: Emergent Properties of the Interpersonal Field addresses the interpersonal field in clinical psychoanalysis and psychotherapy, especially the emergent qualities of the field. The book builds on the foundation of unformulated experience, dissociation, and enactment defined and explored in Stern's previous, widely read books.

Stern never considers the analyst or the patient alone; all clinical events take place between them and involve them both. Their conscious and unconscious conduct and experience are the field's substance. We can say that the changing nature of the field determines the experience that patient and analyst can create in one another's presence; but we can also say that the therapeutic dyad, simply by doing their work together, ceaselessly configures and reconfigures the field. "Relational freedom" is Stern's own interpersonal and relational conception of the field, which he compares, along with other varieties of interpersonal/relational field theory, to the work of Bionian field theorists such as Madeleine and Willy Baranger and Antonino Ferro. Other chapters concern the role of the field in accessing the frozen experience of trauma, in creating theories of therapeutic technique, evaluating quantitative psychotherapy research, evaluating the utility of the concept of unconscious phantasy, treating the hard-to-engage patient, and in devising the ideal psychoanalytic institute.

Relational Freedom is a clear, authoritative, and impassioned statement of the current state of interpersonal and relational psychoanalytic theory and clinical thinking. It will interest anyone who wants to stay up to date with current developments in American psychoanalysis, and for those newer to the field it will serve as an introduction to many of the important questions in contemporary psychoanalysis. Psychoanalysts and psychotherapists of all kinds will profit from the book's thoughtful discussions of clinical problems and quandaries.

Donnel B. Stern, Ph.D., a psychoanalyst and psychotherapist in private practice in New York City, serves as Training and Supervising Analyst at the William Alanson White Institute, and Adjunct Clinical Professor and Consultant at the NYU Postdoctoral Program in Psychotherapy and Psychoanalysis. He is the founder and editor of "Psychoanalysis in a New Key," a book series published by Routledge.

"Stern's great ability to make very complex concepts comprehensible is once again in evidence in this marvelous book of rare depth. This is the book every 'insider' will want to read and secretly wish they had written.

It is replete with delightful clinical vignettes that reveal the author's method of working: free, creative, unconstrained by preconstructed models, and always open to whatever emerges in psychoanalytic session (or, as Bion would put it, to whatever 'evolves' in the session). Rarely have I felt my heart race whilst reading clinical material and such an urge to read on as though these were the final pages of a thriller. For me, this is a truly exhilarating read that creates a wider field in which even the reader becomes co-protagonist.

The scenes and events described are ones that come to life and are lived out during the session, creating a new reality.

I thoroughly enjoyed Stern's delightfully lively and creative indepth description of the field concept. He succeeds in lending a poetic tone to concepts that create a new paradigm for psychoanalysis.

Stern shows in a vivid manner how the analytic field comes alive in each and every session.

I would like to underscore Stern's skill at creating a 'field' with the many authors who have contributed in various ways to the development of this very concept. What is more, the author reveals his capacity to extend the dialogue and implicitly also the field with theorists who hold different perspectives: my personal thanks go to Stern for proposing a 'family' of thinkers I had not had the chance to place on my own family tree of concepts.

Stern writes in such a way as to make the authors in his cast come alive to the reader: he succeeds in breathing vitality into what we knew only in a rather arid way, transforming it, one might say, into today's language and into live holographic presences.

It is within the freedom of the field that new uncensored ideas and concepts can emerge.

In short, if a book may be described as food for thought, this one is a veritable banquet!"

—**Antonino Ferro,** MD, President of the Italian Psychoanalytic Society

"Donnel Stern's *Relational Freedom* is a welcome contribution to the field of psychotherapy and psychoanalysis in which he reinvents the concept of emergence as the experiential component of the interpersonal field, and brings the concept to life in his many, in depth, clinical discussions. What I find truly remarkable about this book is that it offers a way of encompassing relational theory, field theory, Bionian concepts, and modern Freudian thinking, while so many others deal with these perspectives as if they are at war with one another."

—**Thomas Ogden**, MD, Personal and Supervising Analyst, Psychoanalytic Institute of Northern California

"In this exciting and wide-ranging new book, Donnel Stern takes the reader on an exhilarating tour of the contemporary psychoanalytic landscape. For many years, a leading figure in the theoretical articulation of the Interpersonal dimension of Relational theory, Stern here compares and contrasts his own way of viewing the psychoanalytic process to those of Contemporary Freudians, Object Relationists, Bionian Field Theorists and others. Stern's capacity to articulate complex theory is remarkable, and his discussions are always punctuated with powerful clinical examples that further explicate his perspective. He is the consummate teacher and anyone interested in understanding where psychoanalysis is heading today must read this maybe several times over!"

—**Jody Messler Davies**, Ph.D., Editor in Chief Emeritus of *Psychoanalytic Dialogues*

PSYCHOANALYSIS IN A NEW KEY BOOK SERIES
DONNEL STERN
Series Editor

When music is played in a new key, the melody does not change, but the notes that make up the composition do: change in the context of continuity, continuity that perseveres through change. Psychoanalysis in a New Key publishes books that share the aims psychoanalysts have always had, but that approach them differently. The books in the series are not expected to advance any particular theoretical agenda, although to this date most have been written by analysts from the Interpersonal and Relational orientations.

The most important contribution of a psychoanalytic book is the communication of something that nudges the reader's grasp of clinical theory and practice in an unexpected direction. Psychoanalysis in a New Key creates a deliberate focus on innovative and unsettling clinical thinking. Because that kind of thinking is encouraged by exploration of the sometimes surprising contributions to psychoanalysis of ideas and findings from other fields, Psychoanalysis in a New Key particularly encourages interdisciplinary studies. Books in the series have married psychoanalysis with dissociation, trauma theory, sociology, and criminology. The series is open to the consideration of studies examining the relationship between psychoanalysis and any other field—for instance, biology, literary and art criticism, philosophy, systems theory, anthropology, and political theory.

But innovation also takes place within the boundaries of psychoanalysis, and Psychoanalysis in a New Key therefore also presents work that reformulates thought and practice without leaving the precincts of the field. Books in the series focus, for example, on the significance of personal values in psychoanalytic practice, on the complex interrelationship between the analyst's clinical work and personal life, on the consequences for the clinical situation when patient and analyst are from different cultures, and on the need for psychoanalysts to accept the degree to which they knowingly satisfy their own wishes during treatment hours, often to the patient's detriment.

Vol. 26
Relational Freedom: Emergent Properties of the Interpersonal Field
Donnel B. Stern

Vol. 25
Micro-trauma: A Psychoanalytic Understanding of Cumulative Psychic Injury
Margaret Crastnopol

Vol. 24
Understanding and Treating Patients in Clinical Psychoanalysis: Lessons From Literature
Sandra Buechler

Vol. 23
The Interpersonal Tradition: The Origins of Psychoanalytic Subjectivity
Irwin Hirsch

Vol. 22
Body-States: Interpersonal and Relational Perspectives on the Treatment of Eating Disorders
Jean Petrucelli (ed.)

Vol. 21
The One and the Many: Relational Approaches to Group Psychotherapy
Robert Grossmark & Fred Wright (eds.)

Vol. 20
Mended by the Muse: Creative Transformations of Trauma
Sophia Richman

Vol. 19
Cupid's Knife: Women's Anger and Agency in Violent Relationships
Abby Stein

Vol. 18
Contemporary Psychoanalysis and the Legacy of the Third Reich: History, Memory and Tradition
Emily A. Kuriloff

Vol. 17
Love and Loss in Life and in Treatment
Linda B. Sherby

Vol. 16
Imagination from Fantasy to Delusion
Lois Oppenheim

Vol. 15
Still Practicing: The Heartaches and Joys of a Clinical Career
Sandra Buechler

Vol. 14
Dancing with the Unconscious: The Art of Psychoanalysis and the Psychoanalysis of Art
Danielle Knafo

Vol. 13
Money Talks: In Therapy, Society, and Life
Brenda Berger & Stephanie Newman (eds.)

Vol. 12
Partners in Thought: Working with Unformulated Experience, Dissociation, and Enactment
Donnel B. Stern

Vol. 11
Heterosexual Masculinities: Contemporary Perspectives from Psychoanalytic Gender Theory
Bruce Reis & Robert Grossmark (eds.)

Vol. 10
Sex Changes: Transformations in Society and Psychoanalysis
Mark J. Blechner

Vol. 9
The Consulting Room and Beyond: Psychoanalytic Work and Its Reverberations in the Analyst's Life
Therese Ragen

Vol. 8
Making a Difference in Patients' Lives: Emotional Experience in the Therapeutic Setting
Sandra Buechler

Vol. 7
Coasting in the Countertransference: Conflicts of Self Interest between Analyst and Patient
Irwin Hirsch

Vol. 6
Wounded by Reality: Understanding and Treating Adult Onset Trauma
Ghislaine Boulanger

Vol. 5
Prologue to Violence: Child Abuse, Dissociation, and Crime
Abby Stein

Vol. 4
Prelogical Experience: An Inquiry into Dreams & Other Creative Processes
Edward S. Tauber & Maurice R. Green

Vol. 3
The Fallacy of Understanding & The Ambiguity of Change
Edgar A. Levenson

Vol. 2
What Do Mothers Want? Contemporary Perspectives in Psychoanalysis and Related Disciplines
Sheila F. Brown (ed.)

Vol. 1
Clinical Values: Emotions That Guide Psychoanalytic Treatment
Sandra Buechler

Relational Freedom

Emergent properties of the
interpersonal field

Donnel B. Stern

LONDON AND NEW YORK

First published 2015
by Routledge
27 Church Road, Hove, East Sussex, BN3 2FA

and by Routledge
711 Third Avenue, New York, NY 10017

Routledge is an imprint of the Taylor & Francis Group, an informa business

© 2015 Donnel B. Stern

The right of Donnel B. Stern to be identified as author of this work has been asserted by him in accordance with sections 77 and 78 of the Copyright, Designs and Patents Act 1988.

All rights reserved. No part of this book may be reprinted or reproduced or utilised in any form or by any electronic, mechanical, or other means, now known or hereafter invented, including photocopying and recording, or in any information storage or retrieval system, without permission in writing from the publishers.

Trademark notice: Product or corporate names may be trademarks or registered trademarks, and are used only for identification and explanation without intent to infringe.

British Library Cataloguing in Publication Data
A catalogue record for this book is available from the British Library

Library of Congress Cataloging in Publication Data
Stern, Donnel B.
Relational freedom: emergent properties of the interpersonal field / Donnel B. Stern.
pages cm
Field theory (Social psychology) 2. Interpersonal psychotherapy. I. Title.
HM1033.S747 2015
150.19'84—dc23
2014044705

ISBN: 978-1-138-78840-4 (hbk)
ISBN: 978-1-138-78841-1 (pbk)
ISBN: 978-1-315-76557-0 (ebk)

Typeset in Times New Roman
by Swales & Willis Ltd, Exeter, Devon, UK

Printed and bound in the United States of America
by Edwards Brothers Malloy on sustainably sourced paper

To Kathe, for a lifetime.

Contents

Acknowledgments   xiv

1 Introduction: emergent properties of the interpersonal field   1

2 The interpersonal field: its place in American psychoanalysis   35

3 Field theory in psychoanalysis, part I: comparing Madeleine and Willy Baranger, and Harry Stack Sullivan   64

4 Field theory in psychoanalysis, part II: comparing Bionian field theory and contemporary interpersonal/relational psychoanalysis   83

5 Relational freedom and therapeutic action   108

6 Witnessing across time: accessing the present from the past and the past from the present   133

7 Unconscious phantasy and unconscious relatedness: comparing contemporary Freudian and interpersonal/relational approaches to clinical practice   155

8 Implicit theories of technique and the values that inspire them   165

9 Psychotherapy is an emergent process: hermeneutics and quantitative psychotherapy research   187

10 The hard-to-engage patient: a treatment failure   206

11 Curiosity: dealing with divergent ideas in the ideal psychoanalytic institute   220

References   233
Index   249

Acknowledgments

First and foremost among those who have helped me with this book is Phillip Blumberg, Ph.D., a great friend who has also been an excellent and generous editor and an unfailingly astute advisor. Phil has read virtually everything I have written, often at multiple stages of its development, for as long as I have known him. Everyone should have such a friend. Barbara Pizer and Stuart Pizer, also good friends, read Chapter 1 at least twice and helped me see the direction I should take. I am grateful to the long-time members of my study groups, who read most of these chapters and discussed them with me, and with whom I have learned so much about psychoanalysis and have had such a good time: Rachel Altstein, Charles Amrhein, Kim Bernstein, Lisa Director, Alexandra Eitel, Stefanie Solow Glennon, Robert Grossmark, Orna Guralnik, Arthur Heiserman, Jill Howard, Shelly Itzkowitz, Peter Lessem, Robert Millner, James Ogilvie, Jean Petrucelli, Maggie Robbins, Deborah Rothschild, Alan Sirote, Alan Slomowitz, Sarah Stemp, and Don Troise.

I also want to acknowledge the many friends, colleagues, and students I have been lucky enough to have at the William Alanson White Institute and the New York University Postdoctoral Program in Psychotherapy and Psychoanalysis. The atmosphere of these institutions has nurtured me. For a psychoanalyst, it is a great gift to be able to live in a psychoanalytic world. I also wish to express my gratitude to all the people and institutions that made it possible for me to present the chapters of this book to so many people in so many places over the last few years. I learned something from the discussions that followed every one of these presentations.

I am especially grateful to Kathe Hift, my wife and the psychoanalyst who has taught me more than any other, and whose attitude about my work (and me) has been patient, encouraging, and generous.

I wish to thank *Psychoanalytic Dialogues* and Routledge/Taylor & Francis Group for permission to use several of my articles: "Psychotherapy is an emergent process: In favor of acknowledging hermeneutics and against the privileging of systematic empirical research" (2013) 23: 102–115; "The hard-to-engage patient: A treatment failure" (2011) 21: 596–606; "Field theory in psychoanalysis, part I: Harry Stack Sullivan and Madeleine and Willy Baranger" (2013) 23: 487–501; "Field theory in psychoanalysis, part II: Bionian field theory and contemporary interpersonal/relational psychoanalysis" (2013) 23: 630–645; and "The interpersonal field: Its place in American psychoanalysis" (2015). I also thank *Contemporary Psychoanalysis* and Routledge/Taylor & Francis Group for permission to use two articles and a book review: "Unconscious fantasy versus unconscious relatedness: Comparing interpersonal/relational and Freudian approaches to clinical practice" (2010) 46: 101–111; "Curiosity: Dealing with divergent ideas in the ideal psychoanalytic institute" (2009) 45: 292–305; and "Field theory across theoretical boundaries: A review of Lawrence J. Brown's *Intersubjective Processes and the Unconscious: An Integration of Freudian, Kleinian, and Bionian Perspectives*" (2015). *Psychoanalytic Inquiry* and Routledge/Taylor & Francis Group graciously allowed me to use "Implicit theories of technique and the values that inspire them" (2012) 32: 33–49. I thank *The Psychoanalytic Quarterly* and John Wiley and Sons for permission to use "Witnessing across time: Accessing the present from the past and the past from the present" (2012) 81: 53–81. And I thank *The Journal of the American Psychoanalytic Association* and Sage Publications for permission to use "Relational freedom and therapeutic action" (2013) 61: 227–255.

Chapter 1

Introduction
Emergent properties of the interpersonal field

I remember feeling, even as a graduate student seeing my first patients in the early 1970s, that the clinical process took place *between* the patient and me, and that my experience and the patient's were not only our own, but also parts of a larger whole. In my first book (Stern, 1997), *Unformulated Experience: From Dissociation to Imagination in Psychoanalysis*, I recently reread a description of the interpersonal field. It brought back to me those first experiences of that sense of the clinical situation and reminded me of how long the interpersonal field has been central in my mind—longer, even, than I have known it by its name. Here is the passage.

> A fully interpersonal conception of treatment is a field theory. The psychoanalytic relationship, like any relationship, takes place in a field that is defined and ceaselessly redefined by its participants. It is not only the intrapsychic dynamics patient and analyst bring to their relationship that determine their experience with one another. The field is a unique creation, not a simple additive combination of individual dynamics; it is ultimately the field that determines which experiences the people who are in the process of co-creating that field can have in one another's presence. It is the field that determines what will be dissociated and what will be articulated, when imagination will be possible and when the participants will be locked into stereotypic descriptions of their mutual experience. Each time one participant changes the nature of his or her involvement in the field, the possibilities for the other person's experience change as well. . . . The field is the only relevant context.
>
> (p. 110)

Now jump ahead with me nearly two decades, from 1997 to this year. As I reviewed the articles I have written over the last few years, which make up the bulk of this book, I saw that my interests in the recent past, like the more distant past, have revolved around the interpersonal field, and I began to see that the chapters of this book organized themselves around this theme.

Emergence in the third person

One characteristic of the field has always held a particular fascination for me: its emergent properties. The field comes into being between two or more people in a way that cannot be predicted or controlled. It can only be accepted or rejected. To the extent that we can accept it, we sense and understand (and these are not necessarily the same thing at all) something of how this emergent quality informs and shapes the clinical process.

There is a link in psychoanalysis between the unconscious and the quality of emergence. This is not a very well-theorized link, and in fact, it is not at all clear exactly what we are referring to when we invoke it, as indubitable as I think its existence is to most psychoanalysts. Actually, the quality of emergence is itself no better defined than the link that connects it to the unconscious. And so, before going on to discuss the link to the unconscious, which I do later in this chapter, I begin by trying to say what I mean by emergence.

In psychoanalysis, we often experience the phenomena that we understand to "emerge" to be separate from us. That is, we think of emergence in the third person—some "it" emerges, so that the quality of emergence exists apart from subjectivity. Consider, for instance, the frequent appearance of the concept of emergence and the descriptor "emergent" in recent applications of nonlinear dynamic systems theory to the clinical situation (e.g., Seligman, 2005; Boston Change Process Study Group, 2010; Coburn, 2013). The emphasis in this work is not phenomenological—the primary emphasis is not the experience of the analyst or the patient, but on their interaction as a self-organizing system. Emergence in this frame of reference is not really part of our "felt sense" of things, but a characteristic of clinical process itself—clinical process as an object of observation. When the word "emergence" is used in this way, it describes attributes that are *experienced* as if they exist apart from the one who perceives them (even if, as in this case, we must also grant that the observer is part of the phenomenon in question).

Most of the time, psychoanalysts use the word in this third-person sense. We use it to describe aspects of treatment and characteristics of mind. Most of us, including me, continue to write and speak this way more or less routinely; and I will continue to use these meanings here and there throughout this book.

Emergence in the first person: the "felt sense" of emergence

But the way I intend to use the word "emergence" in this introductory chapter, and the way I generally find emergence to be most compelling in my daily clinical work, is not as a reference to attributes of things that feel as if they exist apart from me, but as a way of representing certain parts of my first-person experience, and the patient's, in the consulting room. This is emergence in the phenomenological sense. I have learned from my patients that they and I often have a simultaneous sense of the emergent quality of our experience, although sometimes I have that sense myself without knowing if the patient shares it. In either case, I have learned to value such moments highly, because they herald the appearance of something unexpected.

I have observed for many years that all experience is unbidden. It comes *to* us, we never plan it, and in that sense it is always a surprise (see Chapter 5 and Stern, 1990). Most of the time we are unaware of this unbiddenness. It simply escapes notice.

But the moments in which I have a *felt sense of emergence* are different in this respect. At those times I *feel* the unbiddenness of experience. I have a felt sense of the *arrival* of experience in my mind, of how little my conscious intentions seem to have to do with the whole process. I feel myself as a conduit for experience that comes into being through me. Paradoxically, this kind of experience, more than any other part of my experience—and precisely, I think, because it seems to come to me from elsewhere—feels most thoroughly of my own making. I feel it firmly as mine. My patients' sense of this kind of experience is similar, to the extent to which they have been able to articulate it to me.

A mild sense of emergence is common, an everyday event in my clinical experience. The more intense and gripping experience of emergence is rare. Any sense of emergence, though, mild or gripping, is vital, alive. It is often emotionally powerful, but even when it is not, it is arresting. It carries a sense of mystery, ranging from a feeling of surprise that merely raises the eyebrows, to sudden, intense curiosity, to awe and wonder, and once in a great while, to the numinous or magical.

"Emergence" in this frame of reference describes a certain affective state of things. It is the felt sense of moments that portend the unexpected, or are themselves unexpected. In moments of emergence I am connected to unseen things that feel, despite their invisibility, greatly important to matters at hand. There is a sense of nascence, of budding, of coming-to-be. Jack Foehl, in describing the quality of "depth" in clinical work, brings words to what I am trying to express: in moments of emergence, we are suddenly privy to "a sense of the boundless reaches of what we do not yet know" (Foehl, 2014, p. 295).

I have had experiences of emergence that were private. These generally have happened while I was alone, and I have been aware of this aloneness. I was not only physically by myself, in other words, but I also felt alone—but not necessarily lonely. Many of these times have been in dreams; others have taken place while I was in nature, or overlooking the city from a height. They have happened as I watched a film, read a novel, stood looking at a painting—or as I wrote a paper, finding myself amazed at the appearance in my mind of some expression that captured what I wanted to say in a way that carried me beyond what I had understood in the moment before.

But most of the emergent experiences I have had in the consulting room have not been private in this way. The unseen things I feel connected to in my office, whatever else they may be, are part of the context of my relationship with the particular person who is with me. That much I can tell, even though I can't make out what those things are. It is a feeling of opening-into, of possibility, and so it is generally welcome even when whatever will come next does not necessarily feel pleasant or fulfilling.

Now let me come full circle to my primary subject, the field. The experience of emergence is, to my mind, one of the most important ways any clinician can experience the interpersonal field. Conditions are not always right for it to take place, because it usually (but not always) requires a certain synergy of purpose between patient and analyst, a clinical collaboration that is not always available.[1] (Enactment, as I describe below, is one of the primary obstacles in this regard.) No doubt there are more prerequisites than a collaborative clinical atmosphere, but those other conditions are always unknown to us. We don't know why we have this kind of experience when we do. But in any moment in which my patient and I are working collaboratively, an experience of emergence is possible.

Is "depth" exclusively associated with the internal world?

Like emergence, the idea of depth is both closely associated with unconscious process and only infrequently theorized. Wachtel (2003, 2014), who wrote about the phenomenon in the third-person sense I have already described (i.e., some "it" has depth), concluded that psychoanalysts often lose sight of the fact that the idea of depth is a metaphor, mistaking it instead for a feature of the natural world and thereby creating some unfortunate effects on psychoanalytic understanding. Depth, Wachtel (2003) observed, is equated with profundity: the "farther down" something lies, the closer to the beginning, the more profound, it is. Wachtel's primary objection to this equation is that it leads us to accept unthinkingly the view that earlier, "deeper" events in a person's history are therefore more profoundly influential than events that come later. For my present purpose, while I appreciate Wachtel's point, my primary objection is the equation of depth with internality. We take for granted that the internal is more profound than the external, and therefore more important in the creation of experience and living. Social interaction, wrote Wachtel (2003),

> enter[s] into the psychological equation from the direction of the senses, that is, from the "surface" rather than the "depths." From the vantage point of the depth metaphor, social influences are therefore at risk of appearing "superficial."
>
> (pp. 20–21)

Wachtel also quotes Greenberg and Mitchell (1983), who, in their description of "drive/structure" models in psychoanalysis, make the point that in these models,

> social reality constitutes an overlay, a veneer superimposed upon the deeper, more "natural" fundaments of the psyche constituted by the drives. Any theory omitting or replacing the drives as the underlying motivational principle and, in addition, emphasizing the importance of personal and social relations with others is, from this point of view, superficial by definition, concerned with the "surface" areas of the personality, lacking "depth."
>
> (p. 80)

While today many psychoanalysts, perhaps most, are not adherents of drive/structure models, we all are nevertheless prisoners, to a certain degree, of assumptions contributed by those models. They are our history, and the wide acceptance that the internal life is profound and the social is superficial—and the interpersonal field is certainly social—is one of the artifacts of that history.

None of this is meant to deny the profundity of the internal; the clinical illustration I offer later in this chapter should be enough to do away with any impression that I feel that way. Instead, what I mean to argue is that profundity is not *exclusively* associated with the internal. As Wachtel points out, social influences can also be unconscious. One might say, in fact, that this was the great insight of Harry Stack Sullivan (e.g., 1956), who understood problems in living as the outcome of our dissociation, on the basis of anxiety, of significant parts of social living. We simply do not see, feel, or understand those parts of interactions with others that would call out too much anxiety if we were to grasp them. Just as social phenomena can be unconscious, they can also be emergent. That, as I have said, is in fact my understanding of the interpersonal field. I hope that this point, too, will take on more substance in the clinical illustration.

The felt sense of emergence and the phenomenology of depth: depth as a field concept

Foehl (2014) brings the philosophy of Merleau-Ponty and the thinking of Bion to bear on the phenomenology of depth in psychoanalysis. Foehl's focus on experience—depth in the first person—and his revision of the idea of depth in terms of a contemporary epistemological perspective suitable for grasping the idea as a field concept make his work especially relevant to my consideration of the felt sense of emergence. In his essay, Foehl replaces the vertical, internal-world metaphor of depth with one rooted in relationships: between figure and ground ("form to field"), self to world, and subject to other. It is the relationship between our explicit experience of the foreground (for example, figure, self, or subject) and our less articulated sense of the background (ground, world, or other) that gives us the feeling of depth.[2] The vaguely perceived presence of the background—it is "there" but its meaning is unrealized in this moment—adds a dimension to our explicitly grasped experience.[3] In this way experience gains "an affective resonance and fullness . . . that would otherwise be flattened into either an univocal regularity of 'it is how I see it' or an undifferentiated haze of not specifying what might be experienced" (Foehl, 2014, p. 298).

I imagine "flattened" experience to be like a painting without perspective: its two dimensions allow no movement from the surface of the picture into its background; everything in the picture exists on the same plane. Add perspective, though, as European painters in the Renaissance learned to do, and the eye is free to travel from the painting's surface into any level of the background, and we can in that way discover spatial relations between elements existing at any layer of depth. But we don't need to explicitly formulate every one of those relations to be affected by their presence. Even to view for a moment a painting made with perspective awakens a recognition of the possibilities it offers. Depth is our awareness of the possibility that relations we have not yet imagined will emerge, and it appears only when those possibilities, like three-dimensional perspective, are already present and alive in our experience.

I think this feeling of possibility is closely related to Foehl's "affective resonance and fullness"; and the felt sense of emergence, it seems to me, grows from both. The felt sense of emergence, we might say, is a manifestation of depth.

We can use the phenomenon of enactment to lend this point substance. Enactment is an example of a part of clinical process that we can certainly describe as emergent in the third-person sense, because it arises from unconscious sources; there is no sense of conscious volition. Because the unconscious root of enactment is, by definition, missing from its conscious experience, that experience is typically constricted and often rigid. Enactment feels as if it is just the way things are. One's own involvement with the other—that is, one's motivation to create and maintain the very state of affairs that is later revealed to have been problematic—is invisible. It often feels as if the enactment is the other's fault, as if one is being provoked into an uncomfortable affective state that one would be able to avoid if it weren't for the troublesome behavior of the other, or as if one is reacting to the other in a way that is nothing but reasonable.

And so enactment, despite being emergent in the third-person sense, is perhaps the epitome of the kind of clinical process that, in Foehl's words, is "flattened into . . . univocal regularity." Could any experience be a better illustration of what it means to say (again, in Foehl's words) that, "It is how I see it"?[4] Enactment is defined precisely by that taken-for-granted attitude, that feeling that what is happening in the clinical relatedness means what I think it means, and nothing more. Depth and ambiguity collapse. This point is recognized by analysts everywhere. The Barangers

(1961–62/2008), for instance, write, "It could be said that every event in the analytic field is experienced in the 'as-if' category. . . . [It is crucial that] each thing or event in the field be at the same time something else. If this essential ambiguity is lost, the analysis also disappears" (p. 799).

Now consider the new, spontaneous perceptions of oneself and the other that, when they become available, resolve enactments (Stern, 2004, 2010a).[5] These new perceptions reveal, often quite suddenly, a new and different meaning in what has been transpiring in the clinical relatedness. Sometimes it is the analyst whose perception changes first, sometimes the patient (Stern, 2003, 2004). It doesn't really matter which participant initiates the new perception, because in either scenario the new perception leads the one who develops it to treat the other differently, and that new and different treatment, and the new affective atmosphere that accompanies it, generally awakens in the other participant an awareness of the same new perception. This new grasp of the relationship often arrives with a felt sense of emergence. Simultaneously a new feeling of depth appears in the interpersonal situation or, in a phrase of Foehl's that I like, a "synchronic experience of multiply layered conscious and unconscious processes" (p. 298).

During an enactment, we can say, the foreground and background of experience, or conscious and unconscious, are broken off from one another. Or we can say that they are fused. Either metaphor works, because both portray a consciousness that no longer exists against a background.[6] Things are flattened; there is no depth. There is a sense of certainty about things that are perhaps better left uncertain, because uncertainty allows possibility. The possibility of new meaning is shut down. Things are what they are, nothing more.

But as the new perception of oneself and the other resolves the enactment, conscious and unconscious come back into communication with one another (cf. Ogden, 1992). Foreground disembeds from background, once again existing in relation to it. The possibility that things could be otherwise, or *also* otherwise, returns, and the picture deepens.

In the cellar: a clinical illustration

I turn now to a more detailed clinical illustration of what I mean by the felt sense of emergence. This example is not the report of an enactment and its resolution. It is instead a less difficult kind of moment, the kind of clinical interaction in which the analyst feels basically good about his or her participation and that I have elsewhere called "continuous productive unfolding" (Stern, 2009b).

But first a word of caution. To select a moment, or a case, that describes the quality of emergence is liable to suggest that the material selected is worthy of special note, thereby drawing attention away from the fact that the state of affairs it describes is actually part of everyday analytic work. That is a risk I will have to take to make my point. I have chosen to write about a portion of one clinical session, but in order to underline the ordinariness of the phenomenon I will also say something about the many other moments of this kind that took place in that treatment.

The illustration comes from the treatment of George, a married man in his 70s with grown children, an artist who continues to spend most of his time in the studio creating art. George is capable and intelligent, and obviously creative. He comes to treatment three times per week. On the day in question, about four years into the treatment, he walked into my consulting room and, as usual, sat down in the reclining chair, leaned all the way back, and closed his eyes. It has never seemed necessary to discuss using the couch, because George evolved this posture naturally, and it has always seemed to me to serve the same purpose: it allows him a more intimate kind of contact with his internal world.

On this day, George began telling me about Ted Hughes's English translation of Ovid's *Metamorphoses*, which he was reading at the moment. (George is an avid reader, especially of poetry.) In particular, he was taken with a tale about a nymph who, raped by a river god, turned into water and flowed into her attacker, becoming part of him. George thought there was something both intriguing and sexy about this. By "sexy," he said, he meant that turning into water and flowing into the attacker was sensually appealing and would feel good. He said that he also felt that the feeling of becoming part of someone else was similar to something he sometimes experiences with me, as if I were the river god and he were the nymph.

At the time, I was already familiar with the theme in the transference to which George was referring—the characterization of me as powerful and arbitrary, sometimes sadistic, sometimes loving, and him as smaller, weaker, always loving, and deeply attached to me, resulting in his vulnerability to feeling rejected and hurt. Today he was adding the element of sensual pleasure and outright eroticism, not to mention rape, themes that continued to be developed in many of the sessions that were to come.

I had been through many, many sessions with George in which most or all of the content concerned "the cellar," our shorthand for the sexual abuse of George by a faceless older man, events that may have taken place in the basement of George's parents' house when George was very young, perhaps four or five years old. George had been in analysis once before, 30 years earlier, but the events of the cellar, whatever they were, had barely come up then, and had not been explored. Despite his introspective proclivity, George himself had never really thought about these memories or fantasies—a fact that, at this point, given our immersion in these matters, was startling to him. But despite his present-day interest, there was really nothing in George's mind at this point that he felt he could count on to be a literal memory of such events, and so the scenarios of the abuse that George recounted in great detail could not be taken as factual. They were creations, or re-creations. But that didn't stop them from being highly significant to George, and therefore to me. Nor did that stop those scenarios from feeling to George as if he were not their author. During those many sessions, what he was telling me about was arriving in his mind unbidden.

George and I were "in the cellar" over and over and over again. Sometimes I was a misty kind of observer or witness, barely there at all; sometimes I was simply absent. But my presence, as significant as it was (I will have more to say about that), was not the main event. In the cellar, the focus was on George, who was vivid, and the faceless man, who was shadowy. As the nature of the relationship between these two changed during a session, George's self-states shifted. I could feel it. No doubt I responded with my own self-state shifts. Sometimes George was a helpless, frightened boy being abused; sometimes there was pleasure and perhaps something like love between him and the faceless man; and sometimes he was ferocious, a big, dangerous cat, a predator with long, sharp claws. When he was a cat, or at least in the cat-state, George might feel rage, and he often imagined himself at those moments on the threshold of a mysterious, darkened room within which, he thought, there might be a lot of blood. While the atmosphere at such times could be chilling, I was never particularly uncomfortable. George certainly could be angry with me, sometimes very angry, and there were times, sometimes weeks at a time, when this was the focus of our sessions; but George was never angry at me in the cellar. His cellar rage was not directed at me. Instead, I was a facilitating witness (see Stern, 2009a, 2009b, and Chapters 5 and 6 in this book) to events that generally seemed to me to be self-affirming on

George's part, even the rageful ones. George's fantasies gave shape to affect states—states of self—that I think he needed to be able to experience more explicitly than he had in the past. And to do that, he needed me to be there to know these things with him. My witnessing presence, I believe, contributed to George's capacity to formulate what he told me, and then, eventually, to step back and think about these things for the first time in his life.

The actual physical events that took place in the cellar were seldom clearly discernible to George, although they were sexual in nature. George's visual images of these events were vague. What I can say about George's feelings and fantasied bodily experience was that he could be terrified, sexually aroused, in physical pain, loved and loving, and worried and sad about the possibility of losing the faceless man's interest. Unsurprisingly, there was a good deal of fantasy about penises and long, penis-like objects in his mouth, throat, and anus. George identifies as heterosexual. The idea of sex with men used to intrigue him, but when he tried it he didn't feel aroused. Perhaps George would have been interested in both men and women with or without whatever took place in the cellar—or perhaps he was drawn to sex with men because of what took place in the cellar. Or perhaps both alternatives are true. It doesn't really matter, to me or to him.

Consider all of this as background for what happened on the day George told me the story about the nymph and the river god. I listened to George's thoughts after he told me about the tale, and after he had related the story to his feelings about me. After a while, I said something very simple to him, more or less spontaneously, and from deep within my involvement in the moment and with him. I said, "It reminds me of the cellar." I imagined we were both probably thinking the same thing. Despite that feeling of mystery that comes with the sense of emergence, which I did feel, what I said seemed to me to be uncontroversial.

George was silent for maybe 10 or 15 seconds, and then he said in a low voice, "I'm stunned."

Apparently we had not been thinking the same thing at all. But George's response conveyed to me that, in response to my remark, an emergent experience had come about in his mind, too. I may have offered him the idea, but his intense affective reaction was the shock of recognition. You experience that only when you are faced suddenly with something that summons an answering, involuntary, emergent, and immediate sense in your own mind that this thing belongs to you.

My remark, and the experience that gave rise to it, were the outcome of a jointly created interactive and affective process that had formative properties. I did not *figure out* my way into the connection between the cellar and Ovid's tale; I *felt* my way into it. Even that way of putting it, though, makes what I did sound more consciously volitional than it was. What I said to George grew from living under the spell he and I, without conscious intention, had cast together around our mutual history, the story of the nymph and the river god, and ourselves in this room, in this moment. My experience was the manifestation of the interpersonal field, in other words, not just of my individual capacity to think, know, or understand. Or put it this way: we should *always* understand the analyst's capacity to think, know, and understand in the clinical situation as a phenomenon of the field, not as the creation of the analyst's solitary mind. The analyst does not stand back and observe. She does her best work when living under the kind of spell George and I cast. My thought grew from what was happening between us. It would have been impossible without it.

When George and I are in the cellar, the outside world retreats. It is quiet, the office is dim, and I have noticed that colors tend to darken. There is the illusion that I am there, right there in that cellar. I know something about how it looks, because George has told me the details, and I find that I imagine a version of those details for myself, and I inhabit them. (I am an onlooker to this process of imagining.) The ends of our sessions can be startling. It can be wrenching to return ourselves to the everyday world. That shock testifies to the depth of our involvement, our mutual absorption in the matters at hand. We are thoroughly immersed in a joint fantasy. What comes to exist between us is woven from the strands of George's inner life, from my fantasy of his fantasy life, from George's fantasy of my fantasy, and on and on. *Someone* is weaving this experience between us, but it doesn't feel to George or me that it's either one of *us*. We can say that our mutual experience is the invention of the third (Ogden, 1994a, 2004; Benjamin, 2004), or that it actually constitutes the third, and of course that is true; but as illuminating as that concept is in many clinical contexts, it doesn't shed light on the phenomenon of emergence.

I hope that it comes across to you that process of emergence in this case is not unique, despite the fact that the events between George and me have been particularly dramatic and moving. I could probably use as an example of emergence any treatment of real depth. In fact, the quality of emergence has always been so central to me that I suspect that any one of the many case examples I have published in articles and books, including those in the chapters to follow, could serve as an illustration. Any collaborative treatment contains emergent moments, usually (but not always) during the periods of collaboration themselves (see footnote 1).

It is impossible to know whether George's apparent sexual abuse actually took place. There were various reasons, gleaned from George's history and symptoms, for me to suspect strongly that some kind of traumatic sexual contact did occur. I believe that that sexual contact, the betrayal it represented, and especially the terrible rejection that seems to have brought it to an end (I have not explained that part of the material)—or rather, the ways George has devised to live with these things—has shaped George's life in various damaging and distressing ways. The images, phantasies, quasi-memories, and bodily sensations that George described almost continuously during many sessions, over years, came to him without his volition. Their flow, that is, was itself emergent, and it felt that way to him.

I am convinced that all these things came to George when they did, in the forms they did, and in the order that they did, because he was *telling them to me*. It was the field we shaped between us, not just George's intention to free associate (although George did indeed intend to free associate) that was responsible for the emergence of this material. Just as the analyst's capacity to think, know, and understand is rooted in the field, so is the patient's freedom (or lack of it) to formulate his experience (see especially Chapter 5, in which I refer to this phenomenon as "relational freedom").

More often than not, rather than trying to interpret George's cellar experiences by converting them into some other frame of reference, I accepted them at face value. If I imagined they had symbolic import, I usually kept that thought to myself (my comment that, "It reminds me of the cellar," is an immediate exception to this observation); and if the cellar experiences were vague and hard to understand, I usually did not try to get George to clarify them. George knew perfectly well that I was wondering about what all this might mean, beyond what it signified literally; and of course he wondered, too. But despite sharing that attitude, we usually allowed the material to take us wherever it was going. We were leaves on the stream. It seemed important for the meanings in George's experience to have a chance to emerge by themselves. The atmosphere between us during the sessions when George was in the cellar was not flattened and univocal.

I sensed depth and possibilities for the growth of meaning. It usually felt to me that offering interpretations of our time in that awful cellar would have been heavy-handed, risking intellectualization.

I am hardly claiming that proceeding this way is always best. With other patients, at moments when it seems to further the work, I go about things differently, querying and offering interpretive interventions. But with George, most of the time, at least while he was in the cellar, it seemed best to proceed the way I did. When I did have something to say, my comments were generally intended to expand the material along the narrative lines it already seemed to be following. My interventions, in other words, were frequently—to borrow a useful term from another frame of reference—unsaturated.

I hope that I have communicated in this illustration the quality of felt emergence that frequently characterized this treatment. I hope that this material conveys what Edgar Levenson (1982) writes in one of my favorite passages from his work: Patient and analyst feel that,

> *some* process is going on which they have not initiated or energized. There is the remarkable experience of being carried along by something larger than both therapist and patient: A true sense of an interpersonal field results. *The therapist learns to ride the process rather than to carry the patient.*
>
> (pp. 11–12; italics from the original)

Emergent = unconscious

Briefer versions of Chapters 3 and 4 of this book were first published in *Psychoanalytic Dialogues* (Stern, 2013a, 2013b), where each was accompanied by a number of commentaries. In the second of these articles, the one that appears here in a longer form as Chapter 4, I compared contemporary relational and interpersonal psychoanalysis with contemporary Bionian field theory. In a commentary that accompanied that article, Rachael Peltz and Peter Goldberg (2013) offered a distinction between Bionian field theory and interpersonal and relational psychoanalysis, contrasting what they called the "interactional qualities" of interpersonal/relational clinical work with the "emergent phenomena" of Bionian treatment. This differentiation, even if we take it to describe a difference in emphasis rather than something more absolute, suggests that emergence and interaction do not naturally occur simultaneously;

that is, if one's work and thinking focus on emergence, interaction loses a certain degree of emphasis, and vice versa. In Peltz and Goldberg's account, events in the Bionian field are emergent, while events in the interpersonal/relational field are not. In the remainder of this introductory chapter, I take up this point and answer it.

What is at stake here? Why does Peltz and Goldberg's point matter? The answer grows from the sense we all have that emergent phenomena grow from unconscious processes. This is the link between the quality of emergence and the unconscious that I mentioned at the outset of this chapter, and to which I promised to return. What else could "emergent" mean in psychoanalysis? If the origins of an experience are unclear, and the reasons for its appearance are mysterious, from where else than unconscious process could a psychic phenomenon (speaking from the point of view of the observer, the third person) or an experience (the first-person, phenomenological view) arise?

Today we have more than one conception of what "unconscious" means. The traditional conception of a container of contents hidden away in the mind is less and less compelling. Many of us prefer now to think of unconsciousness as experience that is potential, unmentalized—that is, unsymbolized; and we are likely to think of the means by which experience is made "thinkable" more as a kind of transformation of the very nature of the experience and less as the revelation of previously existing, fully formed mental contents. Winnicott (e.g., 1971), Green (1999), and especially Bion (1962a, 1962b), have opened this area, along with many others who have built on their work (e.g., Botella and Botella, 2005; Ferro, 2006a, 2007; Grotstein, 2007; Brown, 2011b). In particular I think here of theories of mentalization (e.g., Segal, 1957; Mitrani, 1995; Lecours and Bouchard, 1997; Fonagy *et al.*, 2002) and unrepresented states (e.g., Levine *et al.*, 2013). This is also the kind of theory I have proposed in describing unformulated experience (Stern, 1983, 1997, 2010a).

But no matter what model of unconsciousness we use, the quality of emergence is attached to the appearance in the mind of experience that could not be "made" or "known" or "grasped" before. And so to suggest that the quality of emergence is typical of clinicians from some schools, but not from others, is to imply that there are schools of psychoanalysis in which unconscious processes are given short shrift. Of course, given that psychoanalysis is centered on unconscious phenomena, the suggestion that some schools of psychoanalysis are less interested in the unconscious than others is not really just an observation, but a criticism.

Peltz and Goldberg are fellow travelers; they make it clear that they have dual commitments to relational psychoanalysis and Bionian field theory. Nevertheless, in their essay I think these writers fall prey to a common misconception about interpersonal and relational psychoanalysis. In this contemporary misconception, as in the misconceptions held in the past about the interpersonal field by mainstream analysts in North America (see Chapter 2), interpersonal and relational psychoanalysis are sometimes portrayed as environmentally or socially oriented theories that give scant emphasis to the unconscious and to psychic reality, and that therefore sacrifice some significant portion of the "depth" quality of psychoanalytic treatment. Interpersonal and relational analysts, this criticism goes, tend to discuss with their patients what is most easily available; and so treatment tends to be constituted by superficial, rational discussion. Thoroughgoing change, which requires the acceptance and encouragement of less comfortable, rational, and accessible material, is thereby sacrificed.

And so one of my intentions in these introductory remarks is to reply to all such views, not just that of Peltz and Goldberg. I focus on their piece not because its content is unique, but because it is a convenient, thoughtful, and lucid expression of a critical view of interpersonal/relational psychoanalysis that is commonly held by analysts of other schools.

This critical view is sometimes explicitly stated, more often only implied. Peltz and Goldberg's criticism is among the implicit versions; they do not suggest in so many words that an interest in clinical interaction leads to superficiality. But others do suggest just that. More often than not, such claims are made in private conversations, usually conversations with those who feel the same way. But such views do sometimes find their way into print.

Let me quote two recent examples to illustrate what I mean. In another of the commentaries written to accompany that same article of mine on Bionian field theory and contemporary interpersonal/relational psychoanalysis, we read the following from Ferro and Civitarese (2013):

> The clinical vignettes of the interpersonalists sometimes convey the impression that, first, [interpersonal/relational psychoanalysis] is based on an interactionism not guided at all times by a model of the unconscious functioning of the individual and group mind as versatile that of [Bionian field theory], which also takes account of the micrometry of the analytic dialogue; and that, second, [interpersonal/relational

psychoanalysis] sees change as underlain principally by rational understanding and conscious agreement (which admittedly often rest on a reading of unconscious dynamics and on the joint experience of analysis).

(p. 647)

Ferro and Civitarese are entitled to their opinions and to their reading of clinical vignettes written by interpersonal and relational analysts. And I do recognize that they qualify their remarks (I refer to the portion of the last sentence in parentheses). But could any psychoanalyst endorse the suggestion that, in his or her own work, "change [is] underlain principally by rational understanding and conscious agreement?"

My second illustration comes from a recent edited collection called *A New Freudian Synthesis: Clinical Process in the Next Generation* (Druck et al., 2012). In the first of two excellent introductory essays, Druck (2012a) distances the group of Freudian writers represented in these pages from the conflict theory of ego psychology, often identified with Brenner. Druck (2012b) then identifies, in his second piece, the work of this New York-based Freudian group with what he calls "structural theory"—by which he does not mean Freud's structural theory, but theories of developmental difficulty and arrest, heavily influenced by writers from the object relations traditions, especially Winnicott. These "new Freudians" see psychoanalytic treatment as the kind of response to the patient that rekindles the growth and development of mind, which has been inhibited or stymied by the life the patient has led up to that time—especially, of course, his early life. The focus is not on interpretation and genetic reconstruction, but on the analyst's clinical responsiveness to the patient's narcissistic states of mind. Therapeutic action is understood in most of these chapters as the internalization, and therefore the structuralization, of key aspects of the therapeutic relationship.

I read this book with a group of colleagues in a study group. We were all impressed with a problem that keeps popping up in these essays. Most of the writers try to make the case that their way of thinking remains distinctively Freudian—by which they generally mean not only that all the chapters rest on a common core of principles that are identifiably Freudian, but also that this common core is not relational. This is a difficult task, because most of the chapter authors also accept that relational psychoanalysis has made significant contributions that are closely related to their own. And in truth many of the chapters, even most of them, are not difficult for a relational analyst to embrace. But because of the problem of maintaining theoretical identification, most of the chapter authors, in one way or another, argue that what they have to say is not relational in certain key respects.

Norbert Freedman (2012), in one of his final contributions, wrote the book's concluding chapter, which was intended to pull the book together and summarize its message. Tackling the problem of identifying what is uniquely Freudian about the chapters that precede his own, Freedman writes,

> Inherent in this new version of a "Modern Freudian's" vision is also both an appreciation and a differentiation from the contribution from recent relational analysts (cf. Aaron [sic], Benjamin). The role of intersubjectivity as a defining baseline for all analytic work, so much emphasized by these authors, cannot be gainsaid.
>
> (p. 252)

So far, so good. But then Freedman goes on to set up a straw man in order to knock it down: each of the "new Freudian" writers in this volume, he says, "advanced a distinct line of differentiation that eschews *the intrinsic narrowness inherent in the exclusive reliance on action and interaction*" (p. 252; emphasis added). It is clear in context that we are meant to understand an "exclusive reliance on action and interaction" to be characteristic of relational psychoanalysis.

Emergence in the work of interpersonal and relational writers

The most effective rejoinder to assertions of this kind is the presentation of clinical material, and I have already done that. But I don't want to leave the impression that I am the least bit unique among interpersonal and relational analysts in appreciating the inner life and accepting the necessity for quiet and contemplation in clinical process. The quality of emergence is, in fact, central for all psychoanalysts, regardless of orientation. And so I want to demonstrate, before ending this introduction, that I am not alone among interpersonal and relational writers in believing that clinical process is simultaneously interpersonal and emergent, and working on the basis of that understanding.

But whose work shall I feature? Probably all interpersonal and relational analysts conceive the interpersonal or relational field as emergent; but many of them, or most, take the point for granted, seldom making it explicit. That the interpersonal field is an emergent phenomenon, in other words, is for interpersonal and relational writers what water is to a fish: it may seldom be explicitly noted or discussed, but life without it is inconceivable.

I have settled on quoting from my own work and the writings of six other interpersonal and relational analysts: Edgar Levenson, Ken Corbett, Jody Davies, Philip Bromberg, Robert Grossmark, and Jack Foehl. It is arbitrary to choose this particular set of writers. No doubt I could have made different and equally illuminating selections.

I have already quoted Edgar Levenson (1982), dean of interpersonal psychoanalysts, on this subject. Twenty years after he wrote that passage, Levenson (2001) made a similar observation:

> If one can accept that one is tapping into and riding, like a wave, an ineffable process—part conscious, part unconscious, part between people, part autonomous, part rational conceptualizing, and part a mysterious act of mutual creation—then one might wish to augment and facilitate the process without needing to grasp it firmly. As Wilner (1999) put it, "The seeming paradox of unconscious experience is that one cannot be conscious of it without losing the qualitative character of unconsciousness itself—its emergent flow" (p. 621).
>
> (p. 249)

Levenson has maintained his interest in these matters. The following passage (Levenson, 2008) is not directly concerned with the claim that therapeutic action in interpersonal and relational psychoanalysis depends primarily on rational understanding and conscious agreement; but what Levenson says here certainly serves as an economical refutation of the point.

> the analyst need only do his work; the patient will take care of the cure. The changes, when they come, will not have a direct linear cause-and-effect relationship to any analytic input, be it relationship or interpretation. Interpretations do not produce change; they are merely part of the interactional field that leads, always indirectly, to change.
>
> (p. 92)

Relational analyst Ken Corbett (2015) recently wrote a paper in which he offered his own description of the emergent analytic field, especially as manifested in his work with children:

> ... I am often confused, both unwittingly and with intent. Hour-by-hour, I feel myself to be enveloped in a polyphonic field, and I struggle to get my mind into and around the excess. Adding to my confusion, I often court it, indulge it, and mine it to see where it may lead.
>
> I experience this confusion with all of my patients, but it is given particular expression in my work with children, wherein I am often genuinely lost in the potential space of psychic equivalence. I find myself suspended as I am caught in the vista of a child's vision and led toward a *life suspended playing in reality*, playing in a fantastic zone of psychic equivalence, moving as children are wont to move between material reality and psychic reality.
>
> One of the pleasures of working with children is that one gets to work in the land of psychic-equivalence, a liminal space where being hangs suspended between the material and psychic. A spoon is a spoon is a shovel is an evil shovel-monster-man who speaks with an English accent and is set upon devouring the world. Symbols, objects, and characters meld in the alchemy of psychic equivalence. Play is spoken and played with symbols and objects. Characters manifestly take to the field. As the analyst, one speaks within the play sometimes as symbol, sometimes as object, sometimes as character; if you don't speak thus, you are not playing.
>
> (pp. 641–42)

Philip Bromberg (2011a) tells us that "interpersonal novelty," or what he goes on to call "the therapeutic 'internalization' of otherness," is a manifestation of processes in the field that are "unanticipated by both persons" (i.e., emergent) and "belong to neither person alone."

> Interpersonal novelty is what allows the self to grow because it is unanticipated by both persons, it is organized by what takes place between two minds, and it belongs to neither person alone. The reciprocal process of active involvement with the states of mind of the other person allows a patient's here-and-now perception of self to share consciousness with the experiences of incompatible self-narratives that were formerly dissociated. This process, a developing synthesis

of interpersonal interaction and a relational unconscious, lead could be called *the therapeutic "internalization" of otherness.* As long as interpersonal experiences are safe but not too safe, the permeability of the self/other boundary is increased, externally and internally, and psychoanalysis becomes a powerful transformational process. It is through the novelty and surprise of this reciprocal process that the therapeutic action of psychoanalysis takes shape, and it may well be what accounts for the enhanced spontaneity and flexibility of a patient's personality structure that results from a successful analysis.

(p. 104)

Like Bromberg, Jody Davies (2003) describes emergent field processes that contribute to the enhancement of the self of the patient.

> I would suggest that often what creates therapeutic movement in such cases is the almost imperceptible countertransference shift that allows new patient–analyst experiences and therefore new representational images of the patient to emerge for the first time in the mind of the analyst. Much as a parent holds hopeful images of who her child might strive to become in the future, prematurely foreclosed self-experience will often give way to emergent self-experience for the first time in the mind of the analyst. The patient will plant in the analyst's unconscious the seedlings of emergent self-experience, seedlings held there for safe-keeping, while she is free to enact her hatred for, jealousy of, entitlement to, and love of these as yet unintegrated self-organizations. The analyst's task becomes one of discovering and protecting these nascent selves, buried under the landfill of countertransferential blindness. She holds them there and loves and protects them until such time that the patient can discover them for herself, reflected in the analyst's vision, and integrate them for the first time.

(p. 23)

In the course of the article on the phenomenology of depth from which I have already quoted, Jack Foehl (2014) offers a lovely paragraph that might have been written to describe the felt sense of emergence.

> The analyst's role in deepening involves attending to the immersive immediacy of the perceptive moment, where embodied feeling-states might emerge from an unspecified ground, where the gap between

what forms and its context becomes the crucible for new meaning. This entails receptivity to absence as much as presence, to the ways in which formation is always a play between what becomes and what is not yet there.

(p. 301)

In a recent article, Robert Grossmark (2012) suggests that it is natural and desirable for contemporary relational psychoanalysts to bring to bear on their clinical practice Michael Balint's (1968) and Enid Balint's (1993) conception of "the unobtrusive analyst." In summarizing the case of a young man named Kyle, Grossmark (2012) says:

> The ... emphasis on the value of silence, waiting, and regression in a mutual experience are all seen as complementary to contemporary concepts of co-creation and the deep emotional engagement of the analyst with the patient in the analytic field. There is an emphasis on the analyst allowing for the patient's inner world to emerge within the analytic relationship in the idiom of the patient so that the patient can come to own their own sensations, body and mind. Particularly, but not only, with patients like Kyle who are not psychologically alive in a felt and recognizable way, the emergence of these regressed states often comes in the "enactive" register. I emphasize the value of the analyst allowing this process to unfold, to accompany the patient, and to not close it off with interpretations or investigations of the relationship that do not come from within the patient.
>
> (p. 643)

The quality of emergence has always been at the heart of my own interest in psychoanalysis. It was my sense of felt emergence, as a matter of fact, that lay behind the concept of unformulated experience (Stern, 1983, 1997): the idea was that conscious experience is an emergent thing, arising from a less fully articulated state. It was this conviction that led me to think about unconsciousness as potential, unrepresented, unsymbolized experience rather than as fully formed contents somehow hidden away in the mind or disguised. The expressions of the quality of emergence that I offer here mirror what I wrote earlier in this chapter. But because the first two of these passages appeared over 30 years ago, they serve as further substantiation that the recognition of depth and emergence has long been a part of interpersonal and relational psychoanalysis. First, a passage describing clinical process from a paper published in 1983:

> I have said that curiosity means allowing oneself to make constructions. "Allowing" may seem strange wording—or it may sound like some kind of conscious granting of permission to oneself to "go ahead and work on" thinking. To "work on" thinking is precisely the meaning not intended. Curiosity is an active attitude of openness (Schachtel, 1959), not a focused search, at least not to begin with. It means that rather than employing a focused beam of attention, a searchlight to look *for* things in experience, which in one way or another usually seems to result in conventionalizing, one allows the things that are there to impress themselves on one's consciousness. This involves taking one's hand off the tiller and letting what Schachtel (1973) called "global attention and perception" drift as it will. Then, when an interesting construction begins to form itself out of the preattentive material, one may stop and perform a more focused search on and around this construction to fill in the detail and give it the convincing quality Freud (1937) knew it had to have to be useful. Of course, it is no accident that this description of "allowing" is essentially a description of free association; but it is the ideal of free association.
>
> In this view, then, psychoanalysis is not a search for the hidden truth about the patient and the patient's life. It is instead the emergence, through curiosity and the acceptance, of uncertainty, of constructions which may never have been thought before.
>
> (pp. 92–93)

A few pages later in the same paper comes this passage:

> the psychoanalytic process and the creative process have certain communalities. In both, the process is emergent, not predetermined. The outcome is unknowable, and a final outcome is unreachable. In both, an initial stage of receptivity is followed by inspiration, then by the application of directed, ordered thinking. In both, constructions appear, are honed, and then themselves become springboards for the next generation of constructions. Each new construction, if it is useful, has something of the quality of "effective surprise," a term Bruner (1962) uses to describe the result of a truly creative act.
>
> (p. 94)

emergent is opposite of predetermined

Now I jump forward 30 years to an article of mine published in 2013 and reproduced in this book as Chapter 5.

> Our goal in relaxing milder constrictions of the field is the same in kind as our goal in working with dissociative enactment: we want to do whatever is possible to become aware of, and then loosen, constricted interaction, thereby promoting therapeutic action by unlocking the capacity of relatedness to serve as the crucible for the unbidden. But because these events—this relaxation of relatedness—embody an *emergent* quality of the relatedness itself, it is impossible to specify in advance a technique to accomplish it. Events arise from within the analytic relationship in a way that simply cannot be predicted. And so we can almost never describe exactly what needs to be done to expand relational freedom. Such episodes can be encouraged by our openness to the unexpected (an openness that is always and necessarily only partial), but only that much is possible.
>
> (Stern, 2013c, p. 10)

If these passages from contemporary interpersonal and relational analysts do what I intend them to do, they convey that the emergent properties of the interpersonal field are central to the work of analysts from this school.

Retracing the path: the risks that come with commitments to theory

Now let me change course—or rather, let me double back and retrace the same path differently. I want to acknowledge some of the very criticisms of relational and interpersonal psychoanalysis with which I have taken issue. To do this requires that I offer some background.

I did my psychoanalytic training at the William Alanson White Institute in New York City, which was then, and is now, the home and source of interpersonal psychoanalysis. I trained before relational psychoanalysis existed. Today, while White is still the home of interpersonal psychoanalysis, most of us also identify ourselves as relational.

When I trained, my teachers and fellow candidates, while most considered themselves interpersonal, held theoretical and clinical positions that ranged across the entire spectrum of psychoanalysis. Some were fairly conservative, preferring to think more along the lines of the intrapsychic world than the interpersonal one. They conceptualized transference as distortion, did not yet find much informational value in countertransference, and depended on free association, evenly hovering attention, interpretation, and neutrality. On the other end of the spectrum were those who were radically interpersonal, which meant that they tended to focus on present interactional events, especially those in the analytic situation. They were more likely than their conservative colleagues to encourage directness and spontaneity in dealings with patients, often eschewed interpretation for interventions with more explicitly relational aims, and understood transference as selective understanding, not distortion.

But these were the extremes. Only a bare handful of my teachers were either intrapsychic conservatives or confrontational radicals. The vast majority recognized the significance of the analyst's subjectivity, and therefore felt that psychoanalysis took place between two people, both of whose experience was relevant. They believed that analysts needed to understand their patients in their patients' own terms, and needed to talk to patients in a way that their patients could hear. They recognized early the informational value of countertransference, and they emphasized it. Both empathy and the internal world mattered continuously. It was a little early, in the United States (this was the 1970s), for the recognition of the significance of the particular developmental perspective offered by British object relations; but my teachers were among the first to understand these matters and teach them. They recognized the value of both the intrapsychic and the interpersonal positions, and they taught that to me.

It is also true, though, that most of the analysts who have been most focused on the current interactional arena have been interpersonal and relational. I want to avoid any suggestion that an emphasis on interaction is necessarily excessive. I want to avoid that suggestion because I have learned from this emphasis ever since I was a candidate, and I have contributed to it myself, in my writings (e.g., Stern, 2010a), in the years after my training ended. But we can at least agree that, to the extent that an interactional focus *can* detract from our interest in the inner world, and thereby be excessive, it is interpersonal and relational analysts who are most at risk of working that way.

Recently a trio of prominent relational analysts (Cooper, 2014; Corbett, 2014; Seligman, 2014) contributed a symposium on this very topic (see also Grossmark, 2012; Bass, 2014). In their response to the commentaries written to accompany their three papers, Cooper *et al.* (2014) wrote that, "we are concerned that Relationally oriented analysts are missing opportunities for understanding our patients' internal worlds as afforded by contemplative, quiet and even reserved ways of conducting analytic work."

Foehl (2013) makes a similar point. In the following passage, he is discussing the work of the Barangers (1961–62/2008, 2009). As a matter of fact, he is writing in response to an article of mine comparing the Barangers' work with the thinking of Harry Stack Sullivan and others (Stern, 2013a; a longer version appears in this book as Chapter 3). At one point in his commentary, Foehl takes issue with what he believes is my view. Actually, though, I agree with him: what the patient and the analyst say and do are not only participations in the field but also, simultaneously, symbolic representations of those same events. Any moment of clinical process can be grasped from either perspective. Foehl (2013) writes:

> Working with the Barangers on my shoulder, I'm especially attuned to words as symbols in their own right, as products of process and not simply as acts or participatory events. A shifting landscape unfolds, and I listen to the boyfriend, the overheated car, wilted flowers, as commentaries on an evolving field. At these times, unconscious feels between us, but also it's deep inside . . . who?
>
> (p. 510)

Yes, exactly: inside . . . who? Field theory of any variety makes this question hard to answer. But inside, yes: field theory still requires a conception of the individual psyche.

For me, the writings that first leap to mind when I think of the complementarity of field and individual are Klein's and Bion's projective identification (see, for example, Brown, 2011b, pp. 47–82), Sandler's (1976) concept of role-responsiveness and Levenson's (1972, 1983) "transformation" and "fallacy of understanding." The concept of projective identification at this point in psychoanalytic history needs no introduction. Sandler believed that one of the primary functions of transference is to reach the analyst unconsciously in a way that actualizes in the therapeutic relationship an aspect of the patient's internal object relations. Levenson argued that the analyst is routinely "transformed" unconsciously by interaction with the patient into various characters in the patient's inner and outer life.

In another concept linking field and individual, Levenson suggested that the analytic pair inevitably play out between them the very message the analyst offers in her interpretation, so that interpretation without a consideration of its immediate interactive context is incomplete, a "fallacy of understanding" that not only does not have curative properties, but also serves as one more repetition of the very problem the interpretation is an attempt to address. The reverse is also true: that is, it would be just as incomplete to focus on the nature of the analytic relatedness without a simultaneous interest in the unconscious symbolic meanings of what is said. The analyst's attention must zigzag back and forth between attempts to understand the relation of the content of the session to its process, and the relation of its process to its content. And so Levenson (1979) famously wrote, "*The power of psychoanalysis may well depend on what is said about what is done*" (p. 279; italics from the original). But he also wrote elsewhere that, "It is what is done about what is said that matters" (Levenson, 1987, p. 487). This is not a contradiction; both are true.

And so, in retracing my path and acknowledging some of the criticism of interpersonal and relational psychoanalysis with which I have taken issue, I want what I say to be understood in this light: *all* of us—all psychoanalysts and psychoanalytically oriented psychotherapists—accept the necessity for clinicians to absorb themselves—sometimes simultaneously, sometimes successively—in the inner, individual world, and the quiet and contemplation necessary to appreciate it; in the interactive engagement of the outer world, often but not always a noisier part of the work; and in the relation of these two worlds to one another.

In developing my own version of the necessity for quiet and contemplation in the midst of engagement, I have given special emphasis to curiosity (Stern, 1997, 2010a). By curiosity, though, I do not mean a seeking after anything in particular in experience. Curiosity is not a matter of looking *for* something, nor is it mere inquisitiveness. It can appear to be passivity, because there is a great deal of "waiting" involved. For what? Well, in my own experience with patients, I wait for my own unformulated experience to cast up tendrils into my consciousness, tendrils that will begin to bring to my awareness what it is that I am perhaps on the verge of thinking and feeling. I have no choice but to be patient. I could force the matter, of course; but making experience happen before it is ready to happen generally fails to reveal to me what I need to know. The result is intellectualization.

What I am trying to describe in characterizing curiosity in this way is the process of formulating experience. The process of formulation—the waiting, and the active attitude of openness—seems no different to me when the experience to be formulated concerns the nature of my involvement with my patient, or my patient with me, than it is when I am waiting to find out what it is I think and feel about anything else. Engagement, that is, remains engagement, whether the thing engaged is another person, another part of myself, a work of art, a story, etc.

Yes, I am always engaged with my patients. But to be engaged is not necessarily to know the nature of that engagement. I find that there is generally good reason to imagine that my knowledge of any current engagement is only partial. And I cannot know it at will. I must wait for my own capacity to experience it to develop, and that development is on its own schedule. It takes its own time and comes in its own way. Usually, the best I can do is stay out of its way. Or perhaps better: the best I can do is to attend as closely as I can to whatever is arriving in the range of my knowing (see, for example, Stern, 1990, 1997). It often takes what I (Stern, 2010a, 2012; see also Chapter 6) have called witnessing on the part of the analyst. In another book I happened to be reading recently, Ted Jacobs (2013), in describing the recapture of the past—and reminiscent of some of the notes sounded also by Cooper, Corbett, and Seligman—evokes a sense of clinical process very much like my own. Recapture of certain experience, Jacobs writes, requires, "time, patience, silence, and the presence of someone who [understands]—as Christopher Bollas (1989) has reminded us—that news from within comes on its own terms."

Of course, none of this means that we can't make consciously intended contributions to our work. Conscious, disciplined inquiry and inference play a role in every treatment, perhaps even in every session. But we employ them only after the waiting and the receptive attention that allow novel experience to arrive unbidden. Inquiry and inference are tools that we use to shape and polish. But what matters—that must come to us on its own.

If holding a commitment to interpersonal and/or relational theory creates the risk of an overenthusiastic interactionism, more intrapsychically oriented analysts run a risk in the other direction: their commitment to their theory leads them to risk ignoring the present-day impact of their conduct with their patients. Not infrequently I have seen patients whose previous analysts, competent as they otherwise were, simply could not see or accept the influence they were exerting on their patients right there in the consulting room. In the end, what they were missing was not only what was happening in the present. Ironically enough, because they could not accept their contemporary unconscious participation, they were missing the unconscious themes from the past being expressed in the interaction.

I said that I would retrace my path differently. Now I have prepared the ground to do that. What I want to say is simply this: every psychoanalytic theory comes with a different set of risks, risks of excess. Every theory comes with the risk of losing the forest for the trees in a different way. Interpersonal and relational theories come with the risk of giving the inner world too little emphasis; traditional psychoanalysis comes with the risk of giving the contemporary psychoanalytic interaction too little emphasis. In this sense, I am also retracing my disagreement with some of the arguments with which I have disagreed. Peltz and Goldberg (2013) have a point. But because they don't present their observation about interaction in relational psychoanalysis as a risk, but as a more or less inescapable accompaniment of the ideas and practices that comprise this school, they (and the others who have made similar arguments) overstate their case.

I am perfectly content with making the point this way—i.e., as a matter of risk. What I object to—the other way of treading the path—is the suggestion that each theory comes with *inevitable* excesses. Putting the problem this way leads to tendentious relations with those who espouse different ideas: *you* people do *that*. I find that approach disrespectful and inaccurate—not just when it is applied to interpersonal and relational analysts, but to practitioners of any analytic orientation. Yes, it's true, we can find excess in certain parts of the work of clinicians of every stripe. But that excess is not an inevitable consequence of their point of view; it is a *risk* of adopting that point of view. And because it is a risk, it can often, or even usually, be avoided if it is recognized, and if we struggle with it. When we are doing our best work, we are trying to attend to both what is said about what is done, and what is done about what is said. Orientation is not destiny, at least not in this respect.

Returning to emergence

That I believe psychoanalysis and psychotherapy are emergent processes is certainly clear at this point. And it is clear, too, I hope, that I feel that way because I think it is the best description of clinical events. But there is another reason that I take this position. That other reason is not as simple as a fact, and it cannot be reduced to an empirically justifiable argument. It is not really even anchored in psychoanalysis, although it is probably one of the reasons I was drawn to psychoanalysis in the first place. No, the other reason I feel as strongly as I do about emergent processes really seems to boil down to a sense I have always had, not only about clinical process, but about all of life. All living seems, and feels, emergent to me.

I think of it this way: in every moment each one of us is two, one who is living the present moment, and another, always coming into being, who will be able to give conscious representation to some portion of the doing of that living. But never do these two become one—even if, as is often the case, both belong to the same self-state. That is, never do the one who lives and the one who knows and feels the living completely overlap in time. We are always living a moment that we cannot yet feel or represent to ourselves. We must wait to know and feel until—as Proust understood—we have gained enough distance to remember. Frequently, as we live a moment, we exist right on the cusp of representing it to ourselves. In these cases the time lag between living and experiencing is very brief, so quick that, even if we are on the lookout for it, we can hardly sense it.

That is the way we make conscious experience at moments when it is not particularly painful to do so: living and experiencing are nearly simultaneous, but not quite so. But at other times the gap between living and experiencing is longer—seconds or minutes, yes; but sometimes that normal gap stretches into months or years, or even forever, especially when what we would know if we represented it to ourselves is just too awful to bear. Postponement is one way to deal with intolerable pain.

In whatever time passes between living and representation, our experience is what I have called unformulated (Stern, 1983, 1997), existing in a state of potential. And we use the word "dissociation" to refer to the process by which psychic pain has the effect of stretching out the delay between living and representation, so that experience must remain unformulated for defensive reasons (Stern, 1997, Chapters 6 and 7). Dissociation is an ever-present possibility in any personality, although of course the more trauma one has suffered, the more frequently the representation of one's experience to oneself feels intolerable—and so the greater the frequency with which the gap between living and knowing lengthens. In these latter cases, because the part of the mind that does the living is inaccessible to the rest of the personality, sequestered from the sense of self, there can be no representation.

The inevitable existence of the gap between living and knowing, even when psychic pain is not particularly intense and the lag is therefore brief, means that we never know exactly what we are doing, thinking, and feeling, or what we are about to do, think, or feel. In this sense, living and its experience are a continuous surprise. This is true for each one of us individually; but if you add to that uncertainty the fact that our capacity to anticipate the other's experience is at least as limited as our capacity to anticipate our own; and then you consider that the way these two unpredictable sources of subjectivity come together—the way we are each affected by the other's living and its representation—contributes yet another layer of complexity; *then* you have some sense of the emergent properties of the interpersonal field. The possibilities are limitless, and that recognition, when it breaks over you, is breathtaking. The field is a thing of endless mystery.

The chapters of this book

This book is titled with an idea that appears explicitly in Chapter 5 ("Relational freedom and therapeutic action"). When you, the reader, reach that chapter, I think it will be clear why the book has taken its title from it. "Relational freedom" is the state of the therapeutic relationship in which the field is most free to assume whatever shapes and contents it tends toward—that is, when its emergent properties are most free to shape it without the constrictions introduced by unconscious defensive intervention on the part of either the patient or the analyst. In my frame of reference, when the field is free, the *experience* of both patient and analyst is free, as well. Relational freedom, then, leads to the freedom to experience. Thus, the theme of emergence, which I have taken up in this introductory chapter, lies at the heart of the idea of relational freedom; and that is why the subtitle of this book, *Emergent Properties of the Interpersonal Field*, constitutes an elaboration of the title, *Relational Freedom*. Relational freedom is the state of the therapeutic relationship in which the interpersonal field is relatively free to be shaped by its emergent properties.

Now let me offer a brief introduction to the remaining chapters.

Chapter 2, "The interpersonal field: its place in American psychoanalysis." Today the concept of the interpersonal field, while seldom credited to those who created it, is widely used in psychoanalysis. After reviewing how the concept of the field defines interpersonal and relational psychoanalysis, especially in the work of Harry Stack Sullivan and Erich Fromm, I take up the rejection of the idea in American classical psychoanalysis in the decades just after it was proposed by Sullivan and Fromm in the 1930s and 1940s, why that rejection took place, and how the entire discipline of psychoanalysis in North America might have fared if the idea had been more widely recognized earlier than it was.

Chapter 3, "Field theory in psychoanalysis, part I: comparing Madeleine and Willy Baranger, and Harry Stack Sullivan." The theory of the interpersonal field is not the only kind of field theory in psychoanalysis today. Bionian field theory, introduced by Madeleine and Willy Baranger and carried forward in the work of Antonino Ferro and Giuseppe Civitarese, has drawn the attention of psychoanalysts all over the world. Chapters 3 and 4 compare the two varieties of psychoanalytic field theory. In Chapter 3 I compare the thinking of the Barangers with the work of the most influential of the founders of interpersonal psychoanalysis, Harry Stack Sullivan.

Chapter 4, "Field theory in psychoanalysis, part II: comparing Bionian field theory and contemporary interpersonal/relational psychoanalysis" is a comparison of Bionian field theory, especially the thinking of Antonino Ferro, with the field theory, usually implicit, in contemporary interpersonal and relational psychoanalysis. These two chapters are somewhat expanded versions of the originally published journal articles.

Chapter 5, "Relational freedom and therapeutic action," is intended to be a contribution to the theory of the interpersonal field. In this chapter I describe what I call "relational freedom," a phenomenon that for me precedes our capacity for interpretation and makes it possible. It is the relaxation of constrictions in the interpersonal field that creates the possibility for new experience, including new understanding. For me, new relational freedom sometimes opens into the analyst's capacity to offer a new interpretation and the patient's capacity to accept it. From this perspective, therapeutic action is less often the result of the interpretation than it is of the relaxation of the field that preceded it. In fact, interpretation is for me very often only a secondary influence on therapeutic action. In this account, I give particular emphasis to the emergent properties of the interpersonal field by suggesting that field constrictions have the effect, by reducing relational spontaneity, of inhibiting the freedom to experience.

Chapter 6, "Witnessing across time: accessing the present from the past and the past from the present," expands on the idea of witnessing that I introduced in earlier articles (Stern, 2009a, 2009b), which also appeared in my last book, *Partners in Thought: Working with Unformulated Experience, Dissociation, and Enactment* (Stern, 2010a; see Chapters 5 and 6). The theme of the felt sense of emergence in the field is taken up here via an exploration of Freud's *Nachträglichkeit* and its links with metaphor. I introduce in this chapter the idea that, just as trauma in the past inhibits the freedom to fully experience the present, trauma in the present can destroy the capacity to experience the goodness of the past. Trauma is one of those phenomena—probably the primary one—that has the dissociative effect on the psyche of lengthening the gap between experience and representation. Dissociation interrupts the expression of the emergent properties of the field.

Chapter 7, "Unconscious phantasy and unconscious relatedness," is an explanation of why the concept of unconscious phantasy, central to so much psychoanalytic theorizing, is not part of the thinking of many interpersonal and relational analysts. One reason for this difference is that the existence of fully formed unconscious phantasy is inconsistent both with the understanding of unconscious processes as unformulated experience and with dissociation as the primary defense. A second reason comes to light in examining the clinical material that this chapter was originally written to discuss. This clinical material was composed by a clinician who identifies himself as Freudian, and so it is not surprising that the material itself—i.e., the clinical report—was significantly shaped by the clinician's understanding of the formative unconscious phantasy in his patient's mind. At the same time, the analyst's subjectivity was completely missing from his clinical account, revealing the absence of a conception of the field. The way he used the concept of unconscious phantasy—i.e., as if it were "endogenous," without regard to its place in the analytic interaction—was feasible at least partly because of this absence.

Chapter 8, "Implicit theories of technique and the values that inspire them," suggests that many of our theories of technique come about spontaneously (emergently), growing from value commitments that we may or may not have thought through. All theories of technique and therapeutic action, I contend, are basically statements of values, and should be recognized as such. To do so allows us to compare different psychoanalytic positions more realistically than we can if we limit our attention to intellectual commitments.

Chapter 9, "Psychotherapy is an emergent process," examines some of the outcomes resulting from taking the position that psychotherapy is an emergent process that is based on a conception of the continuous, spontaneous flux of the interpersonal field. We should be careful not to privilege empirical, quantitative research findings in describing how psychotherapy should be conducted, and we should not judge psychotherapy outcomes by this standard, either. It is perfectly acceptable to use quantitative research findings as inspirations for new thoughts about clinical practice, in the same way that we use any other findings (e.g., case reports). We should privilege hermeneutics in thinking about psychotherapy: we need to consider ceaselessly the meanings of what we do, and keep open the possibilities. This position, while it is uncontroversial among psychoanalysts, goes against the grain of the culture, which favors evidence-based treatment.

Chapter 10 is a discussion of "The hard-to-engage patient." The treatment I discuss here was a failure, and the chapter is an examination of how such failures can be understood. The primary problem for me with this patient, who I was fond of, was an absence of curiosity and engagement, which I understand as an internal barrenness—which, in turn, is the consequence of a severe constriction of the field, or mutual enactment, i.e., what I have referred to in this introductory chapter as the inhibition of the field's emergent properties.

Chapter 11, "Curiosity: dealing with divergent ideas in the ideal psychoanalytic institute," is a contribution to the ongoing discussion of how best to train psychoanalysts. It is a vexing problem: should we inculcate certain ideas, or teach openness to the variety of psychoanalytic theories? I choose the latter alternative, and I present an argument based on the emergent properties of the analytic field to support my position.

Notes

1 Sometimes, Stuart Pizer (personal communication, 2014) points out, an episode of felt emergence takes place at a moment when a clinical collaboration is not particularly notable—although even at those times, the episode seems to depend on *previous* collaboration. He writes, "I have experienced certain moments of emergence as the yield of a *preceding* period of collaboration. This happened with one patient, for example, after a weekend that followed weeks of collaborative process. On that particular day, though, the collaboration was not particularly foregrounded or explicitly experienced. The immediate impetus for the sense of emergence we both experienced was that she took a step based on the earlier work . . . and we were there."
2 See also Hoffman (1998), whose "dialectical-constructivist" presentation of conscious experience as the outcome of the relation of an explicit foreground to an implicit background is similar in certain respects to what Foehl has to say here.
3 This vaguely experienced background is what phenomenological and existential philosophers such as Merleau-Ponty and Gadamer mean by "being." Being is never fully manifest. It is always *more* than consciousness—but "more" in a way that has no explicit meaning yet. And so we can think of the experience of depth as the impression created by our awareness of the contextualization of consciousness in being. Gadamer (1960) calls being "the infinity of the unsaid" (pp. 443–44; this phrase translated and quoted by D. E. Linge, 1976). He writes that the shape of the unsaid, which changes with the content being expressed in words, plays an important role in establishing the meaning of whatever *is* said.
4 In my frame of reference, what is missing in the experience of enactment is dissociated. Dissociated subjectivity is a significant portion of what I refer to as unformulated experience (Stern, 1997). Remember that Foehl suggests if experience loses the "affective resonance and fullness" of depth, it becomes either "flattened into an univocal regularity" (see the text) or dispersed into "an undifferentiated haze of not specifying what might be experienced" (p. 298). The latter phrase is a good description of what I mean by unformulated experience. What I would say, then, in Foehl's terms, is that enactment leads to a flattening of conscious experience and the maintenance of the dissociated portion in a kind of undifferentiated, unsymbolized haze (see Stern, 1997, Chapters 3, 6, and 7).
5 For clinical illustrations of enactment and its resolution, see Stern (1997), Chapters 5, 7, and 10; Stern (2010a), Chapters 1, 3–6, and 8; and Chapter 5 of the present book.
6 To offer an account of multiple self theory here would distract from my primary argument. But I do think of enactment in those terms. For presentations of that view, see Stern (2004, 2010a).

Chapter 2

The interpersonal field
Its place in American psychoanalysis

The politics of the field

Interpersonal and relational psychoanalysis are both centered on the concept of the field—call it the interpersonal field or the relational field, it doesn't matter. This is a very broadly defined field theory. What I mean when I refer to the concept of the field, and what I believe is implicit in most, and perhaps all, interpersonal and relational writings, is simply that the analytic situation is defined in terms of its relatedness. Analyst and patient are continuously and inevitably, and consciously and unconsciously, in interaction with one another. This interaction has to do with what they experience in one another's presence, and how they behave. The field also determines what each participant can experience in the presence of the other, especially the affective aspects of experience. The field is, on one hand, the sum total of all those influences, conscious and unconscious, that each of the analytic participants exerts on the other. On the other hand, the field is the outcome of all those influences, the relatedness and experience that are created between the two people as a result of the way they deal with one another.

How can the field be both the influences and the outcome of those same influences? The question is really how it could be anything else. Because as soon as there is an outcome in the field—as soon as the field changes to accommodate the influences supplied by its participants—that outcome becomes part of the influence on the next moment of relatedness. Like the influences that pass back and forth, outcomes in the field are not necessarily conscious. And so the sequence continues: each moment of influence in the field interacts with the personalities of those who are influenced to create the next moments of relatedness; and those moments of relatedness, in turn, are part of the conscious and unconscious influences on each participant's experience of the moment after that. The concept of the field is what was unique about views of the early interpersonal psychoanalysts, and it is what distinguished their views from the mainstream psychoanalysis of their day. In the current era the field has become such an intrinsic part of interpersonal and relational psychoanalysis that it is seldom theorized or even explicitly considered.

In this chapter I review some of the most important sources of field theory in interpersonal and relational psychoanalysis, and then discuss some of the politics that have played roles in the dissemination of this crucial idea. I will not explicate other varieties of field theory for the time being. For a review of these developments in Freudian, Kleinian, and Bionian terms, see Brown (2011b). In Chapter 3, I compare the field theory of Madeleine and Willy Baranger to Harry Stack Sullivan's field thinking; and in Chapter 4, I compare the Bionian field theory of Antonino Ferro and Giuseppe Civitarese, among others, to the field theory of contemporary interpersonal and relational psychoanalysis.

Sullivan's conception of the field

The concept of the field in interpersonal theory began in the work of Harry Stack Sullivan, Erich Fromm, Frieda Fromm-Reichmann, and Clara Thompson. Sullivan's work was the most important conceptual influence. For him the field was the arena of what he called "interpersonal relations," and it was, in turn, interpersonal relations that formed the core of his entire system of thought, as well as his understanding of the difference between his thought and the psychoanalysis of his time.

Although field theory was intrinsic to Sullivan's theorizing, central to everything he wrote, constructing a theory of the field was not in itself the point of Sullivan's work. In fact, Sullivan rarely wrote about field theory explicitly. To grasp the way he conceptualized it one must locate his statements on the subject in various places in his writings. One must also draw implications and conclusions about his views of the field from the way he continuously employed the idea. This attitude toward the field concept—i.e., that it is always crucial and yet seldom addressed in so many words—has been maintained over the years in interpersonal and relational psychoanalysis.

One of Sullivan's (1947b) most explicit descriptions of his conception of the field appears in his 1947 article, "The study of psychiatry: Three orienting lectures."

People behave in interpersonal fields. The patterns of their performance reveal the field forces by virtue of the people's susceptibility to these forces; but, unlike . . . iron filings, these people who in their behaving reveal the interpersonal fields are to an extraordinary extent the result of their past experiences with interpersonal fields. It does not make a great deal of difference so far as today's "behavior" is concerned whether a particular particle of iron has always or only very occasionally been subject to a strong magnetic field. The time sequence of historic exposure to interpersonal fields may greatly affect the "traits" which a particular person can be said to manifest in a new interpersonal field. Past experience in interpersonal fields, and the time pattern of such experiences, may greatly affect one's susceptibility . . . in the fields in which one participates . . . The first step towards this science has seemed to be the observation and analysis of behavior in interpersonal fields . . . .

The people in, and in a sense constituting an interpersonal field are more or less aware of the tensions and energy transformations which occur. They have all the primary data there is. If you are one of them and if you are skillful enough, you may be able to observe the progress of events, tensions, and energy transformations well enough to have something to analyze, and on which to base inferences. As your skill increases, you will be able to validate inferences, your provisional hypothesis about events, by influencing the interpersonal field.

(p. 10)

A few years earlier Sullivan (1940) had written this about the field, in his book, *Conceptions of Modern Psychiatry*:

When we speak of impulse to such and such action, of tendency to such and such behavior, of striving towards such and such goal, or use any of these words which sound as if you, a unit, have these things in you and as if they can be studied by and for themselves, we are talking according to the structure of our language and the habits of common speech, about something which is observedly manifested as action in a situation. The situation is not just any old thing, it is you and someone else integrated in a particular fashion which can be converted in the alembic of speech into a statement that "A is striving toward so and so from B." As soon as I say this, you realize that B is a very highly significant element in the situation . . . The situation is . . . the valid object of study, or rather, that which we can observe; namely, the action which indicates the situation and character of its integrations.

(p. 46)

For Sullivan, then, the interpersonal field is a continuous, inevitable, social aspect of human living. It is not specifically a psychoanalytic conception in his frame of reference but an omnipresent, concrete, empirical reality, a sociological and psychological phenomenon that permeates and helps to constitute every moment of every human being's life. It is not possible for a person to exist outside a field. Even when one is alone, one is the product of the interpersonal fields in which one has come to be, and one's experience continues to take its meaning from them, and to contribute to their continuing evolution.

Note that the first, long quotation above begins, "People behave in interpersonal fields." Unlike most other psychoanalytic conceptions of the field, such as that of the Barangers (1961–62/2008, 2009), Sullivan's idea is not limited to the *experience* people have with one another. Sullivan's focus is broader in this respect; he is interested in the field as the medium of people's *conduct* with one another. He is interested, in other words, in the field as the medium of their *ways of behaving, experiencing, and being*.

Sullivan understood participation in the field to be the source of the analyst's interventions. He saw that the analyst could only learn what he needed to know about the patient, and could only intervene in the ways productive to the treatment, if he allowed himself to feel and observe the nature of his involvement with the patient.

Current interpersonal relations, thought Sullivan, have their roots in history but are not properly understood as flies in amber, i.e., as unchanged leftovers of the past somehow orphaned in the present. Murphy and Cattell (1952, pp. 174–75), writing about Sullivan's field theory soon after Sullivan's death, say that,

Strictly speaking, the past as such is not properly used in the formulation of field events; the past has, so to speak, its surrogate, its aftermath, in the present; we cannot mix past events as such in the field forces which are the determination of each individual's conduct. Sullivan was aware of the problem and termed it "the most difficult element in the field theory of interpersonal relations."

(pp. 174–75)

These authors felt that field theory in psychotherapy, up to the time of their article in 1952, had "failed to clarify the fact that it is only the present—rich as it is in heirlooms from the past—*only* the teeming present that counts" (p. 175). Nevertheless, they argued, Sullivan "did as much to bring us face to face with the field realities as any man of this present era" (p. 176).

In Sullivan's frame of reference, psychotherapy is not unique, but rather a special instance of the interpersonal field that occurs everywhere in life. The psychotherapist, then, cannot avoid creating, and then participating in, a field with the patient, and an understanding of this fact was therefore, for Sullivan, the source of psychotherapeutic expertise. The therapist who grasps field theory uses it to observe objectively the nature of her involvement with her patient—not only what she experiences, but the otherwise obscure meanings of what she actually *does*. Sullivan believed that therapists could take this involvement into account, channeling their participation into whatever course best served the patient's interest. "We can improve our techniques for participant observation," wrote Sullivan (1940), using the term he adopted to describe his clinical attitude and approach, "in an interpersonal situation in which we are integrated with our subject-person. This is evidently THE procedure of psychiatry. I urge it as implying the root-premise of psychiatric methodology" (p. 5; capital letters in the original).

Over time in interpersonal and relational psychoanalysis, serious questions arose about whether Sullivan was right about this—that is, whether the capable psychotherapist routinely should be able to observe the important aspects of her own participation. It began to be understood that the analyst was involved with the patient in a way that, while maintaining the behavioral and experiential reciprocity Sullivan describes, did not necessarily allow the analyst's consistent, conscious observation of this reciprocal involvement. A significant portion of the analyst's participation in the field, in other words, not only the meanings of her inner experience but also the significance of her conduct with the patient, began to be understood to take place outside the analyst's awareness; and so the analyst's expertise was therefore no longer defined by her "objective" knowledge of her involvement, but by what she was able to do analytically with the less-than-transparent situation in which she found herself with the patient. (As constructivism increasingly dominated relational psychoanalysis, of course, Sullivan's belief in the analyst's objectivity was itself questioned.) Countertransference began to be understood to be composed not only of the analyst's inner experience, but also of the meanings embodied in his behavior. The analyst's direct, unconsciously motivated participation with the patient in ongoing relatedness began to be seen as inevitable. Theories of therapeutic action evolved into new forms. Change began to be conceptualized as a process in which unconscious enactments were first mutually created by patient and analyst, then explored and negotiated between them.

Edgar Levenson (1972, 1983, 1991), the pioneer in moving from Sullivan's position to the contemporary interpersonal and relational model of the field, described what he called the analyst's unconscious "transformation" by the field and then his struggle to grasp this transformation and use this understanding to the patient's benefit. The analyst could be understood to be involved in the same way with the patient as the patient was with the analyst, including the same lack of awareness of a substantial portion of this involvement. There was a leveling, a democratizing, of analytic relatedness.

Let me just cite a bit more from that early interpersonal literature of the field. Benjamin Wolstein (1959; Bonovitz, 2009) referred in 1959 to the routine unconscious "interlock" of transference and countertransference. Even earlier, Edward Tauber (1954; Tauber and Green, 1959) held that there inevitably existed a spontaneous, preconscious and unconscious, "prelogical" stream of experience in the analyst that was responsive to the interpersonal field and that therefore was inevitably an important source of information about the unconscious parts of the relatedness between patient and analyst, and about both analyst's and patient's unconscious minds. Tauber even recommended that the analyst tell the patient about some of these phenomena, particularly those of the analyst's dreams in which the patient appeared, as a way of perhaps awakening between the two a new appreciation of the unconscious aspects of the field. Wolstein and Tauber are just two of those early interpersonalists besides Levenson who could be cited in this context; for others, see Lionells *et al.* (1995).

Today, this kind of broadened understanding of the analyst's position in the field lies at the heart of both interpersonal and relational psychoanalysis (e.g., Bass, 2001, 2008; Ehrenberg, 1974; Gill, 1982; Hoffman, 1983; Mitchell, 1988; Aron, 1996; Bromberg, 1998; Hirsch, 2014). For these analysts, a capable clinician is therefore not necessarily one who knows the truth, or what is in the patient's mind, or even what is in the analyst's own mind. The analyst has opinions about these matters, of course, and may feel strongly enough about them to argue in favor of them or defend them. But given what she believes is the reality of her unconscious involvement, and the ambiguity of the unconscious (see Stern, 1997), she cannot be sure. She cannot be sure *that* she knows, and she cannot be sure, even if she thinks she does know something, *why* she knows. What kind of unconscious participation might her knowing be? The analyst continuously tries to imagine and reimagine the ways in which the contents of her own mind, and the meanings of her own conduct, may be playing a role in the unconscious aspects of relatedness with the patient. We can say, of course, that the analyst hopes to create thoughtful and emotionally responsive understandings of the patient, herself, and the ongoing clinical process; but she also hopes to maintain a radical uncertainty that, when necessary, will allow her to reimagine these understandings as unconscious participations with the patient.

Let me finish this brief consideration of Sullivan's thinking about the interpersonal field by quoting a passage that Sullivan (1947a) wrote for the tenth anniversary issue of *Psychiatry: Journal for the Study of Interpersonal Processes*, the journal he founded. Keep in mind as we go on from here that this passage from 1947 refers to the contrast between Sullivan's own views and the psychoanalysis of that time:

> it is perhaps timely at this point . . . to comment on the often unnoticed difference between psychoanalysis and psychoanalytically oriented psychiatry and psychiatry as the study of interpersonal relations. In a word interpersonal theory is a field theory, the others are anchored to consideration of the individual as the central fact in his interaction with his environment. Both the interpersonal and psychoanalytically oriented theories pay a good deal of attention to the developmental history of personality—in the first case, defined as the relatively enduring patterns of recurrent interpersonal relations—and to the relationship of past vicissitudes to present peculiarities in living; but with very significantly different frames of reference and techniques for exploring and attempting to effect favorable change.
>
> (p. 434)

Erich Fromm and the early interpersonal analysts

One cannot really overemphasize how influential Sullivan was in the adoption of the concept of the field among interpersonalists. At the same time, the concept of the field would not have become what it did without Erich Fromm, the other guiding light of the early interpersonal group. Fromm was trained at the Berlin Institute, and unlike Sullivan, considered himself very much a psychoanalyst. He shared enough of Sullivan's criticisms of the mainstream psychoanalysis of his day, primarily North American ego psychology, to join with Sullivan and others in the 1940s to form the White Institute. But the two men also often clashed, and when they did, it was frequently over how influential certain typically psychoanalytic ideas and practices ought to be. Clara Thompson (1950, 1964) brought Sullivan's interpersonal relations together with Fromm's psychoanalytic views and was among the first to see and develop the psychoanalytic possibilities that could be developed from Sullivan's perspective.[1] Thompson, too, had traditional psychoanalytic roots. She had been President of the American Psychoanalytic Association fairly early in its history, and then resigned with a group of colleagues from the New York Psychoanalytic Institute over the Institute's treatment of Karen Horney (see footnote 4). Thompson saw that Sullivan's theory of interpersonal relations could be melded with Fromm's thinking to create a field theory that included elements of existential and traditional psychoanalytic ideas.

Other early writers who brought a psychoanalytic sensibility to Sullivan's work (and Fromm's) included Harry Bone, Ralph Crowley, Janet Rioch, Erwin Singer, Rose Spiegel, and Edward Tauber (see Stern *et al.*, 1995). Later, Edgar Levenson (1972, 1983, 1991, 1992), Benjamin Wolstein (1959, 1964), and (in a different, more theoretical way) Ernest Schachtel (1959) found their way to a psychoanalysis rooted in both a traditional analytic sensibility and what each writer took from their reading of Fromm and Sullivan. (For an encyclopedic review of this entire set of developments, see Lionells *et al.*, 1995.)

The early interpersonalists were excited about the focus in Sullivan's work on what happened between people. But they were more interested in psychoanalysis than Sullivan was; they were more like Fromm in this respect. In fact, Sullivan, despite the influence of his writings, most of which were collected and shaped after his death from notes and unpublished manuscripts, may not have been the primary *clinical* influence on the early interpersonalists. In saying this, I don't mean to diminish the impression of Sullivan's influence on the clinical and developmental *conceptions* held by these analysts, or to dilute the enormous influence Sullivan has had on how to think about clinical process, what Sullivan (1954) called "the detailed inquiry." Rather, I mean that it was his conceptual influence and his understanding of the clinical inquiry, and not his personal, clinical example and direct clinical teaching, that carried the most weight with his students and colleagues.

Where did the more experiential clinical influence come from, then? In 1979 or 1980, near the end of my psychoanalytic training, I interviewed the most senior analysts at the William Alanson White Institute, many of whom were my teachers during my analytic training there. I was about 30 years old at the time, and I was fascinated by the history these people embodied. I wish I had notes of those conversations, but I don't. One thing I remember clearly, though, was that none of those very senior clinicians told me that clinical supervision with Sullivan had inspired them, while every single one of them cited as formative their clinical contact with Fromm in supervision and clinical seminars. They all characterized Fromm as charismatic, cantankerous, and honest to a fault, and as one of their most powerful clinical influences. Many of them went further than that, telling me that Fromm was simply their *most* significant clinical influence. He taught them to value aspects of clinical work that were different from Sullivan's careful and thoughtful detailed inquiry: Fromm taught candidates a different kind of field theory, one in which analytic work was no less conceptually interpersonal than it was in Sullivan's model, but which added to Sullivan's understanding a recommendation for the analyst to be, and to encourage, directness, spontaneity, affective vitality, and personal authenticity (e.g., Tauber, 1959). These things mattered more to Fromm than the careful construction of the patient's interpersonal relations. For Fromm, rooted as he was in existentialism, psychoanalysis needed to be a powerful and life-changing *experience* for the patient. Understanding needed to be more than an intellectual grasp. It needed to be emotionally alive. That view has been controversial at certain times in psychoanalytic history (e.g., Ferenczi and Rank, 1925), but it is hard to imagine any interpersonal or relational clinician today taking issue with it. In fact, today affect and authenticity are virtual sacred cows in interpersonal and relational circles. And yet we all know that, even today, analysts often profess such views more effectively than they practice them. Clinically productive honesty and effective clinical spontaneity are reasonably rare and, ironically enough, require great discipline.

And yet Fromm apparently did practice that way, if his writings and the testimony of his students are to be believed. He taught that the analyst should speak to the patient in a way that he described as "core-to-core" (Kwawer, 1975). The creation and preservation of vitality were more significant to him than "data" of any kind ("data" being a word that Sullivan often used to refer to the significant aspects of what a psychiatrist learns about a patient). The analyst's role was to tell the patient the truth. Let the chips fall where they may.

What I learned about Fromm's influence on that first generation of interpersonal analysts is important for my purpose today, because Fromm was not only an existential, clinical iconoclast; he also felt strongly about the necessity for concepts of the inner world and internal structure, and depended heavily on concepts of unconscious process, transference, and countertransference. But despite sharing these commitments with the writers who eventually established interpersonal psychoanalysis, Fromm's influence in that literature is less obvious than Sullivan's because, even though clinical work was central in his life, Fromm's writing, with certain key exceptions, focused on social criticism (e.g., Fromm, 1941, 1947). Fromm never wrote the clinical book he always said he intended to write (but see Fromm, 1955, 1964/1991; Fromm *et al.*, 1970; and to get a sense of his clinical work and presence, see also Feiner, 1975; Kwawer, 1975, 1991; Tauber, 1959; Landis, 1981; Schecter, 1981). And so the literature of interpersonal psychoanalysis in general, and of the interpersonal field in particular, does not reflect the degree of his influence on the fledgling interpersonal group. Fromm's influence on clinical practice and conceptions was enormous, but largely invisible when looking back to that time from our own era.

Sullivan, meanwhile, while his personal influence was probably less powerful, wrote with originality and precision about clinical matters, so that his writings have had an impact that has lasted far longer than the lives of those who knew him personally, and in fact has probably grown over the years. Fromm's influence, on the other hand, existed then, and exists now, in what his students learned directly from him about clinical psychoanalytic work, and in their identifications with him as a clinician—that is, more in the kind of work they did, and that the following generations of their students still do, than in the explicit thoughts most of these practitioners have written down about the nature of psychoanalysis. In the end, though, I believe that Fromm influenced interpersonal field theory as much as Sullivan did.

Politics, love, and loyalties

Sullivan, Fromm, Fromm-Reichmann, and Thompson began to publish their work in the 1930s, escalating their efforts in the 1940s.[2] By the 1950s these analysts and their colleagues had trained a large group of young interpersonalists, who continued the task of developing interpersonal theory, which Sullivan had initially created as a theory of psychiatry, into a body of thought that this second generation of interpersonalists explicitly intended to be a theory of psychoanalysis. And those analysts then taught third and fourth generations of interpersonalists, many of whom are still practicing and publishing today. In the 1980s, many of these contemporary interpersonalists joined with colleagues who had trained in other traditions to create the first wave of relational analysts. Not all interpersonal and relational analysts have agreed on significant theoretical and clinical issues, including their characterizations of one another (see, for example, the exchange between Hirsch [1997, 1998] and Frankel [1998a, 1998b]), but it has always been unmistakable that interpersonalists and relational analysts have a great deal in common, field theory being perhaps the most important of the ideas they share and the most likely to be jointly embraced.

And yet despite a substantial literature on the interpersonal field and a history of 50 years, a wide recognition that the field lies at the heart of clinical practice was not really even considered in the mainstream psychoanalysis of the United States until, at the very earliest, the 1980s. Even in the 1980s, if one were looking for field theory in the American mainstream literature, the only forthright exponent of this way of thinking was Merton Gill (1982).[3] Gill was a lone voice in the mainstream literature of those days, though, and many of us suspected that it was only the prestige he had earned for his earlier, ego psychological work that made it possible for him to publish this new, more social theory in large-circulation psychoanalytic journals, such as the *Journal of the American Psychoanalytic Association*. It was really only in the 1990s that interpersonal field theory began to have a substantial impact on writing in the wider psychoanalytic world in the United States (see Hirsch, 1996). Even today, of course, while the significance of the interpersonal field is widely recognized, the idea remains controversial in some quarters, in which it is sometimes incorrectly claimed that field theory does away with the conception of the individual mind (see, for example, Busch, 2001).

Our commitments to the ideas we love, no matter how reasonable those theories may be, ultimately derive from the deepest kinds of intentions. Because I am a psychoanalyst, it is axiomatic for me that my own deepest intentions, like anyone's, are not simply rational. They are affect-laden expressions of the themes in my life that have had the most to do with defining me and my mind—desires, disappointments, hopes, and fears. One cannot divide such intentions into neat categories. That is, while I can identify my intention to capture clinical and intellectual phenomena in language and thought, my intentions go far beyond anything as rational as that. My intentions, and my theoretical commitments, are personal, historical, somatic, moral-political, and aesthetic. Above all, and whatever else they are, they are passionate. However thoughtful we may also be, we are all significantly nonrational beings. Our relation to ideas is deep, complicated, and affectively charged. And so the history of the field concept in American psychoanalysis, being a history of ideas, is as much a political and moral story as it is an intellectual one, and it is passionate at every step of the way.

My involvement in that story is complicated, as all such matters are. I admired my teachers and mentors, and I loved some of them, and so I was deeply affected by the political impact on them of the issue of the field. From what I could observe, this impact was at least as much emotional as it was intellectual. My teachers suffered over the things that I will describe. And because they did, I did, too. Their suffering became mine. Of course, I suffered for my own reasons, as well. I was, and am, identified with the concept of the interpersonal field, and with the analysts who created and espoused it. This political/moral story was the background of my coming of age in the psychoanalytic world. It provided the context within which I trained, and the psychoanalytic world in which I developed my views.

And so I offer a brief history of some of the political/moral issues that surrounded the creation of the concept of the interpersonal field in the United States, and the failure of American mainstream psychoanalysts, for 50 years, to welcome the idea and its exponents into the establishment. The story concerns most centrally a relatively small group of psychoanalysts, especially at the beginning, when it was only interpersonal psychoanalysts who championed the idea. This small number of analysts grew over the years, and the significance of the issue grew even more quickly than the number of those who espoused it, until today the concept of the field is at least grudgingly acknowledged as central to current theorizing by even those North American psychoanalysts and psychodynamic psychotherapists who do not find it easy to accept it.[4]

When I was a candidate in psychoanalytic training, in the latter half of the 1970s, many, probably most, psychoanalysts of that era's mainstream believed that interpersonal psychoanalysis was too much concerned with "environmental" or sociological issues, and too little interested in the inner life, the intrapsychic world, the unconscious, or the mind. In those mainstream circles, interpersonal theory was often explicitly rejected, not infrequently with the accompanying suggestion that interpersonalists were not psychoanalysts at all.

The rejection was painful. It hurt the interpersonal analysts of that time, it made them angry and defensive, and it encouraged them to circle their wagons and talk mainly to one another. That was a reasonable enough attitude to take, since dialogue with their more traditional colleagues really wasn't possible. Things have changed now, thankfully, to a significant degree. There is more interchange between analysts from these schools of thought than there used to be, although, judging from what one might think we would all embrace as our commonalities, not as much as might be imagined. But at this point the reasons why we do not communicate with one another more often and deeply than we do are primarily historical. That is, at least to my eye, our distance from one another is more a leftover of the past than an expression of currently held attitudes. I have the impression that, among younger psychoanalysts, there is less contempt from contemporary Freudians, Kleinians, and Bionians toward interpersonal and relational analysts, and little resentment and defensiveness from those trained in interpersonal and relational institutes toward their more intrapsychically oriented colleagues. Most members of my generation, though—analysts in their 50s and 60s and older—must contend with some version of the old situation. For us, though we recognize the changes, and feel them, the old issues remain emotionally alive.

The more contemptuous characterizations of interpersonalists that used to be commonly held by other analysts seldom appeared in print. I suspect that is because there was at least some awareness that such views were not reasonably considered attitudes, but prejudices. Consider the outrageous characterization of the White Institute and the Horney Institute as "the fly-by-night institutes" by the New York Psychoanalytic Institute's "Dr. Aaron," the analyst who served as the primary, disguised informant in Janet Malcolm's (1981) book, *Psychoanalysis: The Impossible Profession*.

That kind of actively embraced prejudice is perhaps less objectionable to me, though, than what I believe was probably the other reason for the relative absence of print references to this contempt: a sense that it was simply unnecessary to actively denigrate interpersonalists, because they had no power at all in the rest of psychoanalysis. That is, in the wider psychoanalytic world, the claim of interpersonalists to be psychoanalysts not only posed no threat—it did not even really pose a challenge, at least not one that, in those days, had to be taken seriously. And so there are few scholarly references that convey the depth of the rejection, and for that reason the illustrations that can be cited tend to express a diluted form of the prejudice.

In a famous article in 1991, for instance—not very long ago, really—as liberal a mainstream analyst as James McLaughlin wrote that his own way of understanding unconscious enactment, "while *nominally* an interpersonal perspective . . . facilitates a more balanced attention to the involvement of both parties and to the intrapsychic dynamics in both that specifically shape these interactions" (McLaughlin, 1991, p. 595, italics added).

Now, this is hardly the most scurrilous comment I have ever read. On the other hand, one doesn't usually take the trouble to differentiate oneself from a group of one's colleagues, indicating that one wouldn't want to be identified with them. Instead, when the issue is just a matter of disagreement, the issue is stated straightforwardly, and one's position is made clear. In McLaughlin's passage we get the drift: those who hold an interpersonal perspective aren't members of the same club. McLaughlin wanted to be sure that no one would mistake *him* for one of *them*—even if he sort of sounds that way.

I don't mean to blame McLaughlin in particular. I don't even believe that the passage was intended to be patronizing. I think McLaughlin thought he was merely saying that his point of view, despite including a significant social aspect, was not interpersonal, and was therefore not shallow and social, but remained deep and traditionally intrapsychic. McLaughlin, a liberal thinker who shared much of substance with field theorists, seemed to take it so much for granted that no analyst would want to be described as interpersonal that it probably didn't even occur to him that what he wrote could be objectionable to some of his readers.[5]

Hirsch (1996), who quotes this same passage from McLaughlin on his way to a similar point, explains very well, I think, why mainstream psychoanalytic writers of that time felt this way. He points out that it was not so hard to understand why these analysts often believed that Sullivan's ideas about psychotherapy and personality constituted a temporally flattened and exclusively present-day version of human conduct and experience. After all, it was Sullivan's intention to create a theory of psychology and psychotherapy based on the observation and analysis of interpersonal relations. On top of that, Sullivan embraced the operationism of Percy Bridgman (1955), for whom all ideas and observations, even the most basic, were to be defined according to the operations used to make and measure them. This positivistic view is a limited way of thinking, one that few psychoanalysts of any stripe, including the interpersonalists who came after Sullivan, could embrace. And Sullivan's apostasy didn't stop there. He also positioned himself against the dominant psychoanalytic theory and practice of his day in many important respects. He excluded from significance the concept of biologically based drive and he challenged the inevitable centrality of the Oedipus complex. Hirsch also claims that Sullivan ignored the analysis of transference in his technique. Hirsch is right, I think, that Sullivan did not encourage the intensive involvement of the patient with the analyst, nor did he push to articulate the patient's emotional involvement with the analyst. (Although Fromm did both these things.) On the other hand, Sullivan was vitally interested in the patient's history and his early life, and he was interested in the unconscious ways in which these factors influenced current relationships.

And so there certainly was reason for mainstream analysts of that day to question whether they could accept Sullivan's stance. But the reaction of these analysts went far beyond that. The impression of many of them, I believe, was that Sullivan not only took issue with certain key parts of Freudian psychoanalysis, but also that he really did understand the interpersonal field exclusively as the product of contemporaneous sociological influences, ignoring the unconscious contribution and the past. And that was simply incorrect.

But even this mistaken understanding of Sullivan, Hirsch explains, would not necessarily have been enough, in and of itself, to result in the problem that eventually resulted. That is, this mistaken understanding of Sullivan was not actually the primary reason for the contempt leveled at interpersonalists. The primary reason for that contempt was that, for decades after Sullivan's death, the misunderstanding of Sullivan's views among traditional analysts, inaccurate in the first place, was taken by many of those analysts to be the sum total of the interpersonal psychoanalysis that *followed* Sullivan. The most common assessment by traditional psychoanalysts of interpersonal psychoanalysis, in other words, was doubly wrong: the interpersonal psychoanalysis that eventually began to be formulated by, among others, Thompson (1950, 1964), Levenson (1972, 1983), and Wolstein (1959, 1964), a body of thought that went far beyond Sullivan, was not only incorrectly equated with Sullivan's original views, but with a narrow, "sociological" version of Sullivan's views that had been wrong in the first place.[6]

If both the interpretations of interpersonal psychoanalysis that so often appeared in traditional psychoanalytic circles had been accurate, or at least reasonable—that is, if Sullivan's thinking had been as one-dimensional as these analysts believed it was, and if, decades after the death of Sullivan, his thinking had remained synonymous with interpersonal psychoanalysis (which it was not)—then the dismissive attitude toward interpersonal theory, while it still would not have been an acceptable response to colleagues, would have been at least understandable. But neither of these points held water.

Sullivan's neologisms and idiosyncratic syntax didn't help; his writing didn't sound or read like conventional psychoanalysis. (Not that most of the writers of any psychoanalytic school have been literary stylists!) And so classical analysts of the time, dismissing Sullivan, also dismissed the interpersonal literature that, despite being partly inspired by Sullivan, went far beyond his thinking.

The history I have reviewed to this point may actually have been preceded by a brief period of hopefulness. The following passage is from a recent article by Arnold Richards (2013) on the exclusionary practices of the American Psychoanalytic Association (APsaA).

> [D]espite APsaA's rigidity with regard to medical exclusivity, for a while after 1946 it seemed to be open to a certain amount of ideological diversity. After all, the Sullivanian/Interpersonal analysts of the William Alanson White Institute were members of APsaA by virtue of WAW's complicated relationship with the Baltimore Washington Institute (see Mosher & Richards, 2005, for more on this). But when that relationship ended—another complicated story—so did the hope for diversity within APsaA. The WAW analysts who were

members of APsaA sought independent affiliate status for WAW in the Association, and a committee was formed at BOPS [the Board on Professional Standards, the group in the American Psychoanalytic Association charged with defining principles and standards of psychoanalytic education] to consider their application. The deliberations dragged on for years. Finally Merton Gill, who was a member of the BOPS committee, told the WAW members that it would never happen, and they withdrew their application. Gill made it clear that the issue was more their ideology than the other old bone of contention, analytic frequency. This decision had fateful consequences for the American Psychoanalytic Association. It more or less closed the door on the possibility of amicable ideological differences, and doomed analysts who diverged from BOPS's view of orthodoxy to the status of dissidents at best, and heretics at worst.

(pp. 9–10)

And so interpersonal psychoanalysts, now shut out of the International Psychoanalytic Association and the American Psychoanalytic Association, as well as most psychoanalytic journals, had no alternative but to develop their own institutes, professional associations, and journals. This ostracism had a tendency to reinforce itself. As Hirsch (1996) says, "The interpersonal school's isolation lent itself to being ignored and demonized by the Freudian psychoanalytic mainstream" (p. 378). Starting in the 1930s, and accelerating through the years after that, American Freudian analysts missed many decades of the development of a new and original psychoanalytic point of view. Interpersonalists, for their part, suffered not only from the rejection and contempt they faced from those who would otherwise have been their natural colleagues, but also from the absence of an opportunity to belong to the larger national and international psychoanalytic associations that would have allowed them to exchange ideas with their more intrapsychically oriented colleagues. Later on, with the advent of relational psychoanalysis (Greenberg and Mitchell, 1983; Mitchell, 1988; Mitchell and Aron, 1999), with its deep roots in interpersonal theory, the whole interaction was repeated—although, as we know, this time around the outcome has been different, and better. Relational psychoanalysis, while it remains controversial in contemporary Freudian and neo-Kleinian circles, is taken seriously in those quarters in a way that interpersonal psychoanalysis, in the decades from the 1930s through the 1980s, was not. Recently, with the invitation to the White Institute to join the American Psychoanalytic Association, we have seen more evidence of the difference between our time and earlier, darker days. We have every reason to believe that this trend within our field will continue.

What exactly *was* the relationship of Sullivan's thinking to the interpersonal psychoanalysis that came after Sullivan died in 1949? As I have already said, as influential as Sullivan's work grew to be over time among those who came to think of themselves as interpersonalists, very few, if any, of those early analysts adopted Sullivan's ideas wholesale. These analysts looked at Sullivan's ideas as useful and inspiring, even crucial, but not as a theoretical endpoint. They admired the originality and incisiveness of the way that Sullivan's thinking addressed transactional matters—in both psychological development and clinical practice—that were completely ignored at that time in the wider psychoanalytic community. The world revealed itself differently through this new, transactional lens.

But those who eventually became the early interpersonal analysts also recognized that Sullivan's thinking was never intended to be psychoanalysis. Sullivan was doing something different. He thought of himself as a psychiatrist, not as a psychoanalyst, and, in fact, he actively resisted being labeled as a psychoanalyst. He may very well have believed that his work was an alternative to psychoanalysis; but however much his colleagues and students admired his thinking, those of them who were psychoanalysts, aspired to be, or were interested in psychoanalysis, did not take his views to be sufficient in and of themselves. While these analysts were sometimes quite critical of certain aspects of the dominant psychoanalytic theories of the era, they did not intend simply to replace Freud with Sullivan. What they wanted was to *meld* Sullivan's views with existing psychoanalytic thought. They wanted to create a new *kind* of psychoanalysis, one in which the interpersonal relations they had learned about through Sullivan played a larger and central role. Sadly, although that is what has eventually happened, few members of the first two generations of interpersonal analysts lived to see it.

What was missed?

What did North American mainstream analysts miss during the 50 years in which the concept of the interpersonal field was excluded from their conceptualizations? The historical notes I have just presented tell us something about that, I think. Interpersonal theory, partly because of Fromm and the influence he exerted, was a *psychoanalytic* theory; but few analysts from the American Psychoanalytic Association, most of whom were not reading interpersonal writing, knew that. As Hirsch (1996) observes, the early interpersonalists, along with Sullivan, rejected the centrality of drive and the Oedipus conflict; but they did elaborate distinctive interpersonal understandings of unconscious processes, the unconscious aspects of the analytic relationship, and the internal world. As far as I am concerned, it is possible to be a psychoanalyst without embracing drive and the inevitable significance of the Oedipus. However important these conceptions may be, they are parts of particular psychoanalytic theories, not attributes that any theory must have if it is to be called psychoanalytic. Drive and the Oedipus, to my mind, are not the essence of psychoanalysis.

There are other ideas, however, that *are* something like psychoanalytic essences. It is not possible to be an analyst and to do psychoanalytic work without conceptualizing unconscious processes, transference and countertransference, and the internal world. And the early interpersonalists were psychoanalysts in these respects: their work was rooted in their ways of conceptualizing these phenomena.

Contemporary American mainstream psychoanalytic thinking has become notably "interpersonalized." Evidence of this shift appears in virtually every issue of the very journals from which earlier generations of interpersonal writers were excluded. The trend has progressed far enough that, as a friend and colleague of mine (Blumberg, personal communication, 2013) points out, certain aspects of contemporary Freudian theory and practice remain "inscrutable" and "historically incoherent" if one does not relate them to the interpersonal theory that preceded them. In the same paper that I have been quoting, Hirsch (1996) points out that contemporary Freudian writers who address the basic nature of the analytic relationship often present ideas notably similar to earlier interpersonal conceptions—but without necessarily citing their interpersonal predecessors.

I believe that the mainstream writers Hirsch discusses were not consciously inspired by earlier interpersonal ideas; I believe that they did not necessarily know they were influenced by these ideas. I certainly don't intend to accuse anyone of intentionally depriving their predecessors of credit. These mainstream writers no doubt believed that they were developing their ideas about relationship independently. Given how little direct exposure most of them had to the interpersonal literature, that is easy to imagine. I believe that, in line with the absence of citations of their interpersonal predecessors, these writers actually did not read the interpersonal psychoanalytic literature. I believe they developed their ideas about clinical relatedness on their own, apart from the influence of interpersonal writings—at least apart from *direct* influence.

But the absence of direct, consciously accepted influence is not necessarily the same thing as the absence of all influence. It seems most likely to me that the mainstream contributions to thinking through the interpersonal field grew from a *Zeitgeist*, an intellectual groundswell more like an atmosphere than a specific set of scholarly references. This atmosphere grew, it seems to me, from interpersonal writings and sensibilities that had worked their way into the life of even the conservative part of our psychoanalytic culture.[7] Many mainstream analysts, perhaps even most, knew interpersonal ideas were there, but really knew very little about them. The largest portion of the influence, I think, took place outside the range of formal scholarship. I think this point probably applies most to North American Freudians, who were traditionally ego psychologists. The field developments in Kleinian and Bionian circles took place elsewhere and independently, first in South America in the 1960s (de Léon de Bernardi, 2000, 2008) and then in Italy; and only later, quite recently, were these developments imported into North America. That importation continues today. In this more recent North American Bionian literature, though, as in the Freudian literature, the fact that psychoanalysts of other schools had been contributing to theories of the field for many decades has gone largely unrecognized.[8] I leave it to readers, then, to decide whether the point I am about to make should apply to both the North American Kleinian and Bionian literature and to the North American Freudian literature, or only to North American Freudian writing. (Of course, I know that some readers will feel that it applies to neither!)

What I want to say is this: I believe that there is a case to be made that a significant portion of the North American mainstream psychoanalytic writers who have championed the significance of interpersonal transactions have become what they beheld. Like all such becoming, which is not due to the conscious, linear acquisition of explicitly stated knowledge, but to the absorption of unformulated influence (identification, if you will), it seems to make the most sense to imagine that the process took place without explicit awareness. While this kind of influence, because it is invisible, is very hard to credit properly, it is notably effective in the creation of ways of thinking that seem to be new but are not. Such ideas, since they are not visibly linked to their sources, can seem to have been created entirely within the minds of those who convey them. No doubt such writers often, even usually, sincerely believe that there are no significant predecessors of their views; in these cases, probably the majority, we can accept their ignorance that their thoughts were presaged by others.

But we are psychoanalysts, and so we also imagine cases in which writers are unconsciously motivated not to grasp the ways they have been influenced. To be indebted to a predecessor can feel confining, and the effect on one's narcissism can be less salutary than the perception that one has created something *de novo*. The one who is influenced, in other words, by "creatively misreading" the "strong poets" who have come before (or, in this case, creatively "not reading" them), can avoid what Harold Bloom (1973) famously described as "the anxiety of influence," and can feel instead that the new idea is wholly his or her own. We know from Bloom that this process is rampant among poets. And we know, too, that creative misreading should not be dismissed as nothing but secret coattail-riding, as if it were inconsistent with originality. Avoiding the acknowledgment of one's predecessors may not be good scholarship, but it is perfectly consistent with the production of significant contributions. That has been the case in literature, and it has been the case in psychoanalysis.

In any case, when one reads the psychoanalytic literature, it can seem as if a large proportion of psychoanalysts, from all schools, really "always knew" that the analyst and the patient continuously influence one another unconsciously. It can seem, that is, as if many of us, from many schools, always accepted the concept of the interpersonal field—or at least it can seem as if we all accepted it as soon as it came along. But of course that isn't true.

I have suggested that the ostracism of early interpersonal psychoanalysis by the dominant psychoanalysis of the time carried a cost for the mainstream of the day, because these analysts missed important developments that would have allowed them to take account of the therapeutic potential of the analytic relationship decades earlier than they began to do so. But I don't believe that this clinical and intellectual cost to the analytic establishment was the most significant injury done by this ostracism. Nor do I believe that the greatest injury was the damage done to the early interpersonalists, despite the personal and professional significance of their ostracism to the many individuals whose thought and work never received the attention it should have.

No, the greatest injury, I believe, was the damage done to the field of psychoanalysis as a whole, at least in the United States. It was not until the landmark book by Greenberg and Mitchell, *Object Relations in Psychoanalytic Theory* (1983), and then the enunciation of relational psychoanalysis by Mitchell (1988), that the early interpersonalists' ideas (now, in Mitchell's new relational theory, brought into conversation with object relations theory and self psychology) became a widely acknowledged alternative to conservative Freudian theory in the United States. And it was not really until a number of years after the first single-authored book by Mitchell in 1988 that relational psychoanalysis began to have an impact among contemporary American Freudian analysts.

By that time, psychoanalysis in the United States had already endured four or five decades of criticism by the culture at large, and had been either rejected or dismissed by a larger and larger proportion of those in the mental health field itself. Imagine how differently all this might have transpired if the institutional powers in American psychoanalysis had not represented the field of psychoanalysis during the latter half of the twentieth century in the way they did—a way that one might characterize, without resorting to hyperbole, as hidebound and out of touch, frozen in the same shape it had held for decades. What if, instead, there had been an effort, in presenting psychoanalysis to the world, to combine intrapsychic views with a recognition of the clinical significance of the present context, in interaction with the past—that is, the field? Imagine the American public image of psychoanalysis having included, in the 1960s and 1970s, an acceptance of the significance of the analyst's subjectivity, in addition to the traditional focus on the patient's.[9] Imagine psychoanalysts not having been analogized as coldly rational surgeons, doing whatever it took to excise diseased parts of the mind (were surgeons themselves ever complimented by this metaphor?), but instead as particular individuals who valued their personal contributions to the relationships they established with patients. Imagine having included in the portrayal of psychoanalysis the possibility of understanding treatment as an interaction between two particular individuals struggling toward relational change. Imagine having replaced, in the American public mind, the image of the analyst who knows the contents of the patient's mind, and is merely waiting for the opportunity to demonstrate it to the patient, with the image of the analyst as a collaborator, someone who may suspect but does not know the unconscious meanings of the patient's experience—or even his own—until these meanings are discovered/created in the interaction between the two participants.

Imagine, that is, having given the American public a reason to question the image of psychoanalysts as arrogant, out of touch, and rigid, offering instead the picture of analysts who are affectively present and interested in learning about their patients and the relationship they develop with them. Imagine, in other words, having included in the public portrayal of psychoanalysis in the United States an image derived from the analyst as part of the interpersonal field.

I hasten to acknowledge that the public images of psychoanalysis in this country have never been fair, or even realistic. Psychoanalysts as a group were never as rigid and authoritarian as their images in the culture at large (although certain individual analysts, of course, did fulfill this image). And analysts of all kinds, it goes without saying, can be affectively present.

But in the 1960s and 1970s there was little theoretical justification in the literature of mainstream psychoanalysis for working in an affectively present way that relied on the analyst's subjectivity. To think that way required some kind of concept of a field. Until the idea became available that no one, including the psychoanalyst, can avoid being unconsciously involved with the other, it was possible to believe that the analyst should judge his or her own professional conduct exclusively by a concept of proper technique. Analysts could preserve the belief, quaint in field theory, that their job was to figure out what kind of behavior (or lack thereof) would promote the psychoanalytic process, and then just go ahead and behave that way, without regard to the place of that behavior in the experience of the patient. Here is Roy Schafer (1992), for instance, someone I admire enormously for other reasons, describing what the analyst should say to a patient who "talks back"—that is, someone who tells the analyst what he or she thinks of what the analyst has said:

> [T]he analyst treats the analysand in the same manner that many literary critics treat authors—with interest in what the analysand says about the aims of his or her utterances and choices, but with an overall attitude of autonomous critical command rather than submission or conventional politeness, and with a readiness to view these explanatory comments as just so much more prose to be both heard as such *and* interpreted.
>
> (p. 176)

From the perspective of a psychology of the field, then, despite the fact that public portrayals of psychoanalysts were often caricatures, perhaps it is also true to say that there was a certain amount of truth in portrayals of psychoanalysts as silent, rigid, and authoritarian.

Whether or not it is fair to come to that conclusion, though, organized psychoanalysis—and in the United States, since the beginning of the discipline, that has meant the American Psychoanalytic Association—has never done enough to challenge these portrayals. That is partly because there has never been (and there is not, even now) sufficient agreement in American mainstream circles that the portrayal of the psychoanalyst as a participant in a jointly established interpersonal field is not only acceptable, but desirable.

There have been many reasons for the historical decline of psychoanalysis in the public mind and the professional world of the United States, and we all know perfectly well that not every one of those reasons had to do with the rigidity of organizational psychoanalysis and its attendant rejection of the field concept. But if that rejection had been avoided, or at least moderated, things would have turned out better for American psychoanalysis as a whole. There is no telling how different the status of psychoanalysis in American culture might be today, and how much more of its original influence the field might have maintained in the American mental health field. Today, interpersonal and relational psychoanalysis are healthy, perhaps healthier even than their mainstream cousins. But a great deal of damage has been done, and what might have been the possibility for a different kind of participation of psychoanalysis in American cultural life has been lost. I do maintain the hope that we can convey a different image of our discipline to the American public. We have wasted much of whatever opportunity we may have had; but I nevertheless nurture the hope that, at least partly because of the broad acceptance of some concept of the field that has developed over time in our discipline, we may perhaps reach for whatever portion of that opportunity remains. The next years will be interesting ones in North American psychoanalysis.

Notes

1 Thompson's work on this subject and others (see especially her early contributions to the psychology of women), most of which was originally published in the 1940s and 1950s, is available in the volume of her selected papers that appeared in 1964. Not all of these articles can be accessed on Psychoanalytic Electronic Publishing (PEP), though, because some of the journals that would accept interpersonal writing in those days (the mainstream ones would not) are still not part of PEP—e.g., *Samiksa*, the journal of the Indian Psychoanalytical Society.

2 Reference to the work of Sullivan, Fromm, and Thompson appears elsewhere in this chapter. Most of Fromm-Reichmann's work is collected in two volumes (Fromm-Reichmann, 1955, 1959).
3 Other mainstream writers of that era (e.g., see collections by Jacobs [1991] and McLaughlin [2005], which were published later but contain articles from the era being discussed) exemplified a field mentality, but without necessarily giving explicit expression to the idea. Mitchell (2000) urges that Loewald be recognized as a field theorist (see Chapter 5, footnote 2).
4 There are relevant historical points to be made here, in addition to those made in the text. I did my psychoanalytic training at the William Alanson White Institute in New York City, which has long been known as the source and home of interpersonal psychoanalysis. White has a long and complicated relationship with the American Psychoanalytic Association (APsaA), which, since its inception early in the twentieth century, has been the dominant psychoanalytic organization in the United States. Most of the founders of the White Institute were members of APsaA until they left their institute—the New York Psychoanalytic Institute—over that institute's treatment of Karen Horney. Horney's course at New York Psychoanalytic, which concerned cultural factors in psychoanalysis and her own ideas about treatment (both perspectives were highly controversial among the classical analysts of that era), was extremely popular with candidates, and apparently because of this, her course was moved from the first year to the fourth year, over her objections. Those who made this decision are said to have hoped that this action would diminish Horney's influence on candidates just beginning their training.

In response to this action, the story goes, a group of senior analysts, young analysts, and candidates left the institute and walked down the avenue singing "Go Down, Moses (Let My People Go)." They eventually banded together and formed a new institute, the American Institute of Psychoanalysis, headed by Horney. But within a very brief period, Erich Fromm was denied teaching privileges at this new institute, ostensibly because he had a Ph.D., not an M.D. (Matters may have been more complicated than that, although the question of Fromm's degree was apparently a genuine controversy.) At that point, Clara Thompson, Erich Fromm, and others left the Horney institute and joined with Frieda Fromm-Reichmann and Harry Stack Sullivan to form the William Alanson White Institute.

That was in 1946. The relationship between the White Institute and APsaA has been painful and complicated ever since.

I will mention some of this history in the remainder of this chapter. For the moment, let me just add a recent installment, a quite different and more positive development. Between two and three years ago, the APsaA Executive Council and the Bureau on Professional Standards each unanimously agreed to invite the White Institute to join APsaA, and to join on its own terms. APsaA decided that the White Institute training model was an acceptable variant of the Eitingon Model, which is the model in use by all APsaA institutes.

The members of the William Alanson White Psychoanalytic Society and Institute met and talked about the invitation intensively for the following two years. There was a good deal of controversy. In May of 2014 the Council of Fellows of the White Institute, which is the Institute's governing body, and to which I belong, voted to accept the APsaA invitation.
5 Interpersonal and relational analysts have always read the literature of the wider psychoanalytic world—the work of McLaughlin, yes, but much more conservative members of the mainstream, as well. Starting with the establishment of the William Alanson White Institute in 1946 and continuing at the New York University Postdoctoral Program in Psychotherapy and Psychoanalysis (and elsewhere), candidates studying interpersonal psychoanalysis, and then relational psychoanalysis, also studied Freudian psychoanalysis as well as object relations theory and self psychology,

and more recently, the contemporary Kleinians, Bion and those influenced by him, Lacan, and other contemporary French analysts. In my time in training, I was taught to learn and respect all the schools of psychoanalysis, and the lesson took. The attitude of interpersonalists, and later the relational group as well, has usually been respect, maintained despite disagreement. While some individual mainstream analysts, even during those years, had the same attitude toward interpersonal and relational thought, the same cannot be said about institutional mainstream attitudes. Only now are some mainstream institutes in the United States beginning to teach interpersonal and relational thinking.

6   I am not taking up Sullivan's defense; that isn't my point here. But if I were inclined to disprove the claim that Sullivan simply neglected the internal world and psychic structure, I would present a number of his relevant ideas, among them these: his conception of the self-system and character; his three modes of experience (prototaxic, parataxic, and syntaxic); the first "personifications" (good-me, bad-me, not-me; good mother, bad or evil mother); and developing from those first personifications (and sounding very much like internal objects), "the complement of eidetic people which each of us carries with us and lives with" (1948, p. 248); and "parataxic distortion," Sullivan's term for the unconscious construction of present relationships along the lines of significant relationships from the past.

7   Of course, the early interpersonal writings themselves can also be imagined to have arisen from unarticulated influences. My point is that they came first, and opened the possibility for their assimilation by the Freudian mainstream in North America.

8   Brown's (2011b) *Intersubjective Processes and the Unconscious* is a case in point, because Brown's project is the description of field theory, although from a Freudian/Kleinian/Bionian perspective. His book deserves to be addressed in some depth in this chapter, both for that reason and because of Brown's failure to address interpersonal and relational field theory. This long footnote, which is really a mini-essay or a small chapter within a chapter, takes up these issues. Postponing the reading of this note until after reading the chapter, or forgoing it altogether, will not diminish the reader's grasp of the argument made in the text.

First, let me acknowledge Brown's recognition that relational theories of intersubjectivity preexisted his own Kleinian/Bionian/Freudian conception of intersubjectivity (see Brown, 2011b, pp. 9–10). Even in Brown's single paragraph of acknowledgment, however, there is no recognition of the interpersonal contribution, which came first. But the recognition of relational forms of intersubjectivity does not lead Brown to treat any of the earlier forms of field theory as contributions. Brown seems to make this choice largely because he does not accept that interpersonal and relational psychoanalysts are as committed to the place of the unconscious in psychic life as Freudian/Kleinian/Bionian analysts are.

Of course, we would all agree that Brown's description of unconscious processes is not typically interpersonal or relational; but that fact does not imply that relational analysts are any less interested in the unconscious than is Brown himself. But Brown implies just that—that is, that relational analysts *are* less interested in unconscious processes than he is—when he contrasts his own view of intersubjectivity to relational views of the same phenomenon on the grounds that his own intention—as opposed to that of relationalists—"is to stay focused on the unconscious dimensions" (p. 10).

This, it seems to me, is an expression of the same dismissive attitude about interpersonal and relational psychoanalytic attitudes toward the unconscious that I took issue with in Chapter 1. In this instance, the attitude serves to justify Brown's decision not to consider interpersonal and relational contributions to psychoanalytic views of intersubjectivity. What might be treated as part of the natural context for Brown's views—and I would argue ought to be so treated—instead goes unaddressed.

This outcome is made especially ironic by Brown's observation that the analytic field was an idea that "in retrospect we may see as an important notion that went unnoticed at the time" (p. 109). But Brown does not mean to refer here to the early field theory of the interpersonalists that I have covered in this chapter. Not in the least. Instead, he means to refer to what he feels was the stifling of *Freudian* work that he feels presaged the view of intersubjectivity he presents in his book! He writes that,

> For example, Otto Isakower's thinking . . . about the two-person aspect of the analyzing instrument . . . largely lay fallow because political forces of the day [the 1930s and 1940s] marshaled against a full appreciation of Isakower's ideas, due to doubts regarding the creative use of countertransference (Lothane, 2006), thus effectively driving the notion of the two-person field into a theoretical purgatory in American psychoanalysis.
>
> (p. 109–10)

I have no doubt that Brown is right: the thoughts about intersubjectivity that can, in retrospect, be mined from Isakower's work were no doubt discouraged in the 1930s and 1940s. But consider that these thoughts were only *hints* of an idea of the analytic field—and on top of that, that they were hints only visible, in Brown's own view, from the present day. And then consider that the early interpersonalists *did* explicitly propose a field theory. Is the rejection of the entire message of the interpersonal school not a far more notable event than the lack of recognition of *hints* of intersubjectivity in the Freudian canon, hints that were not necessarily even recognized at the time?

The disregard of interpersonal and relational literature continues in the particular topics covered by Brown's book. In chapters previously published as articles in various journals, Brown writes as if his take on his subject matter is new, when the same attitude has been part of the relational literature since the inception of that point of view in the 1980s, and in the interpersonal literature since long before that. Let me offer just two examples, culled from many. In each of these vignettes, I will cite only some of the earliest expressions of interpersonal psychoanalytic views that presaged the kinds of ideas presented by Brown. I proceed that way in order to show that interpersonal ideas of this kind have existed for a number of decades. But it should be understood that, in the case of each of these examples (and many others), these early citations have become themes in the literature and teaching of interpersonal psychoanalysis, inspiring numerous contributions along the same lines.

Example 1: Chapter 8 is titled, "The triadic intersubjective matrix in supervision." Brown writes that,

> We have been tracing the evolution of intersubjective concepts in the analytic relationship which has developed over the last century from an initial "one-person" emphasis to a "two-person" focus and finally to an appreciation of the intersubjective field. [I must resist here the temptation to observe again the irony of referring to "two-person" psychoanalysis and "the intersubjective field" without intending to include interpersonal and relational psychoanalysis.] Despite this progression in conceptualizing the analytic dyad, change has been slower to develop in our thinking about the supervisory relationship. It is only recently that analysts have begun to address the triadic dimensions of supervision.
>
> (p. 178)

And yet interpersonal and relational psychoanalysts, because of their awareness of their continuous participation in an interpersonal field, have been considering processes transpiring between all three of the clinical participants—patient, supervisee, and supervisor—for several decades. See especially the book edited by Caligor *et al.* (1983), which was in turn inspired by the earlier work of Searles (1955) on parallel process. The following illustrative passages come from Caligor (1981).

When in the midst of the parallel process, both the candidate and the supervisor, each is struggling through for himself—each is at his own growing edge. The implications: Obviously, in parallel processing, the controlling variable is the supervisor. For the parallel process to be truly usable in teaching-learning in supervision, the supervisor must be aware of himself, what he experiences in the supervisory relationship. If the supervisor is not "inside" and actively participating in the process but rather functions cognitively and separate from the ongoing process, a didactic approach, the focus inevitably falls on the candidate's countertransference to his patient, his "inability" or "negative attitude" toward learning in supervision. The supervision becomes a morass.

(p. 20)

Where there is parallel process, there is always transference and countertransference operative for the patient, analyst candidate, and probably supervisor as well.

(p. 21)

Caligor was one of the interpersonal analysts most interested in these questions in those days, but his orientation to supervision was neither unusual nor controversial (at least among interpersonalists) in the early 1980s, and it has become common in the decades since then. It goes without saying that contributions such as Caligor's are not identical with the proposal made by Brown that patient, supervisee, and supervisor form a triadic intersubjective field in which a joint unconscious phantasy is created. But ideas like Caligor's are certainly closely enough related to Brown's to be considered as forerunners, and therefore as relevant to Brown's thesis. It is not the difference between the interpersonal contribution and Brown's ideas, in other words, that is responsible for the omission of these ideas from consideration in Brown's book.

Example 2: In Chapter 9, "On dreaming one's patient: reflections on an aspect of countertransference dreams," Brown proposes that the analyst's dreams about the patient may be informative, and he comments that, "Until very recently, such dreams have tended to be seen as either reflecting unanalyzed difficulties in the analyst or unexamined conflicts in the analytic relationship" (p. 195). Yet since Edward Tauber's classic (1954) article on this subject, countertransference dreams have been treated as informative in the interpersonal literature, and in every interpersonal supervision experience. In that 1954 paper, Tauber has this to say (the word "parataxis" is Harry Stack Sullivan's term for nonrational experience that cannot be known directly by the experiencer or communicated to someone else, i.e., Sullivan's understanding of the unconscious):

> the question must be raised as to whether the therapist does not enter the parataxic areas of the patient's life much more often than he realizes, if he dares to recognize this. The distinction as to when this unconscious operation is of value or not has to be explored further. One point that seems indisputable is that once the intrusion is made, the therapist must be able to assume responsibility for his actions and thoughts with honesty and without defensiveness.

(p. 335)

Tauber's thinking is not Brown's. There is certainly a difference. But in this 1954 article (and in a book that expanded on the article [Tauber and Green, 1959]) Tauber is describing jointly created unconscious experience and communication of a sort that bears a similarity to the kind of shared unconscious phantasy that, for Brown, composes the analytic field.

The same might be said of many early interpersonal contributions. I think of Wolstein's (1959) "transference-countertransference interlock," for instance, which is a description of the jointly maintained unconscious relatedness between patient and analyst; or Levenson's (1972) unconsciously provoked "transformation" of the analyst into a participant in the patient's family drama. All of these contributions, and many others, derived from an understanding of the analytic situation as a jointly constructed field of relatedness in which the most clinically significant aspects were unconscious.

Brown is hardly the only Freudian, Kleinian, or Bionian analyst who takes this kind of attitude toward interpersonal and relational psychoanalysis. I offer these examples (there are others) of Brown's treatment of interpersonal and relational psychoanalysis not because his attitude is unique. It certainly isn't. The kind of exegesis I have carried out here could be applied to many texts. Brown's book reflects an attitude that is not unusual among analysts with the kinds of theoretical commitments he holds. And so the reason I have taken the trouble to offer these remarks is not that I think Brown's book is particularly deserving of criticism on this issue.

On the other hand, I do think the book offers a particularly clear example of prejudicial mainstream attitudes toward interpersonal and relational psychoanalysis. Unlike many of his Freudian, Kleinian, and Bionian predecessors, Brown does not treat interpersonal and relational psychoanalysis the way he does on the basis of a rejection of the concept of the field, as was so common in past decades (see the text); and that makes his treatment of interpersonal and relational field theory that much more notable.

In many other respects (that is, other than Brown's treatment of interpersonal and relational thought), as a matter of fact, I admire Brown's book, find it instructive, and have enjoyed reading it. It currently appears on most of my course syllabi. It is my admiration for the book, and my interest in its arguments, actually, that makes my disappointment in its neglect of the earlier forms of field theory in psychoanalysis particularly keen.

For the sake of completeness, I want to cite the role of ignorance in maintaining the kinds of prejudices that I have described. I am sure that there are important things I do not know about Freudian, Kleinian, and Bionian theory, things that make it more difficult for me to think in those terms than it is for people for whom that kind of language is a native tongue. I also suspect that part of the reason Brown and his colleagues do not cite interpersonal and relational psychoanalysis is that they are not familiar with it. Lack of familiarity has two effects: outright ignorance is one; the other is that simplistic interpretations, which always tend to be prejudicial, are easier to maintain in the absence of close acquaintance with the ideas in question.

My psychoanalytic education was comparative, leading me to have at least some appreciation for all forms of psychoanalytic thought. I don't have the impression that that was the case in mainstream psychoanalytic institutes, at least not in the past. We can hope that will change.

But ignorance is not the primary factor here. Brown intended to write as he wrote. I feel fairly sure that he would answer the questions I have raised by saying that his idea of intersubjectivity is different than mine, because it grows from a greater emphasis on unconscious process in Freudian, Kleinian, and Bionian thinking. I think he would say that this difference is the reason he did not consider interpersonal and relational field theory in his book. But of course that point is precisely what I am disputing.

9 I don't want to stray from my course here, but I do want to acknowledge that important stirrings of interest in countertransference came not only from interpersonalists—e.g., Edgar Levenson (1972), Harold Searles (1965, 1979), Edward Tauber (1954), Benjamin Wolstein (1959), Lawrence Epstein and Arthur Feiner (1979)—but also from analysts of the object relations school—e.g., Otto Kernberg (1965), Paula Heimann (1950), Margaret Little (1951), Heinrich Racker (1968), Sarah Tower (1956), and Donald Winnicott (1949). I want to emphasize two points about these two groups of writers: (1) the classical literature acknowledged exclusively the latter group, while writers from both groups were cited frequently in the interpersonal, and then the relational, literature; and (2) only the interpersonal, and then the relational, perspectives included the view that the analyst was a particular individual, interacting consciously and unconsciously with another particular individual.

Chapter 3

Field theory in psychoanalysis, part I

Comparing Madeleine and Willy Baranger, and Harry Stack Sullivan

In this chapter and its companion, Chapter 4, I compare the contemporary field theory that has arisen in South America, Italy, and elsewhere with the field theory of interpersonal/relational psychoanalysis, primarily a North American invention that has also inspired analysts elsewhere. I will often consider interpersonal and relational psychoanalysis as a single school of psychoanalytic thought, and when I do, I abbreviate them as IRP. I refer to South American and European field theory as Bionian field theory (BFT), a terminology I adopt in order to differentiate this body of work from the field theory of IRP. BFT, especially the writings of Antonino Ferro but also including the work of many others, has attracted enormous interest in both American and international psychoanalytic journals and meetings over the last two decades.[1]

This chapter focuses on comparing the work of the intellectual ancestors of these two kinds of field theory: Harry Stack Sullivan, the progenitor of IRP field theory; and Madeleine and Willy Baranger, who most BFT writers credit with inventing their field conception. What is the relation of Sullivan's "interpersonal field" to the Barangers' (1961–62/2008) "bipersonal field" or "intersubjective field" (W. Baranger, 1979; M. Baranger, 2005)? Because the Barangers' work continued into the 1990s, I also make observations about the relation of their thinking to contemporary work in IRP.

The field theory of Harry Stack Sullivan

The writings and teachings of Harry Stack Sullivan were the most influential and inspirational influence on the early interpersonalists, and one of the defining characteristics of Sullivan's thinking was field theory. Via his reading of sources such as the Chicago School of Sociology

(Charles Horton Cooley, George Herbert Mead) and the field theory of his day's physical sciences and experimental embryology (see Murphy and Cattell, 1952; Tubert-Oklander, 2007), Sullivan brought field theory to his colleagues, and eventually to the rest of psychoanalysis.[2]

Sullivan's field theory was woven into his theory of interpersonal relations, which he constructed over the years of the 1920s to the 1940s. Sullivan died in 1949, which is significant for the purposes of this chapter, because the Barangers' most important publications appeared from the early 1960s into the 1990s. Sullivan and the Barangers, then, the sources of their respective schools' conceptions of the field, not only belonged to different cultures and different schools of thought, but to different generations.

As I have already written in Chapter 2, Sullivan did not set out to create a field theory. His aim was to study what he described as interpersonal relations. Sullivan certainly did understand these relations to occur in a field, but unlike Kurt Lewin, for whom the field itself was the object of study, Sullivan understood the field as the medium in which his primary object of study took place. And therefore, while the field was central in everything Sullivan wrote, he did not explicitly theorize its nature. It's a bit like the attitude of a zoologist toward air: all the animals the zoologist studies must breathe, but this fact is largely taken for granted. (Of course, the difference is that there is no controversy over the fact that air is the medium of life, whereas, as I showed in Chapter 2, the idea of the field, when it was introduced into psychoanalysis, was greatly controversial.) This attitude—that the field is always crucial and yet seldom addressed in so many words—has been maintained over the years in IRP. One could nevertheless make the case that the work of many IRP writers (e.g., Jessica Benjamin, Philip Bromberg, Darlene Ehrenberg, Irwin Hoffman, Edgar Levenson, Stephen Mitchell) actually centers around their conception of the nature of the field. Yet unlike BFT analysts, who have contributed a large and substantial literature devoted to theorizing explicitly about the analytic field, IRP writers have not made field theory a focus of their work—none of them, that is, has referred to his or her work as a contribution to field theory. The theories of these modern IRP writers are broad psychoanalytic points of view, theories of the nature of clinical process and, more generally, human relatedness; and so it is the vocabulary of those subjects that they use. One might say that in this respect, contemporary IRP writers share Sullivan's intention and method: the concept of the field is so thoroughly imbricated with their other ideas that it does not occur to them to precipitate it out of solution and give it separate consideration. Add to this point the fact that relational psychoanalysis is as deeply influenced by the English object relations theorists as it is by interpersonal psychoanalysis. In the mix that became relational theory, Sullivan's field theory combined with Fairbairn's and Winnicott's ideas, and with Kohut's self psychology. If one wished to do so, one could describe a field theory, largely implicit in IRP, based on the equally implicit field theories of Winnicott, Fairbairn, and Kohut.

For a description of Sullivan's views about the field, including several long quotations in which Sullivan describes his conception of the field, see the section of Chapter 2 entitled "Sullivan's conception of the field."

In the contemporary IRP conception, the most important property of the field is its dynamic, constitutive function. The field shapes the experience and conduct of its participants, and that influence affects the analyst in just the same way that it influences the patient. The fact that the field is a dynamic structure/process means that the nature of its constitutive influence is in continuous flux, leading to change in the experience of each participant. This position, originated by Sullivan and broadened and deepened by Levenson (1972, 1983, 1991), and then by other writers as well (e.g., Ehrenberg, 1974; Gill, 1983; Hoffman, 1983; Mitchell, 1988; Aron, 1996; Bromberg, 1998), lies at the root of the thinking of all IRP analysts today.

I have already mentioned that Sullivan introduced field theory into psychoanalysis. The point is worth repeating, though, because apparently it is not as widely known outside IRP circles as I would have thought.[3] Ferro and Basile (2009b), in their editors' introduction of a compilation of essays on the analytic field, write that, "The concept of the analytic field originated in the 1960s from an insight by two Franco-Argentinian analysts, Madeleine and Willy Baranger." They add, "For a long time, the idea of the analytic field remained confined to the geographical area of Latin America" (p. 1).

When I came across this passage I was surprised; but I had just begun to learn about BFT, and I explained to myself that the reason for the absence of reference to Sullivan and the several decades of interpersonal psychoanalysis that preceded the 1960s was probably that the field theory of the Barangers and those who followed them was so very different from the field theory of IRP. I imagined that it would not have occurred to Ferro and Basile, despite the similarity in terminology, to link the two kinds of theory. But then I read Ferro and Basile's description of the Barangers' field theory, which comes on the heels of these editors' claim for the Barangers' priority:

> Exploring the relational vertex in psychoanalysis, these two authors [i.e., the Barangers] realized that the "analytic dyad" creates a dynamic field—that is, a situation between two persons "who remain unavoidably connected and complementary" as long as they share the analytic situation and are "involved in a single dynamic process. In this situation, neither member of the couple can be understood without the other," for in the analytic field all the current and emerging structures depend on the interaction between the two participants.
>
> (p. 1)[4]

To the extent that this description, with its quotations from the Barangers, represents what Ferro and Basile understand as the heart of psychoanalytic field theory, one has to take issue with their claim that this kind of thinking originated with the Barangers. Ferro and Basile's description could just as well have been written about Sullivan, or about any IRP writer's work. We shall see that there are important differences between Sullivan and the Barangers, but this passage expresses with particular clarity what IRP and BFT share.[5]

The field theory of Madeleine and Willy Baranger

Madeleine and Willy Baranger, having relocated from France to Argentina early in their careers, and then to Uruguay, became highly influential in South American psychoanalysis during the 1960s and 1970s. Their innovative work had its roots in a number of sources outside psychoanalysis proper: *gestalt* psychology and philosophy; the work of Merleau-Ponty (1942, 1945), himself one of the seminal *gestalt* theorists; Kurt Lewin's (1935, 1936, 1951) influential thinking on field theory;[6] and the early writings of Bion, especially his work on groups (1961). But only a few of the Barangers' articles were available in English until the last few years, when their first and most important statement of field theory (Baranger and Baranger, 1961–62/2008; revised in minor respects for republication in Spanish in 1969; translated into English on the basis of this revision) and a collection of their articles (Baranger and Baranger, 2009) finally appeared in English translation.[7]

In quoting Ferro's impression that the Barangers introduced field theory to psychoanalysis, I have already also quoted from the Barangers' (1961–62/2008) most influential article. Some of those words appear in what follows. In this passage, which appears at the outset of the Barangers' paper, it is clear what the Barangers have in common with Sullivan, but it also begins to be clear how they diverge from him: it is immediately apparent that they, like those who inherited and broadened Sullivan's views, pay much more attention than Sullivan did to the unconscious aspects of the field and to unconscious communication.

> There is nothing new in admitting the error of one-sidedness in early descriptions of the analytic situation as a situation of objective observation of a patient in a state of more or less pronounced regression by an analyst-eye that restricts itself to recording, understanding and sometimes interpreting what is happening in the patient.
>
> Direct observation and progressively deeper studies of the countertransference, the unconscious means of communication that develops in the analytic situation with particular ease and intensity; the latent meanings of verbal communication: all these factors imply a very different and much broader concept of the analytic situation, in which the analyst intervenes—in spite of the necessary "neutrality" and "passivity"—as a fully participant member.
>
> Therefore, the analytic situation should be formulated not only as a situation of one person who is confronted by an indefinite and neutral personage—in effect, of a person confronted by his or her own self—but as a situation between two persons who remain unavoidably connected and complementary as long as the situation obtains, and involved in a single dynamic process. In this situation, neither member of the couple can be understood without the other.
>
> (pp. 795–96)

Essential ambiguity

In this early paper the Barangers (1961–62/2008) go on to define what they call "the field of the analytic situation" or "the bi-personal field." They define it in terms of space (e.g., an analysis would develop differently if the couch were in the middle of the room instead of against the wall), time (e.g., frequency and duration of appointments, an open-ended future for the analytic work with any particular patient) and functional arrangements (e.g., the commitments to the roles of analyst and patient made by the participants at the beginning). They lay particular emphasis on the necessity to preserve the "essential ambiguity" of the analytic situation: "It could be said that every event in the analytic field is experienced in the 'as-if' category" (p. 799). It is crucial, that is, that "each thing or event in the field be at the same time something else. If this essential ambiguity is lost, the analysis also disappears." Why? Because unlike everyday life, in which "we try to relate to people on the basis of their objective reality and not according to our subjective projections; in the analytic situation we try to eliminate as far as possible any reference to our objective personality and leave this as indefinite as possible" (p. 799). For example,

> If the patient were to experience the analyst exactly as the analyst is (for example, if the patient were to consider the analyst only as his or her analyst), the transference phenomenon would be suppressed, which is obviously inconceivable, and for the same reason any possibility of analysis would be suppressed.
>
> (p. 799)

This point holds, say the Barangers, for every aspect of the field: not only the meanings of the presence, bodies, and conduct of its participants, but its space, time, and functional arrangements. In the bi-personal field, nothing can be only "what it is."

In contemporary IRP, a distinction between what is objectively real and what is transferential has been replaced by a conception of transference as a construction or a selection from the possibilities (e.g., Gill, 1983; Hoffman, 1983). The Barangers' work is not constructivist; but there nevertheless exists basic agreement between contemporary IRP and the Barangers on the point that limiting reality to a single version is deadly to psychoanalysis. In IRP terms, the "essential ambiguity" of the Barangers is expressed as the desirability of preserving experiential uncertainty; one tries never to lapse into the comfortable sense that one *knows*, or has one's finger on the truth.

As a matter of fact, in laying out a case for constructivism, Mitchell (1993), too, referred to "essential ambiguity." Hoffman (1998) has either used this phrase or one that carries the same meaning; and I have used the phrase myself in print, more than once. But Mitchell, Hoffman, and I are using "essential" in a different way than the Barangers, who intend the word to convey that it is crucial to maintain an *intentional* ambiguity. Ambiguity is a goal. Mitchell, Hoffman, and I, on the other hand, mean the phrase to refer to the hermeneutic position that ambiguity is *unavoidable*, so that "essential" refers to ambiguity as an *essence*. It is desirable to maintain one's awareness of it—but whether one is aware of it or not, it is there. And therefore the goal is not ambiguity itself but one's awareness of it—the ongoing sense of uncertainty about what one knows and does not know that marks one's acceptance that experience is inherently ambiguous.

According to the Barangers, the ambiguity of the analytic situation is largely due to the fact that the bi-personal field is not really a two-person structure, but a tri- or multi-person situation; and this multi-person structure, in turn, is the outcome of the splitting "prevalent in the patient's regressive and neurotic situation" and present to a lesser extent in the "partial regression" (1961–62/2008, p. 798) allowed by the analyst in her own mind for the purpose of analytic work. Analyst and patient, then, are each potentially more than one, and so the analytic relationship is a situation in which "[at least] one [member] is physically absent and experientially present" (p. 798). While the concrete, bi-personal field remains present in the background, helping to structure the analytic situation, the analysis is generally carried out in a triangular situation—which, for them, results in that specifically psychoanalytic kind of essential ambiguity in which nothing is "only itself."

Both the Barangers' and contemporary IRP's views about the desirability of ambiguity exceed Sullivan's reach, because Sullivan's version of reality, as one would expect, given the era in which he thought and wrote, is uni-dimensional, defined in traditional, objectivistic, empirical terms. As a matter of fact, Sullivan's intention, pursued in the service of clarity in communication, is to drain as much ambiguity as possible from the interpersonal field. For Sullivan, ambiguity has no redeeming value.

But the Barangers' understanding of analytic experience as multi-dimensional and ambiguous is quite amenable to contemporary relational writers. This is particularly clear when one keeps in mind that the Barangers' argument that analysis is a multi-person situation is based on their observation of the ubiquity of splitting. One of the ideas most characteristic of contemporary IRP thinking is, in the most general sense, the fragmentation of the self bequeathed by postmodernism, and in a more specifically theoretical sense, the multiple self. In fact, one way to understand "essential ambiguity" in relational terms is to describe it as the recognition that self-states are continuously shifting in and out of awareness in response to affectively charged events in the interpersonal field, and that the recognition of this unstable, ambiguous state of affairs encourages the analyst to maintain a particularly close attunement to her own and the other's experience. States of being that are not currently shaping consciousness remain present in a potential or unformulated way in the background of the mind. Each self-state is a different way of creating relatedness, and so, in IRP terms, we can understand the Barangers' "essential ambiguity" as the ever-present potential in the next moment for a shift in self-state to simultaneously shift the nature of the object (and the self).

Unconscious phantasy

The Barangers' primary theoretical commitment was neo-Kleinian. Given the time in which they wrote, I expected to find that unconscious phantasy would perhaps be the factor that most clearly differentiated IRP and BFT. But it turns out that the differentiation is more complex than I had imagined.

The Barangers' (1961–62/2008, pp. 803–9) conception of unconscious phantasy was particularly influenced by Bion (1961), who argued that psychotherapy groups develop what he called *basic assumptions*— "group phantasies," such as "fight" or "flight." A group phantasy is not the contribution of any one person, but is instead created and held by the whole group, which is thus also influenced and shaped by the phantasy. This conception of Bion's, as a matter of fact, is a good approximation of what the Barangers mean by the jointly held phantasy that defines the analytic field.[8] Bion is responsible, for instance, for the idea that while the group phantasy is constructed from the phantasies of the individuals in the group, it is more than the sum of these individual contributions. This point came to be a defining feature of the Barangers' view, and marks a significant divergence of their view from Sullivan's field concept.

The Barangers were also indebted to Isaacs's (1948) landmark article, in which unconscious phantasy is understood as a structuring influence on experience and is largely (but not completely) detached from the necessary connection it has with drive in Klein's thinking. The Barangers take the detachment of drive and phantasy a step further, so that there really seems to be little, if any, necessity to cite drive in their understanding of phantasy.

The Barangers do not offer a detailed alternative theory of unconscious phantasy, though. Instead, it seems to be their view that unconscious phantasy is an internal elaboration of past experience, and of hopes, expectations, and dreads about the future. How one has lived and hopes and fears to live, not drive, seems to be the source of phantasy; and phantasy, in turn, is one of the most important influences on what experience will come to be. In the course of the session the analyst tries to identify the joint phantasy organizing the field, which suggests that phantasy expresses the current state of the field and, on another level, of the patient's inner life. Part of the clinical significance of the patient's phantasy therefore lies in this expressive function, from which the analyst learns what she needs to know; but the structuring function of phantasy has perhaps even greater significance. The function of phantasy in shaping inner reality, and eventually in shaping the field, as well, is crucial.

All psychoanalytic theories have some conception of unconscious regularity, some way of understanding the contribution that the unconscious makes to the structuring of conscious experience. For IRP, unconscious regularity consists of patterns of relatedness that, for dynamic reasons, remain outside awareness. Mitchell (1988) writes that, *"The most useful way to view psychological reality is as operating within a relational matrix which encompasses both intrapsychic and interpersonal realms"* (p. 9; italics from the original). All experience, in one way or another, is influenced by its place in, and contribution to, this matrix.

The relational matrix has a structuring influence on experience that is analogous to the structuring influence that unconscious phantasy has for Isaacs, and even more for the Barangers. It is therefore much easier for an analyst with IRP commitments to feel at home with the Barangers' conception of phantasy than with the earlier, drive-based, Kleinian version.

But despite all this, the Barangers' uncoupling of drive and phantasy is not what was most innovative about their theory of phantasy. It is not even what is most comfortable about their theory for IRP analysts, virtually all of whom eschew the position that biological drive lies at the core of motivation. The most unique and inspired aspect of the Barangers' use of phantasy was their integration of this nondrive-based notion with their interpersonalized understanding of the analytic situation, and it is this way of defining the field that has had the greatest influence on the BFT analysts who have come after them.

The Barangers believed that the field should be understood as a jointly created unconscious phantasy, but this phantasy of the field was not a simple additive combination of the phantasies of analyst and patient. It was instead understood to be something new, something unique to these two people in the particular time and place in which they came together. It is this jointly constructed phantasy that the BFT analyst immerses herself in, studies, and interprets, and it is change in this field that is responsible for eventual change in the patient.

The question of the analyst's conduct

And yet the Barangers' embrace of the centrality of phantasy does, in the end, lead to what I believe is a significant divergence between their work and the work of Sullivan and contemporary IRP. To grasp what the Barangers think about this issue requires some digging. We can begin with the observation that, at the very least, the Barangers certainly do not simply accept the IRP view—that the analyst is inevitably unconsciously and reciprocally involved in the interaction with the patient, and that therapeutic action has to do with the way these unconscious involvements, usually called enactments, are dealt with. In the IRP view, while the two analytic participants obviously have different responsibilities, the *nature* of their involvement with one another is the same in both directions.

The Barangers do describe the unconscious phantasy of the field as a joint creation; but they also often distance themselves from certain aspects of this position. This happens over and over again in their papers. In their first article on the field, for instance, they (Baranger and Baranger, 1961–62/2008) write, "The basic phantasy of the session is not the mere understanding of the patient's phantasy by the analyst, but something that is constructed in a couple relationship." So far, so good. This appears to imply an acceptance of joint creation. But the passage continues as follows:

> We have no doubt that the two persons have different roles in this phantasy and that it would be dangerously absurd for the analyst to impose his or her own phantasy on the field, but we have to recognize that a "good" session means that the patient's basic phantasy *coincides* with the analyst's in the structuring of the analytic session (italics added).
>
> (p. 806)

It seems that mutual construction is acceptable only as long as the two phantasies are the same. But we do not know exactly what this means. How are the phantasies the same? In what respects? The authors go on to suggest that when the phantasies of patient and analyst do not coincide, the analyst should accept that this is a patient she cannot treat. It seems that, while the processes going on in the couple may very well result in a jointly constructed unconscious phantasy, those couple processes cannot diverge too much from one another. This idea suggests only a limited acceptance of the joint construction of meaning, and the solution to be adopted when the phantasies do not coincide (not treating the patient) is quite different than the frank and routine acceptance in IRP that analytic relatedness requires relational negotiation and struggle (of course, while maintaining the context of a professional relationship).

The point about coinciding phantasies is not repeated in the Barangers' later papers, and so we do not know if they continued to hold it. It is also true that there are many places in the Barangers' papers where they are eloquent about what sounds much more like the mutual construction of IRP. I am inclined to believe that the Barangers were embarking on a pioneering effort to revise psychoanalysis, and that they had not yet resolved (and perhaps never did) the conflicts between the old psychoanalysis and the new one they were creating.

At the very least, though, we must say that the Barangers were worried about going too far. A few pages after the passage I have just cited, they opine that the projective identifications of the patient must be given free rein, while the analyst's must be (and can be) controlled: "the analyst has to use [the patient's projective identification] . . . , but in small doses and by way of experimental exploration" (p. 808). The projective identification "must be allowed to be massive on one side (the patient's) but kept very limited on the other (the analyst's)" (p. 808). The analyst's introjection of the patient's projective identifications "has to be limited and controlled to avoid feelings in the analyst of being inundated by the situation" (p. 809). These passages are reminiscent of some of the early classical writings on the use of countertransference—for example, Fliess's (1953) recommendation that the analyst limit countertransference experience to "trial identifications" with aspects of the patient's mind.

The question, of course, is how to do such a thing. (I had the same questions about Fliess's recommendation when I first read it as a candidate.) If projective identification and introjection are unconscious processes, which of course the Barangers believe they are, then where does the analyst get the leverage to exert conscious control over them? The Barangers do not answer this question.

The same is not true of behavior or conduct, of course. That is, we all agree that, at least to some degree, the analyst can control her own conduct. The Barangers, however, take a strong stance on this point: the analyst, they believe, always has the choice and the responsibility not to allow her countertransference experience to emerge in conduct. The analyst, that is, has the choice and professional duty not to engage in enactment. Here is a typical statement of this kind, from later in the Barangers' work (Baranger *et al.*, 1983):

> Due to his function, and from the outset, the analyst is committed to truth and abstinence from anything *acted out* with the analysand. In the analytic situation there is no formalized, computable operation but a situation in which the analyst is committed, flesh, bone, and unconscious. He is so intrinsically, not contingently, because of the fact that an analyst listens and reacts: this implies that countertransference will be prohibited in its expression and condemned to an internal unfolding in him.
> (p. 70; italics from the original)

The Barangers, that is, believed that the analyst's commitment to the analytic role was sufficient to allow the analyst to rein in her countertransference enactment by conscious choice, thereby restricting countertransference to the realm of inner experience only.

Of course, challenges to this traditional understanding of transference and countertransference analysis, and to the possibilities inherent in the analyst's commitment to the analytic role, were the very heart of the relational turn—the work of Levenson (1972, 1983, 1991), Wolstein (1959), and Gill (1983), and eventually all of contemporary IRP. It seemed to these writers that inner experience inevitably bled into the analyst's outer conduct, so that the separation between countertransference experience and enactment, upheld with such confidence by earlier analysts (including the Barangers), could no longer be maintained. As a result, contemporary IRP analysts have concluded that analysts' only realistic course is to accept the reality of their unconscious, enactive involvement with patients, including those very difficult enactments—I repeat, in *conduct*—that are often the most significant parts of treatment. From this perspective, the analyst, by accepting that he has no choice but to occupy this position, creates the best situation to further clinical goals. This is a stark difference between the work of the Barangers and contemporary IRP.

For the Barangers, then, the field is limited to the realm of experience—a fact which should not surprise us when we remember that the field is for the Barangers a jointly constructed unconscious phantasy. And even within the realm of experience, countertransference can be, and must be, modulated in intensity. But for Sullivan, even though he believed, like the Barangers, that the analyst should be able to prevent the involvement of her conduct in the countertransference, and for contemporary IRP analysts, who do not accept Sullivan's view in this respect, the field is both experiential *and* behavioral, both the inner life *and* external conduct. The analyst remains accountable, of course, for conducting herself in a disciplined, professionally responsible way designed to serve the patient's interests—but within these broad parameters, the analyst's unconscious involvement with the patient cannot be restricted to the operations of mind.

Because the Barangers belonged to a psychoanalytic world rooted in the concept of unconscious phantasy, they probably would have maintained their position even if they had known about the IRP alternative. As far as I can see, there is no reason to believe that the Barangers would have embraced the relational turn if, later on in their work, in the 1980s and 1990s, they had learned about it.

Enactments and bastions

This difference in conceptions of the involvement of the analyst's conduct illuminates what is otherwise one of the most significant points of contact between the theories under discussion: the relation between bastions and enactments.

To appreciate the concept of bastion (sometimes translated as "bulwark"), consider that for the Barangers (1961–62/2008), "what is important in the dynamic of the treatment is not the emergence of emotions, wishes and past anxieties, but their emergence in one way and not another. They need to emerge in a new and vivid context and not paralyse it." The field, that is, must be free to change in response to current circumstances; it must be free to evolve into the future, unfettered by rigidities, stereotypies, repetitions of the past.

> [W]hat is most important is the mobility or crystallization of the field . . . The field moves, and the analyst can intervene in it effectively when the patient "takes a risk," but such risk-taking is prevented by an aspect of personal life or phantasy that for the patient is a

personal bastion (and is generally the unconscious refuge of powerful phantasies of omnipotence).

This bastion varies enormously from one person to another, but is never absent. It is whatever the patient does not want to put at risk because the risk of losing it would throw the patient into a state of extreme helplessness, vulnerability, and despair (p. 814).

The bastion may be some sort of perverse activity (in an unfortunate passage, the Barangers suggest that one of the most frequent examples is homosexuality); a sense of intellectual or moral superiority; a relation with an idealized love object; an attachment to an ideology, money, or a profession; or a sense that one is special in some way, perhaps a member of some social aristocracy. If the patient is not willing to give up this (usually) grandiose phantasy, which requires putting it at risk in the analysis, the field stagnates, immobilized by being split into pieces, one of which must remain rigid and unchanging, and the treatment stalls.

> The field of the analytic situation is the opportunity, through repetition in a new context of the original situations that motivated the splitting, to break up this defensive process and to re-integrate the split off sectors of experience into the whole of the patient's life. This is why it is necessary to break down the internal bastions.
>
> (p. 216)

In the Barangers' (1961–62/2008) original paper on the field, the link between their concept of bastion and the IRP understanding of enactments is not as clear as it is in papers written just a few years later (e.g., Baranger and Baranger, 1964). In the first paper, the Barangers do cite approvingly Racker's (1968; the Barangers cited the original publication, in Spanish, 1960) work on the countertransference micro-neurosis, commenting that,

> the interpretive process as a whole tends to permit the mobilization of the transference–countertransference neurosis and thereby the gradual modification of all the patient's aspects involved in it, meaning the patient's whole person. In parallel, the process consists, for the analysts, of freeing aspects of themselves that are involved in the countertransference situation and paralysed in the countertransference neurosis.
>
> (p. 817)

A few years later, the Barangers (1964) write about the analyst's involvement on a level closer to clinical experience:

> If there is no complicity [in preventing analytic consideration of the bastion] on the analyst's part, then the patient's bastion is just a difficulty for the analytic work or a "resistance," but it is not a bastion in the field. The patient tries one way or another to breach the fundamental rule, and the analyst strives to reintegrate into the general movement the content avoided by the patient. However, when such complicity is present, communication is divided: a sector of the field crystallizes, comprising the patient's resistance and the analyst's counter-resistance, unconsciously communicated and operating together, while on another separate level an apparently normal communication goes on.
>
> (p. 9)

As is so often the case in their writings, the Barangers present the clinical situation in a way that IRP analysts recognize as closely related to their own views. There is no doubt that, in their thinking about the significance of bastions, the Barangers accept the analyst's unconscious involvement with the patient. They recommend that analysts adopt what they call "the second look" (W. Baranger, 1979; Baranger *et al.*, 1983; M. Baranger, 1993), by which they mean an examination of the treatment situation with an eye toward the identification of patterns of involvement in which both analyst and patient are implicated. Without this "second look," and without modifying her approach on the basis of what she learns in this way, the analyst cannot intervene effectively to set a stalled field into motion once again. If we accept the broad IRP definition of mutual enactment, i.e., that mutual enactment is the unconscious participation in the treatment of both analyst and patient, then in IRP terms we can perhaps classify as an enactment the Barangers' understanding of the analyst's complicity in the expression of a bastion in the field.

But I think there is a difference between these views, and that difference has to do with the understanding of conduct. For however deeply the analyst and the patient may be unconsciously involved with one another in the Barangers' scheme, this is *involvement in the realm of phantasy* (and this goes for the work of Racker, as well). The Barangers (and Racker) maintain throughout their work these divergent understandings of phantasy and conduct. In this understanding the analyst's unconscious complicity in preventing examination of the patient's bastions simply does not (and should not) shape the analyst's conduct.

Now, this point becomes more and more complicated the longer one considers it. Is it really possible to completely differentiate the analyst's involvement with the patient on the level of unconscious phantasy from her involvement with the patient on the level of conduct? Must it not be the case that the analyst's phantasy involvement has *some* inescapable implications for the kind of conduct he engages in with the patient? Would the Barangers agree? Would Racker? I don't know the answer to this question. Perhaps they would. But even if they did, the difference in *emphasis* would remain. There is clearly more room in IRP than in the Barangers' views for there to be a continuous, inescapable, unconscious influence on the analyst's behavior with the patient. And if the meaning of the analyst's conduct is routinely at least partly unconscious, then her influence on the patient is also at least partly unconscious. And therefore, it seems to follow that IRP theory encourages the analysts who use it to ask themselves, more often than BFT analysts ask themselves, about the nature of their involvement with their patients. How might the course of the session, the nature of the relatedness, and the patient's experience be influenced by unconscious contributions from the analyst?

Affect

One point that I have not made about the work of the Barangers and contemporary IRP, and that should at least be mentioned, because it moderates the difference I have described, is the similar, central role of affect in the two views of clinical process. I might cite any of a number of the Barangers' papers that emphasize their sensitivity to the moment-to-moment emotional tenor of their work. Perhaps the most elegant and eloquent is Madeleine Baranger's (1993) compelling and moving discussion of the rootedness of the analyst's listening and interventions in her affective experience of the field. Of course, neither the Barangers nor IRP analysts are unusual in this respect; many analysts, of all stripes, value the nuances of affect in the session. Who could argue against such a point? But it is worth noting that the Barangers (and their contemporary BFT colleagues, too, such as Ferro and Civitarese) have in common with IRP analysts the inclination to argue *for* it. These are analysts for whom interventions, if they are to be mutative, cannot be the manifestations of a theory of technique but must instead grow out of clinical relatedness. The necessity and desirability for the analyst to be affectively embedded in the field are no less evident in the Barangers' work than in contemporary IRP. Being part of the analytic field entails more than mere presence; it requires a depth of involvement.

Conclusions

Given that both Sullivan and the Barangers were field theorists, it is not surprising that there are notable similarities in their work. These similarities are the context that give the differences between them their significance.

Sullivan used field theory to make the clinical thinking of his day consistent with what he saw as the cutting edge of social science. Field theory in Sullivan's thought was an application of general principles of psychology, psychiatry, sociology, and linguistics to a specific case, the psychotherapeutic situation. Because Sullivan took the tack he did, he understood conduct—what two people did with one another, and the *way* that they did it—as the heart of the interpersonal field. When later IRP analysts came along, it was natural for them, having grown at least partly from Sullivan's position, to take the position that not only the contents of the analyst's mind, but the analyst's conduct was routinely affected by the analyst's unconsciously motivated participation in the interpersonal field.

The Barangers, on the other hand, wrote a field theory that was quite specific to the psychoanalytic situation and its unique characteristics. They took the position about the analyst's conduct that had always been taken in psychoanalysis up to that time—i.e., they considered it practical and possible (and correct) for the analyst to decide upon and control her experience (to some degree) and her conduct (more or less completely), using her commitment to the analytic task and role to shape her experience and behavior always in the service of the patient's interests.

In the next chapter, we shall see where this divergence has led. For BFT analysts, as for all Kleinians, including the Barangers, the interpretive process and the analyst's part of the clinical process have remained more or less synonymous. Questions of technique and therapeutic action continue to revolve around the nature of the analyst's interpretive participation. The container/contained model that has become so influential since the work of Bion does indeed draw a different kind of attention than before to the relationship between the analyst and the patient. But the events of the relationship are usually understood to have their mutative impact via their influence on the analyst's interpretive process.

Sullivan's acceptance of the analyst's involvement on the level of conduct, on the other hand, opened the possibility of relational effects in therapeutic action. If what has to be disentangled in the therapeutic relationship is not limited to inner events, events of the mind, but is also a matter of the way analyst and patient deal with one another, then therapeutic action is also liable to depend on the analyst's conduct. How the analyst conducts herself with the patient is liable to be as significant as her interpretations to the outcome of the treatment.

Notes

1 I create these two groups and the acronyms that designate them for heuristic purposes. The members of each group have important theoretical commitments in common, but of course I also recognize that each of these broad categories also contains writers and clinicians who feel quite differently about various aspects of psychoanalysis.

2 Murphy and Cattell (1952) offer this characterization of the kind of influences Sullivan absorbed from the physical sciences:

> Classical physics . . . consisted largely of pushes and pulls. If a particle happened to be pulling on another particle, that was so to speak just a question of the external relations, the foreign policy, of the two particles; it did not bear upon their internal affairs. The study of electromagnetism during the nineteenth century gradually showed the inadequacy of this conception. The interactions between events give definition and form to the events; the event is an aspect of a context, a field, not definable in terms of its inner essence.
>
> (pp. 162–63)

The same authors imply that Sullivan was aware of the embryological work of Spemann and Weiss, "who showed that the growing embryo is not an assemblage of particles, but a mass governed in its growth by a definite field structure, with organizing poles and the dependence of any given cell upon its location and the forces acting upon it" (p. 163).

Oddly, in his writings and lectures Sullivan, as far as I know, only once mentioned Kurt Lewin, who brought field theory to academic psychology; and even that one mention was peripheral.

3 Tubert-Oklander (2007) and Fiscalini (2007), the only other writers I know who have commented on the appearance of the field concept in the work of Sullivan and the Barangers, both recognize Sullivan's precedence. That takes nothing away from the Barangers, who developed their ideas independently.

4 The quotations within this quoted passage are unreferenced. They are taken from Baranger and Baranger (1961–62/2008). For citation, see the more complete quotation in the text, below.

5 Ferro and Basile's oversight is consistent with what seems to have been the common understanding of Sullivan's work among Argentine analysts of Sullivan's time. Marco Conci (personal communication, 2012) reported to me that M. Baranger, in a conversation with him in Athens in 2010, said that she and her husband, and other Argentine analysts such as Pichon-Rivière, had heard about Sullivan, but that they did not include his work in their thinking because they did not believe he belonged to the psychoanalytic tradition—and certainly not to the Kleinian tradition in which they had been trained. The same was true of Bleger and Etchegoyen, other prominent Argentine analysts who admired Sullivan in certain nonpsychoanalytic respects. Conci (2009) tells us, for

instance, that Etchegoyen (1990) described Sullivan as "undoubtedly one of the greatest psychiatrists of our century." This South American view of Sullivan as interesting and important but irrelevant to psychoanalysis is not hard to understand, since Sullivan's ideas could not have been much more different from the Kleinian psychoanalysis of his day than they were. Furthermore, Sullivan was not, and did not wish to be considered, a psychoanalyst. But in the United States, despite Sullivan's attitude, many members of Sullivan's wide following nevertheless understood his ideas as both psychoanalytically informed and a contribution to psychoanalytic thought; and interpersonal psychoanalysis arose from his views (see, for example, Levenson, 1992).

6 I know of only one citation of Lewin in the Barangers' work; but Tubert-Oklander (2007) and de León de Bernardi (2008) tell us that the Barangers' most significant mentor, Enrique Pichon-Rivière, whose influence the Barangers cite frequently, was an avid reader of Lewin. De León de Bernardi (2008) credits Pichon-Rivière, who eventually left psychoanalysis for social psychology, with introducing *gestalt* thinking to South America.

7 For introductions in English to the work of the Barangers, see de León de Bernardi (2000, 2008) and Brown (2010, 2011b). In addition, Brown, and Reis (1999a, 1999b, 2006, 2009, 2010) are each in the process of developing their own versions of a view of psychoanalytic interaction in the work of Klein, the London Kleinians, the Barangers, Bion, and Ferro. (Brown includes Freudian views, Reis less so.)

8 Brown (2011a), among others, reports that the Barangers were the first to apply Bion's group phantasy idea to the psychoanalytic dyad. While there is agreement about that point, introducing Bion's idea into psychoanalysis is not synonymous with introducing field theory to psychoanalysis. As I have argued, that distinction belongs to Sullivan.

Chapter 4

Field theory in psychoanalysis, part II

Comparing Bionian field theory and contemporary interpersonal/relational psychoanalysis

This is the second of two chapters on the field concept in psychoanalysis (see Chapter 3). The impetus for both articles is the centrality of the idea of the field in contemporary interpersonal and relational psychoanalysis (IRP), on one hand, and in Bionian field theory (BFT), on the other. How is the idea of the field used in these two schools? Does their joint use of this key word signify a similarity in their approach to clinical psychoanalysis?

Chapter 3 was devoted to a comparison of the field theory of Harry Stack Sullivan, and of Madeleine and Willy Baranger, the influential intellectual and clinical sources of field theory in IRP and BFT, respectively. This chapter moves on to compare the more contemporary writings of IRP and BFT.

Prominent interpersonal and relational writers are well known to most North American readers, and their work is easily available in English. BFT writers, on the other hand, concentrated first in South America, primarily in Uruguay and Argentina, and then, since the 1990s, also in Italy, with a smaller number in the United States. One problem for a reader limited to English, as I am, is that much of the work of BFT writers has not been translated from Italian and Spanish into English. Those who have been translated, of course, have had the greatest influence in English-speaking countries.

The most widely known, prolific, and influential BFT writer is Antonino Ferro (1996, 1999, 2002b, 2006b, 2007, 2009; Ferro and Basile, 2004, 2009b), and therefore, when I discuss BFT, it is usually Ferro's work I am addressing. Ferro's thinking, because of its widespread influence, represents the modal views of BFT theorists more than the work of any other single writer. But there is also the fact that Ferro has made a special effort to describe the details of his theoretical position. In Ferro's hands BFT is not only a theory of the analytic field; it has become an overarching theoretical scheme, a way of conceptualizing all of clinical psychoanalysis.

Besides Ferro and the Barangers, contemporary Italian and South American writers whose work contributes to BFT and appears in English include the writers represented in the volume on the analytic field edited by Ferro and Basile (2009a), César and Sára Botella (2005), Chianese (2007), and Civitarese (2008, 2012, 2014). For a sense of the larger literature in Italian and Spanish—and it is quite large—see the reference lists in Ferro's books and articles. Among Americans, Ogden (1994b, 2005) and Grotstein (2000, 2002, 2007, 2009) are important contributors. Levine (in press) offers a brief, useful introduction to Ferro, and Brown (2010, 2011b) and Reis (1999a, 1999b, 2006, 2010) bring together some of this material with other Kleinian and (in Brown's case) Freudian thinking to address their (Reis's and Brown's) versions of intersubjectivity.

Similarities

Abstraction and experience-near clinical content; co-creation and collaboration

IRP analysts are generally averse to understandings primarily rooted in logical necessity. One important reason for this attitude is that conclusions that are not phenomenologically compelling for the patient may owe what seems to be their inescapable quality to their conformity with the analyst's theory. BFT analysts share this strong preference for experience-near understanding. A great deal of the clinical process that Ferro reports is co-created: the stories he and his patients tell are negotiated and constructed collaboratively. More than once Ferro compares his understanding of clinical work in the analytic field with Winnicott's squiggle game, in which each partner adds spontaneously to what the other has created. In another spot Ferro (Ferro and Basile, 2009b) says that the analytic field can be described as a movie made jointly by two directors, analyst and patient, each of whom also continuously makes his or her own film of this joint movie. To the extent that BFT is about joint elaboration of the stories that arise in the field, as Ferro writes, the contents of BFT clinical sessions, like IRP, are experience-near, collaboration is a highly significant ideal, and abstraction is infrequent. These characteristics also jointly differentiate IRP and BFT from mainstream Freudian psychoanalysis, in which it has long been held (e.g., Freud,

1937) that, while logical necessity is of course not the preferred grounds for an interpretation, it is nevertheless acceptable when a more affectively convincing reason is not available.

It can be argued that one reason why IRP and BFT have these attributes in common is that they are both field theories. Field theory discourages abstraction and encourages experience-near understanding, because its explanations are not based on theories of the enduring psychic structures of the past, but on its portrayal of field processes in the present (Lewin, 1935, 1951). Those processes are understood as the outcomes of the past, but field theory does not require the construction of their histories. It requires only that one identify the relevant, formative influences in the here and now. For similar reasons, analytic collaboration and co-construction are also natural to field theory, because field processes implicate both participants in all events, at all times.

A complication about co-creation arises, however, because of the different ways that the analyst's involvement with the patient is conceptualized in IRP and BFT. I will return to this subject below (see "Selecting interpretations: the fallacy of understanding?").

The role of affect

One of the ways that a focus on experience-near clinical process shows itself in both IRP and BFT is the emphasis on affect shared by the two schools. The aim of Ferro's method is what Bion would call the transformation (or alphabetization, in Ferro's term) of beta elements (primitive sensory and emotional states that have yet to be symbolized) into alpha elements (symbolically represented experience) and the new capacity for symbolic thought that such transformation is said to allow.[1] In one expression of this point, and referring to the field rigidities that his form of treatment is meant to destabilize, Ferro (2009) writes,

> [U]pstream of the calcified areas of the stories and the history, there is the processes of alphabetization of protoemotional states, in which, starting from lumps of emotional alexia, we proceed to lumps of dyslexia, and ultimately to the reading, containability, and transformation of emotions that have a name and a status. The field must contract the patient's "illnesses," and it is only once this happens that genuine transformation will be possible.

Compare this to the following passage from Bromberg (2011a), which, albeit in a different kind of language, is quite similar in its expression of the centrality of affect in the context of analytic relatedness.

> Every time a patient and analyst can each access and openly share their dissociated affective experience of something that is taking place between them—some cognitively unsymbolizable aspect of their mutual experience that is felt but is unthinkable—the process of state-sharing through which this takes place begins to enlarge the domain and fluency of the dialogue.
>
> (p. 136)

Unformulated experience/unmentalized experience/ symbolization

In neither IRP nor BFT is dynamically unconscious mentation understood to be hidden away or distorted, as in traditional psychoanalytic models. IRP and BFT have in common that they are based neither in repression nor in an understanding of unconscious contents as formed and ready to be revealed when defensive operations cease. Rather, in both IRP dissociation theory and in the BFT theory of the transformation of mental contents (i.e., Bion's theory), symbolic experience has yet to be constructed. In unformulated experience (Stern, 1983, 1997, 2010a), Bion's understanding of unmentalized experience, and César and Sára Botella's (2005) BFT work on the symbolization of experience and "mental states without representation," symbolic experience is not yet shaped, or formed; it exists in either a primitive, unmentalized state (Ferro, the Botellas) or as potential that has not yet been actualized in symbolic form (Stern, Bromberg). I have already mentioned that Ferro describes the creation of symbolic experience as "alphabetization" or transformation; the Botellas call it "the work of psychic figurability"; and I refer to it as the process of formulating experience (Stern, 1983, 1997, 2010a).

Symbolization and field processes; transformation; therapeutic action as the growth of mind or self

In both IRP and BFT, the process of symbolization is either facilitated ("catalyzed" might be a better word) or inhibited by field processes, and vice versa. That is, in both sets of ideas, field processes are responsible for the selection of which experiences can be symbolized and which cannot; and in both IRP and BFT, the reciprocal is also true: the symbolization of experience plays a role in determining which events take place in the field (in Ferro's [e.g., 2009] terms, the cast of characters that appears, and what they do). Symbolization and field processes each continuously influence the forms the other takes.

Ferro adopts Bion's clinical model, according to which the analyst serves as a "container" (that is, performs a containment function) for certain mental contents of the patient, contents transferred to his mind via projective identification. Then, via reverie, the same reveric characteristic of mothers containing and processing their babies' primitive sensory and emotional experience, the analyst contains and "cooks" (a word with a certain charm in this context, and one that Ferro is fond of using) the patient's experience, thereby encouraging the transformation of protoemotional and protosensory experience into symbolically represented forms that can be used to think with. Eventually, like the baby with the mother, the patient becomes able to perform for himself the same transformation of mental content that the analyst has transformed for him. Therapeutic action is understood as the encouragement, via internalization of the analyst's capacity for reverie, of the patient's capacity more regularly and subtly to transform his own experience in this way. Symbolically represented experience is often described by Bion, and routinely by Ferro (e.g., 2009), as *waking dream thoughts*, which is a term meant to signify the process according to which primitive experience is linked with images or *pictograms* (Aulagnier, 1975/2001). In this sense, we are always potentially involved in transforming protosensory and protoemotional experience into symbols to be used in thought, and so we are always dreaming, even while awake: "The pictographing of protoemotional states entails giving a name to something that was previously nameless" (Ferro, 2009, p. 217).

The existence of these basic emotional pictograms, though, remains hypothetical; like drive and unconscious phantasy, they cannot be directly known in experience and must be inferred from what we can observe. But Ferro, and in Ferro's view Bion as well, believes that human psychology works in a way that makes the continuous process of creating pictograms undeniable. Pictograms are basic and stable building blocks of meaning (that is, they do not change over time in the way that stories do), to be combined according to *narrative transformations* that, in their turn, are determined by one's choice of *literary genre*.

A good example of Ferro's understanding here is what he describes as the "casting" of "characters." The field is represented in stories constructed consciously and unconsciously by analyst and patient together. Elements of meaning in ongoing stories—people, yes, but also significant objects, weather, animals, almost anything—are the story's characters. The casting of a new character by the patient is evidence of an expanded capacity for symbolic representation.

And so therapeutic action in BFT is understood in terms of the repair and growth of the mind, and these reparative events are mediated by the analyst's transformation of the patient's mental contents. Ferro (2006a) writes,

> The focus is no longer on a psychoanalysis that aims to remove the veil of repression or to integrate splittings, but on a psychoanalysis interested in the development of the tools that allow the development and creation of thought, that is the mental apparatus for dreaming, feeling and thinking.
>
> (p. 990)

The most original and significant of Ferro's contributions may be his description of these transformative mind events in a language derived from his combination of narrative theory and the conception of the analytic field identified with Bion and the Barangers. For my present purpose—that is, for the purpose of describing how symbolization is linked to field processes, and vice versa—it is enough to say this: for BFT analysts, the transformation of mental contents and the growth of mind come about via the relational events that transpire in the analytic situation.

There has been a substantial change in theories of therapeutic action all over the world since the days when historical reconstruction and insight were primary. In many quarters, theories of the growth of mind and the transformation of experience have replaced older concepts of change. One of the primary analytic theories with which these newer ideas have been associated is that of Bion and the contemporary analysts carrying his work forward. We have just seen that one of the conceptions most characteristic of BFT is that the events of the bi-personal field mediate the growth of mind.

It is less widely appreciated, though, that contemporary IRP, independently and according to different principles, has moved in the same direction over the last several decades. Most, and perhaps even all, contemporary IRP writers, that is, take the position that events in the field determine the contents of consciousness and the degree to which the mind is free and can grow; and they also take the same position we have just seen in BFT about the effect of new symbolization on the field: that is, new formulations of experience make new and different relational events possible.

Once again, it seems to me that this similarity can be at least partly attributed to the fact that both IRP and BFT are field theories. I have already noted that all field theories, beginning with Lewin's (1935, 1951), tend to direct interest away from explanations of the present based on the persistence of the past, and toward understandings based on present events as the outcomes of contemporary configurations of the field. Analytic events are not understood as rigidities left over from an earlier time—as in older theories of transference, for instance. The influence of field theory on the strong tendency in IRP to focus clinically on processes in the here and now is not widely noted, because the field-theory roots of IRP are seldom explicitly recognized today.

And so, as in BFT, historical reconstruction and insight about the past play a distinctly subsidiary role in IRP theories of therapeutic action, which focus instead on growth in the present. This growth is sometimes ascribed to the mind, as it is in BFT (see especially Bromberg, 2011a, and below). Sometimes it is ascribed instead to the self. In either case, though, it is an increasing capacity for symbolization that is at stake in IRP, just as it is in BFT, and this symbolization is understood as a transformation of experience based on events in the field.

Jessica Benjamin's (2004, 2009) work on the analytic third is one good example of an IRP theory of therapeutic action based in transformation of the field, which then changes the mind. Benjamin's work is rooted in an understanding of human relatedness as the relationship of two separate subjectivities. If two people are to recognize one another as separate subjectivities, and thereby avoid the breakdown into enactment or impasse, a co-created or shared intersubjective third is required. It is only thirdness that prevents the dissolution into twoness, or complementarity, a state in which intersubjectivity, or mutual recognition of the other, is absent.

For Benjamin, therapeutic action is the conversion of complementarity, or "doer–done-to relations" (see also Benjamin, 1990) into thirdness and mutual recognition, via what Ghent (1990) described as "surrender."

In surrender, one does not feel the sense of failure and domination that accompanies submission, but instead willingly and knowingly gives over to the other, or in Benjamin's frame of reference, to the third. This understanding of therapeutic action, too, is based in a kind of transformation in the here and now, and not in insight about the past or historical reconstruction. And this transformation, like BFT, represents the growth of mind.[2] Here is one of Benjamin's (2004) own statements of that theme.

> Rather than viewing understanding—that is, the third—as a thing to be acquired, a relational view sees it as an interactive process that creates a dialogic structure: a shared third, an opportunity to experience mutual recognition. This shared third, the dialogue, creates mental space for thinking as an internal conversation with the other.
>
> (p. 22)

I have already quoted Bromberg (2011a) making the similar point that symbolizing experience in the here and now, experience that had been felt but could not be thought, has a therapeutic impact by enlarging the domain of the dialogue between patient and analyst, and the capacity of the patient to think elsewhere, as well. Actually, the growth of mind is the heart of Bromberg's work, a point underlined by the appearance of the phrase in the title of his most recent book, *The Shadow of the Tsunami: And the Growth of the Relational Mind* (Bromberg, 2011a). Many other IRP theorists, myself among them, could be cited in the same vein.

While Benjamin has perhaps had the most to say about IRP concepts of the third, others have also contributed (Ogden, 1994a, 2004; Gerson, 2004, 2009; Aron, 2006). Gerson (2009), reminiscent of the way BFT authors describe the field as a joint unconscious phantasy, created by both analyst and patient but not reducible to individually contributed elements, says that the "analytic third," a "specific form" of the broader category of the "relational third," "illustrates that in all relationships unconscious structures are created that transcend the individuality of the two participants" (p. 1342). And just as in BFT the analytic situation is said to shape the events between analyst and patient into a relationship of container and contained (see the section below, "Selecting interpretations: the fallacy of understanding?"), Gerson says that the unconscious structures of the analytic third "are partially determined by the context within which the relationship exists" (p. 1342).

Differences

IRP and BFT, then, do seem to be linked by meaningful similarities, and it seems plausible to link these similarities to the field theory shared by the two perspectives. But the difference between the two ways of thinking and working are as notable as their similarities.

Internal worlds, external worlds, and the analytic relationship

Because the roots of BFT lie in the theory of unconscious phantasy, it should not be surprising that BFT virtually exclusively concerns the inner world. This point can be confusing, though, because the BFT position that the field is a joint creation can suggest (misleadingly, as it turns out) a dialogue between inner and outer. It is around the question of what the relation of inner and outer should be in psychoanalysis that IRP and BFT diverge most profoundly.

The Barangers (1961–62/2008, 2009; see Chapter 3) gave particular emphasis to the point that their version of the analytic field was a joint unconscious phantasy. Ferro seldom describes the field in the language of unconscious phantasy, but he does adopt the Barangers' conception of the field as jointly created. Yet at the same time Ferro could not be clearer that psychoanalysis is always and only about the internal world. The field is not the combination of inner and outer, but inner and *inner*—the internal, phantasy worlds of analyst and patient. (And we shall see that, even when we restrict consideration to the inner worlds of patient and analyst, there are significant limitations to the degree of interaction.) In one passage, Ferro (2009) writes that he favors:

> a kind of listening that deliberately, as it were *ad absurdum*, assumes a zero degree of external reality in any communication from the patient, thus making the session a privileged space and a unique opportunity for the transformation of the mental functioning of patient and analyst alike.
>
> (p. 211)

The most significant way this approach translates into practice is the *oneiric paradigm* (e.g., Grotstein, 2000, 2002; Ferro, 2009), in which the entire session is understood as a dream, and the analyst's most important activity becomes the process of transformation in dreaming, which operates at all time [sic] by way of a particular filter that precedes each of the patient's communications with the words: "I had a dream in which . . . "

(Ferro, 2009, p. 210)

Ferro regards everything the patient says—everyday incidents, reports of dreams, memories, *everything*—as indications of his reaction to the analyst's previous interpretations. Ferro believes that the most important part of the analyst's job is to interpret what the patient says in these terms, and then to modify his own approach to the patient on the basis of this running commentary. Consistent with a longstanding theme in Kleinian technique, Ferro ceaselessly looks for some way to intervene that responds to his current understanding of the patient's response to his interpretations.

I sometimes have difficulty in accepting this insistence on the conversion of everything the patient says into an expression of the inner world. But I remind myself that Ferro is not taking an epistemological position here. He is hardly claiming that external reality should not be considered at face value under other circumstances. He is taking a specifically clinical psychoanalytic position: it is only within the session that the patient's commentary on external reality must be understood as an expression of the inner world. This thought softens my objection, but I do still have significant misgivings, which I explain below.

Let me offer a brief and simple illustration, one that I think Ferro could very well have offered himself. On entering the session, my patient mentions that on his way to see me he bought a hot dog on the street, but that he was unhappy to find that the vendor had run out of mustard. I think of the patient saying instead, "*I had a dream in which* . . . I bought a hot dog on the street, but I was unhappy to find that the vendor had run out of mustard." I find myself open to possibilities of meaning that might not have occurred to me so readily otherwise, especially possibilities having to do with the place in the inner world of what might otherwise have seemed to be only my patient's observation of the external one. I might be more aware than I would have been otherwise, for example, of the frequency with which the patient feels emotionally deprived. I know this is a theme for him. Am I the agent of his deprivation? Perhaps the roles could be assigned the other way around, so that he is the depriver, imagining that the vendor enjoyed not giving the patient what he wanted. In any case, the patient and the vendor—and the hot dog, and the mustard, too—are all characters in Ferro's sense, because all of them represent sensory-affective experience in a form that can be thought. And what about what the patient says as his commentary on my recent clinical behavior? In the last session did I say something that makes the patient feel cheated or disappointed? Does *he* want to deprive *me* as a result? Or is the significance of the absent mustard due to mustard's role as a spicy condiment, so that perhaps something in the last session fell flat, i.e., was I unresponsive in some way? Did the patient perhaps feel that something was missing in my response to him? Ferro might use understandings such as these by making a "saturated," or explicitly transferential, interpretation (e.g., "I guess what I said must have sounded pretty bland," or "There must have been something important missing from what I said").

But remember that the analyst's purpose is not the revelation of transference, affect regulation, mutual recognition, or the expansion of freedom in the relationship between patient and analyst, but the transformation of meaning via narrative transformation of the field. For Ferro, the unpacking of the analytic relationship via interpretation simply is not the point. Nor are the relational aspects of therapeutic action that have become so significant for contemporary IRP analysts (e.g., Ehrenberg, 1992; Hoffman, 1998; Benjamin, 2004, 2009; Davies, 2004; Bromberg, 2011a; Stern, 2010a). Yes, it is crucial to Ferro to keep track of the current state of the analytic relatedness. And yes, explicit interpretation of the transference (a "saturated" interpretation) is sometimes the intervention that Ferro believes best serves the purpose of adding to the narrative currently active in the field and thus to the transformation of the patient's experience. But at other times, a saturated interpretation is not the best way to do this. And when a saturated interpretation is not the best course, it is not for the traditional reason—that is, Ferro does not decide to offer an "unsaturated" interpretation[3] as a way of negotiating the patient's resistance. No, this is a completely different point of view. For BFT, it is not important, in and of itself, to reveal the hidden parts of relatedness. What is important is to create meaning, to further the narrative currently alive in the field and to learn how the patient is responding to the analyst's interpretations. Revealing the nature of the transference/countertransference, or introducing new possibilities to the relatedness between patient and analyst, sometimes accomplishes those things. But these courses of action are not the goals of BFT; they are merely two of the ways that protoemotional elements can be transformed into waking dream thoughts. The BFT analyst's feelings toward, and perceptions of, the patient, and the patient's feelings and perceptions of the analyst, are to be used to make the analyst a better interpreter, a better transformer of meaning. The analytic relationship is always important in BFT, but as a means to an end, not as an end in itself.

And so Ferro creates and adjusts his interpretations, saturated or unsaturated, on the basis of his understanding of the patient's reaction to what he has just done (or what he did yesterday, or ten minutes ago). Let's say that Ferro understood my patient's report of the hot-dog-with-no-mustard incident as a complaint that Ferro's recent interpretations had not been very satisfying, that they had not been sufficiently tasty or nutritive. And let's say that Ferro wanted to offer an unsaturated interpretation of this state of affairs. In response to the patient's report of the hot dog incident, Ferro might say sympathetically, "That's not fair! A hot dog without mustard isn't worth much!" Or, if he thought that the remark was a way of telling a story about being insulted by some recent comment Ferro made, maybe he would say, "No mustard? It's enough to make you want to knock somebody's block off!" Or, if he thought that the patient told the story because of some kind of feeling of being alone in the session (i.e., without his mustard), "Now that's sad. That's one lonely hot dog." Or maybe, if the point seemed to be the patient's helplessness to do anything to get what he wanted from the analyst, Ferro might say, "Who would have thought the hot dog guy would end up with that kind of power?" All of these interpretations (because that is what Ferro would call them) would be offered with the intention of increasing the meaning in the narrative composing the field, in the same way that Winnicott added to the image being mutually created when he played the squiggle game with a child.

I should add, too, that Ferro would say these things only if he felt they were personally resonant contributions to the ongoing themes being developed in the field. Ferro does not create his interventions in a calculated way; what he says, that is, is not chosen with the intention of creating a certain effect. It is not Ferro's kind of language to say that he must "mean what he says"; but I have the distinct impression that this phrase conveys what he means. The BFT analyst, like the IRP analyst, intends clinical participation to be personally authentic.

Ferro's exclusive focus on the inner world, and the freedom and playfulness of his affective responsiveness to his patients, can be immensely productive. Any reading of his clinical material indicates that. One cannot miss how spontaneous, related, warm, and intuitive he is as a clinician. Over and over again it is clear to me, in reading Ferro's work (and Civitarese's [2008], as well), that he and his patients are close and familiar with one another in a way that I cannot help but imagine is good for the work. There is plenty of humor, but one also senses that the clinical atmosphere is serious and collaborative.

But any clinical choice burns bridges to other possibilities, and Ferro's (and BFT's) exclusive focus on the inner world is no exception. To understand everything the patient says as a dream makes the external world into nothing more than a means of expression and deprives trauma of a meaningful place in the genesis of human problems.

IRP analysts think differently than this about the relation of internal and external worlds. The IRP position, enunciated by Stephen Mitchell (1988) in his description of the "relational matrix" (his term for what in this article is being called the analytic field), and practiced by virtually all IRP analysts, is to think dialectically (see especially Hoffman's [1998] "dialectical-constructivist" or "psychoanalytic constructivist" views). Every phenomenon is contextualized by, and gains part of its meaning from, what it is not. The alternative to whatever occupies the foreground constitutes the background, and the meaning of each is shaped by the other. The inner world and the outer world constitute one of the most significant of these dialectical pairs. Others commonly encountered in clinical practice are past and present, conscious and unconscious, verbal and nonverbal, good object and bad object, symbolized and unmentalized, and so on. For an IRP analyst, psychoanalysis gains its best opportunities not from focusing primarily on the influence of the inner world on the outer one, and certainly not from a focus on the external, but on the continuous interaction of these two kinds of meaning, and their mutual constitution of one another. Our grasp of the external world, of course, is deeply influenced and informed by the internal one. But the internal world is also shaped by the events in the world outside it, and especially by trauma; and in the IRP view this interaction is so continuous and complex that, in practice, the two worlds are completely entwined with one another.

Co-creation?

It can appear that the BFT analyst is a fully fledged participant, contributing his own subjectivity in a way that, like the IRP analyst, is symmetrical ("mutual" is the word used in IRP [Aron, 1996]).[4] It can appear that way because the BFT analyst does actively participate in creating the field, and acknowledges doing so; but BFT analysts believe, it seems to me, that they are something more like handmaidens—or perhaps better, particularly active muses—serving the transformative processes of the patient's mind. The field is understood to be co-created, but only in the terms of the container–contained model—and that means, at least by the standards of IRP, that the two participants are not actually mutually creating what comes to exist between them. The analyst is not responsible for the shape of the field in the same way that the patient is. The analyst's own, separate affective involvement with patients is not the subject of BFT interest, as it is in IRP.[5] Ferro (2002a) certainly does suggest that the analyst must allow his experience to be *responsive* to the patient: "the analyst . . . must allow himself to be involved—in effect captured—by the forces of the field" (p. 48). The analyst, in other words, must let himself have his nonrational, affective response to the patient. Such responsiveness, in interaction with the storylines originated by the patient, creates the field.

But responsiveness is not the same thing as independent participation; it is not initiative. BFT analysts believe that they do not directly participate in creating the narratives that make up the field. It is considered desirable and entirely possible in BFT for the analyst to work freely within the analytic role, *without* contributing his own stories. Later in the same article from which I quoted just now, for example, Ferro (2002a) writes, "it is the patient's projective identifications and emotions, and these *alone*, that must enter into stories" (p. 57; italics from the original). This expression of the point is particularly clear, but it is not rare: statements that only the patient should projectively identify are common in BFT work. The compassionate acceptance in BFT of the analyst's sometimes unwitting projection into the patient does not weaken the point; it is instead a statement of the exception (the analyst's compassionately accepted failure) that proves the rule.

There are occasions on which BFT writers do more than this with enactments, something more like the mutuality of IRP (for example, see Civitarese, 2008, Chapter 4). This wrinkle does not change the point, but it does complicate it: the difference between IRP and BFT on this aspect of clinical work is not absolute, but a matter of degree.

I have already mentioned that the question of the analyst's emotional involvement with the patient is for me one of the most confusing aspects of BFT, and now perhaps it is clear why. The language used by BFT writers is often the language of co-creation, and yet the analyst's freedom is generally limited to his response, in affect and phantasy, to the patient. The analyst usually should not *initiate* meanings, or narratives; and in BFT it is considered possible to live up to this requirement. The IRP analyst, on the other hand, believes that it is impossible for the analyst *not* to contribute his own meanings and stories—although much of this part of the analyst's activity is unconscious. In fact, it is the primary task of the treatment in IRP to sort out and work with, and through, the interplay of the patient's meanings/feelings and the analyst's.

Selecting interpretations: the fallacy of understanding?

As I have already pointed out, IRP and BFT share the perspective that new experience in psychoanalytic treatment is not uncovered but created. But the two groups differ over the processes by which this newly created experience comes into being. This difference, in fact, may be the most important clinical divergence of IRP and BFT.

Most IRP writers are constructivists (Mitchell, 1993, 1997; Stern, 1997, 2010a, 2012; Hoffman, 1998, 2009): they understand conscious experience to be in a continuous process of coming into being. The unconscious, in this frame of reference, is not fully formed, requiring only discovery or revelation to become conscious; it is instead unformulated or potential experience, a vaguely organized, primitive, global, nonideational, affective state. This does not mean, though, that anything goes. Like the hermeneutic philosophers who have inspired some of their views in these matters, IRP analysts are not relativists. They make a point of saying that reality is indeed "there," and that reality therefore constrains what we can think, feel, and perceive while remaining sane and truthful. But reality, being multiple and manifold, usually leaves a certain degree of indeterminacy or ambiguity, to be resolved by the way we construct conscious experience.

The most crucial events from moment to moment, then, both inside and outside the consulting room, are those that resolve the ambiguity of unformulated experience into some explicit, conscious shape. Most IRP analysts, and perhaps even all, would agree that the factors responsible for resolving that ambiguity are relational phenomena, the very events that comprise the analytic field. For IRP, remember, the field is made of the and interactions of the patient's and the analyst's conscious [un]conscious experience and conduct. The more freedom exists in the [field] between patient and analyst, the wider the reach of the self and the capacity of the minds in the field to think and feel without inhibition, distortion, or constraint. This freedom grows as a result of finding and symbolizing the dissociated experience that motivates and comprises the enactments between patient and analyst.

And so IRP analysts are continuously curious about the motivations and intentions behind their own participation. They are ready to find evidence in any of their experiences or understandings of their unconscious involvements with their patients. This attitude began in the work of Edgar Levenson, whose first book, *The Fallacy of Understanding* (1972), took its title from its assertion that unless the analyst recognizes that each clinical understanding can also be an unconscious participation with the patient in the very themes of the interpretation, the interpretation will do nothing more than continue to enact the same problem it describes. Ever since the appearance of this idea, IRP analysts have continuously questioned themselves about their participation in clinical process, trying to imagine what they might be enacting with their patients, simply in the course of conducting the treatment.

BFT analysts have a different attitude about their clinical participation. While explicit about embracing constructivism (see Civitarese's [2008, Chapter 5] excellent presentation of this point), they believe that, in the very act of setting up the analytic situation, the roles of analyst and patient are being defined in the terms of container–contained. The container–contained configuration is inherent to the analytic relationship, a natural consequence of two people being together in search of the understanding of one of them (which is not to dismiss the significance of the analyst's understanding of him- or herself). That is, simply by virtue of adopting the roles of analyst and patient, the analyst becomes the container and the patient the contained. The assumption of these functions by patient and analyst happens, so to speak, "by itself"—by which I mean without any necessary conscious intention on the part of either the patient or the analyst. In this vein, Ferro (2009, p. 210) writes that,

> the operations of historical reconstruction . . . or the unveiling of unconscious phantasies are important not only in themselves but also in so far as they . . . become the occasion for and vehicle of development

of the container and the α-function, *even if this takes place without analyst and patient being aware of it* (italics added for emphasis).

The position that the container–contained configuration is an inherent part of the analytic situation explains the frequency with which BFT analysts assert that the patient (and not the analyst) offers projective identifications and the analyst (and not the patient), via reverie, transforms the projective identifications into a more differentiated form of experience. However, it is worth noting that the analyst's capacity for containment can be drawn into troubles in the analytic field, and maintaining it can be a struggle. Containment occurs, that is, when things are going reasonably well, or smoothly. Given that state of affairs, the container–contained roles of patient and analyst follow naturally, unlike the situation that is believed by IRP analysts to obtain in their treatments, in which mutual, personally derived unconscious influence never ceases to influence the shape of analytic events and the roles taken by the participants, even when things are moving along without any obvious problem.

By virtue of this definition of the roles of analyst and patient, it seems, BFT analysts can generally depend on their understandings to be constructed in the service of their patients. BFT analysts generally write as if their choice of interpretation, because it is the outcome of their containing function, can usually be trusted to be rooted in the intention to digest the patient's projective identification.

IRP analysts, on the other hand, wonder about the significance of the choice. Which intervention attracts the analyst, and why (i.e., what unconscious influences might be involved)? What can be learned about the analytic relationship by considering these questions? What new freedom might become available if the analyst does not simply settle on a way of proceeding and forge ahead, but, in the midst of choosing a course for the immediate future, continues to question himself about the significance of what he is drawn to do?

Ferro assigns meanings to patients' communications with an intelligence, exuberance, and spontaneity that are both likeable and admirable. But I could and would not do what he does, at least not as often as he does it, even though I aspire to his manner. Why? Because very often his interpretive choices, if I were to make them, would strike me as arbitrary. (Putting it this way—that is, emphasizing the subjectivity of my preference—is important, because I certainly don't mean to say that Ferro, given his theoretical commitments, should feel about his choices the way I do. I will try to say why I have the preferences I do, and I am willing to argue that this choice may be best for others, as well—but I intend to avoid claims of objective correctness.) He writes as if he trusts his own clinical instincts implicitly; he decides on an interpretive tack on the basis of what occurs to him, and he generally does not seem to wonder about the place of this choice in what is unfolding unconsciously between him and the patient. He reacts spontaneously. Of course, in one way, so do we all—or so we aspire to do. But on the basis of what I have read, I believe that BFT analysts have more immediate confidence than IRP analysts do that the understanding that comes to mind is a simple and unalloyed expression of clinical care for the patient.

Ferro has offered the example I am about to quote in at least two articles. The passage below is from Ferro and Basile (2009b).

> An experienced colleague asks me for a consultancy due to a dramatic situation he is going through. I get the first bits of information over the phone—as he lives in a nation in the far North. In the last few weeks, both he and his family have been protected by body guards because of the threats made by one of his patients.
>
> This patient, I am told by my colleague during a session, has threatened him because analysis caused him to lose the joy of living, made him get married, become a father, find a job in a bank, but all this prevented him from finding "true life." He lost all the women he could have had, had to give up the custom-built cars he used to own when he was young, the travels he could have made. In short, the price was too high, and now he wants to get back at his analyst by killing him after slaughtering the analyst's family. The analyst incidentally tells me that the patient continues to get some special creams from Switzerland to treat a worrying rash.
>
> What speaks to me as *chosen fact* is the rash, the red skin, a tangential element, i.e., the "redskin." A redskin who terrifies all the pale faces (white men). But I wonder why. A redskin cannot be so scary.
>
> I enquire about the age of both the patient and the analyst.
>
> The patient will turn 40 and, around the same time, the analyst will turn 50.
>
> Here is the key: the "redskin" of the patient, with his flaming arrows, sets fire to the "redskin" of the analyst. The very same redskin

with which the analyst had lost contact and which caught fire upon the crisis of his fiftieth birthday (and the fortieth of the patient).

A life spent working in a bank, a life spent in the consulting room, is quite unacceptable to the redskin (the redskins!) who claims revenge and makes threats. A painful mourning process, for the many existential potentials given up, has to be carried out. A mourning process of accepting reality is preceded by telluric shocks of anger.

Having tactfully helped my colleague to reestablish contact with his own "redskin" has enabled him to contain the patient's redskin without fearing his own so much, so that each of them was able to find a way to give some relief and space to his own redskin.

(p. 16)

For those unfamiliar with working this way, this illustration can be surprising, even shocking. In conventional terms, Ferro's selection of the "redskin" idea seems arbitrary, based only on his internal reactions to it. He gets to his interpretation via a *selected* or *chosen fact*: the patient's rash and the cream he uses to calm it down. Many analysts would feel that this "fact" is "chosen" out of the blue. The IRP analyst might worry that accepting this kind of arbitrary-seeming inner prompting as the basis for one's interventions, without wondering why this very particular and rather odd detail—the patient's rash—suddenly seems uppermost in the analyst's mind, is liable to be a step down a slippery slope to the blind enactment of exactly what ought to be symbolized.

It would be one thing if Ferro were treating the redskin idea as an expressive metaphor—that is, if he *first* had the thought that the patient had not really come to terms with growing up and sacrificing some of the powerful experiences of youth to do so. If he *then* came up with the metaphor of the redskin, as an expression of this theme, those of us who work differently would probably be more comfortable.

But that is precisely the point. The theory of mind that Ferro is using—a version of Bion's—leads Ferro to believe that what he needs to do is to allow the patient's (in this case, the colleague's) projective identifications to contact his mind in a way that stimulates his own responsive production of pictograms, and eventually waking dream thoughts. The reason Ferro does not start out with an observation and then create a metaphor for it is simply that he does not believe that is the way the mind works. The production of thought proceeds concretely, via images and waking dream thoughts; and it matters not at all whether these images are rational or sensible representations. Such considerations are simply irrelevant, as they were in Keats's idea of *negative capability*, which Ferro cites nearly as often as reverie in his explanations of what the analyst's mind does with the patient's projective identifications. In criticizing Coleridge and others who sought to formulate theories and categorize knowledge, Keats (1899) wrote,

> it struck me what quality went to form a Man of Achievement, especially in Literature, and which Shakespeare possessed so enormously— I mean Negative Capability, that is, when a man is capable of being in uncertainties, mysteries, doubts, without any irritable reaching after fact and reason.
>
> (p. 277)

In Ferro's view, if thought develops far enough, an abstract observation may come about. But in the BFT worldview, and especially Ferro's, metaphors do not illustrate more general points; general points, if they take place at all (and they do not necessarily, and need not—remember the role of unsaturated interpretations), are not the source of metaphor, but instead are metaphor's eventual *result*. Metaphors come first. In fact, to call waking dream thoughts metaphors in the first place is not quite right. They are more like concrete representations; they are direct expressions. Typically there is no space, or very little space, between waking dream thoughts and what they symbolize, no "as if" quality. For Ferro, it is not "as if" the patient and the supervisee are redskins. They *are* redskins.

To be more precise, I should really say that Ferro often, but not always, *works as if* the vocabulary of images and characters are direct representations, not metaphors. That is, addressing these phenomena this way often suits his clinical purposes. He also can understand images and characters as metaphors, of course, and he sometimes works with them that way, as when he playfully engages patients with unsaturated interpretations that are really more like sly acknowledgments of some aspect of the analytic relationship, a kind of metaphorical communication in the language of imagery, one that the patient is "in" on. For instance, having heard from the patient how bad his dinner was the night before, and sharing a little, implicit joke with the patient about the correspondence between the bad dinner and Ferro's bad interpretations of the day before, Ferro might say something wry about the person who cooked the dinner, knowing perfectly well that the patient will take the communication as a direct but humorous acknowledgment by Ferro of his responsibility. But these exceptions should not obscure the point that characters and images for Ferro are generally treated as symbolic expressions no further removed from what they represent than dream images feel to the dreamer. Most of the time, it is as if the analyst is working *within* the dream, constructing a mutual inner reality and sharing it with the patient the way it feels to a dreamer as he dreams. The analyst may "know better" in some other epistemology that is not clinically relevant. But that is just the point: it is not relevant. In the session, the analyst lives in the world being jointly created in phantasy with the patient.

I said that the reason Ferro does not start out with an observation and then create a metaphor for it is simply that he does not believe that that is the way the mind works. What I should really say is that Ferro does not believe that this is the way the mind works *in the world in which clinical events take place*. But the point, whittled to its proper size, is still significantly different from the way most IRP analysts usually understand symbolic representation.[6]

Despite being surprised by the ease with which Ferro accepted his own nonrational thought in the redskin example, I feel a kinship with this way of thinking and working. Its reliance on the analyst's intuition and clinical conviction appeals to me and reflects what I often do. It is noteworthy that the clinical outcome of the "redskin" interpretation was excellent, suggesting that Ferro's understanding took account of the powerful affects in the field. It is also noteworthy that Ferro does, in fact, consider one aspect of what may have been his unconscious participation—in this case, a facilitative unconscious participation. It turns out that Ferro's birthday, his 60th, was at about the same time as the patient's 40th and the colleague's 50th. Ferro implies that he, too, is a disappointed redskin, and that he was therefore able to grasp the patient's and the colleague's meanings.

And that is the way the BFT literature often reads: unconscious participation is routinely involved, but it is generally facilitative in nature. The more troubling kind of enactments that are described in the IRP literature are virtually never reported in the BFT literature, and the enactments that are reported are seldom, if ever, portrayed as seriously disruptive. It is impossible to say whether this relative calm is a real difference between IRP and BFT, or whether more disruptive enactments are underreported in BFT (as I have the impression they may be in other literatures).

Cultural differences

When I first read the "redskin" example, I was shocked at that use of language. But that reaction was short-lived, because of course I recognized immediately that Ferro used this word, "redskin," in complete innocence of how it signifies in North America—especially since he tells us that, as a child, he admired Geronimo. But this example does bring home the reality of cultural difference.

One thing that has impressed me over and over again in reading the clinical literature of BFT is the greater acceptance that I see in the United States and Canada, by both analyst and patient, of the analyst's authority. Prior to the 1960s, I have the impression that American patients, for the most part, felt secure being in the hands of analysts who believed they knew the contents of their patients' minds, and who conveyed that knowledge in interpretations that they expected their patients to accept. Of course, reluctance on patients' part to accept their analysts' interpretations was common enough, usually understood as privately motivated resistance; but patients' attitude toward their analysts' authority was much less ambivalent than it is today.

I don't mean to accuse North American analysts from earlier times of accepting in some unthinking way what Lacan calls being "the one who knows." That is, I don't mean that analysts were any less thoughtful then than they are now. I am referring to a sociopolitical change that, today, makes the naked expression of authority frequently objectionable in North America, and makes suspect any interchange constructed largely according to authority relations. It is a truism that it simply doesn't mean the same thing in our culture today that it meant in the 1950s to be a doctor, a policeman, a teacher, a religious leader—or a psychoanalyst.

My personal opinion is that this change is not entirely due to what I would like to be able to believe in: the effective deconstruction of authority relations, so that authoritarianism (authority embraced for its own sake) is easily differentiated from rational authority (authority that is based on expertise and that gives itself up when the expertise is learned by the other). It seems to me that today authority relations are more subtle than they were in the past, and tend to be expressed indirectly. Authority is continuously confused with authoritarianism, resulting in kneejerk rejection of authority that, in fact, may not be problematic. It is more often the *appearance* of authority than its actuality that has become distasteful. One shouldn't *look* as if one is wielding authority. There are many individuals who are sincerely concerned with the reality of authority relations, of course. But when it comes to authority, the widest current in the culture, I fear, if not the deepest, has to do with appearances. American psychoanalysis, like the rest of the culture, has been affected by both the sincere desire to deconstruct authority and the more superficial desire not to appear authoritarian.

But in Italy the sense that authority should not be visible seems not to have come about to the same degree. In clinical examples presented by Ferro, he often says things to patients that make me marvel at the degree to which he expects patients to accept what he has to say, no matter how little his comment may be conventionally related to what the patient has just said—and the degree to which patients do, in fact, find what he says useful.

Of course, the response to me from a practitioner of BFT would probably be that what I have noticed simply illustrates how deeply Ferro and his patients are cohabiting the field, so that they understand each other even when, to an outsider, what they say doesn't signify in conventional terms. I accept that claim to some degree; I would even want to claim that my own exchanges with patients sometimes sound just that way. But I also think that it is likely that this kind of interchange, when it occurs with the frequency with which it seems to happen in BFT, requires an acceptance of straightforward authority relations that is rare today in the United States and Canada: in Ferro's work, it seems that the analyst is the expert, and the patient is there to find out what the expert sees and knows. The fact that what the BFT analyst "knows" is not some kind of fixed thought in his mind, but comes about in a fluid way as the session moves along, does not change my impression about the role of authority.

To wonder about a greater degree of authority in Italian analytic relationships than in those in the United States and Canada may seem to amount to a denial of the joint construction of the field that is so close to the heart of BFT. I hope I am not read that way. Fields can be jointly constructed with different degrees of authority between their partners. Collaboration probably requires that the partners agree about the distribution of authority, but collaboration certainly doesn't require its absence. In my reading of their clinical illustrations I see that BFT writers, especially Ferro, have consistently collaborative relationships with their patients.

IRP analysts have been those at the forefront of concern about authority in the consulting room (e.g., Hoffman, 1996; Mitchell, 1997; Fairfield *et al.*, 2002; Hirsch, 2014). And so my noting of this issue may have something specific to do with my embeddedness in a particular intellectual and clinical community. But I suspect it goes beyond that. I think that working the way that Ferro does is easier in Ferro's culture than it is in ours.

Coda

Should we conclude, from the IRP perspective, that BFT is missing something in giving less consideration than IRP does to the analyst's continuous unconscious involvement with patients?

When one understands the differences between psychoanalytic approaches, the criticisms one might make of one school from the perspective of the other are blunted by an appreciation of the fact that each school arises from its own distinctive view of the world. Unless one takes issue with the worldview, the differences seem necessary. If one accepts Bion's theory of the mind, along with the position that the container–contained model is inherent in the analytic relationship, then it seems inevitable that the analytic field is a transformational environment in which the analyst can trust his own mind to "cook" the patient's projective identifications. In IRP, on the other hand, analyst and patient, while they obviously do have different roles, are also involved with one another in the same way that any other two people in a relationship are mutually involved. The analytic field is a continuous interaction of inescapable, reciprocal, emotional influence, conscious and unconscious. Given this view of the world, analysts must continuously reimagine the ways in which their participations comprise an unconscious enactment with the patient of affectively saturated themes that need to be symbolized.

Notes

1 These conceptions were originally Bion's, of course. Ferro uses them in his own way, attributing a meaning to them that seems more allied with natural science, such as cognitive psychology, than they had in Bion's thinking, which seems more allied with philosophy. In Ferro's hands, beta and alpha elements are like levels of the organization of experience, something like Bucci's (1997) modes of representation. In this chapter I use these terms as Ferro uses them.
2 I am bringing out the similarity here for heuristic reasons, but there are significant differences, of course. Benjamin's version of the field, the third, is a direct manifestation of curative processes, because it is what allows doer–done-to relations to be transcended and what makes intersubjectivity possible. The BFT field, on the other hand, has no such role. It is better understood as the site of both the problems and the cure. As I have already quoted Ferro in the text, the field must "contract the patient's illness," and then

be cured of it. It is also apposite that, unlike Ferro's conception of the analytic field, Benjamin's third has nothing to do with unconscious phantasy.

3 An unsaturated interpretation is a participation by the analyst that, while it may address themes active in the analytic relationship, does not directly address the transference–countertransference. Instead, it furthers the patient's narrative in that narrative's own terms. See examples below.

4 Of course, the *roles* of analyst and patient are no more mutual in IRP than they are in BFT or any other psychoanalytic school. What is mutual in IRP is the impact of the personhood of each participant on the other, especially the unconscious impact.

5 I want to be sure not to be misunderstood on this point. When I refer to the IRP analyst's separate affective involvement with patients, I don't mean to suggest that IRP analysts knowingly introduce their own personal themes to the field. The personal affective involvement I am referring to, which IRP analysts believe is inevitable, is a spontaneous emotional responsiveness, sometimes only going on outside awareness. Yet, by searching out and addressing the resulting mutual enactments, IRP analysts believe that such involvements on the analyst's part offer access to unsymbolized aspects of the patient's experience that would otherwise be impossible to reach.

6 It is also worth noting, though, that BFT is not the only psychoanalytic perspective from which it has been observed that, under certain circumstances, symbols do not have metaphorical status and instead are one with what they represent. Loewald (1978) wrote about this in the case of language: "Words in their original or recovered power do not function then as signs or symbols for . . . something other than themselves, but as being of the same substance, the same actual efficacy as that which they name; they embody it in a specific sensory-motor medium" (p. 203).

Chapter 5

Relational freedom and therapeutic action

The freedom to experience

Novel conscious experience is unbidden (Stern, 1990). It arrives in our minds and bodies without an accompanying consciousness of effort or memory of process; the means by which we create it are not available to our inspection. We do not have access to what we would need in order to construct a phenomenological account of the genesis of the experience we create.

There is a strangeness about the unbiddenness of novel experience, and about the hidden unfolding of its process, a strangeness we seldom notice. We have so little sensuous or even cognitive contact with what takes place in our minds to create novelty that it is in some ways as if it belonged to someone else. When experience is unbidden, we are unfamiliar to ourselves; our minds and bodies are not simply our own, at least if possessing ourselves means knowing what we possess. In itself, this fact is strange; yet what is perhaps even stranger is that it seldom registers. In order to be aware of how *un*familiar we are to ourselves, it is usually necessary to pay explicit, conscious attention to how little we have to do with selecting and shaping the conscious contents of our minds. We must remind ourselves, actively and with conscious purpose, that those contents generally appear spontaneously and suddenly, out of what feels like nowhere. Experience is just *there*. Despite the fact, though, that we must agree that we have no prior acquaintance with much of what we find in our minds and feel in our bodies, we do not feel most of this novel experience as alien or "other" to us, nor does the ongoing process of creating, observing, and containing such experience have an alienating impact. Quite the contrary. The process feels natural, and its products, in the very moments of their arrival, feel as if they belong to us, as if they are part of us. They do not feel as unfamiliar as, in fact, they are. If anything, and oddly, or at least contrarily, they usually feel *familiar*. The whole process seems utterly unremarkable. Unbidden, novel experience is like the air we breathe: it is outside us or beyond us, but, at the same time, it is completely of a piece with living.

What I am describing is the *freedom to experience*, the freedom to use our minds. But when we are free in this way, we never know what our minds will do; and so perhaps it would be better not to describe the freedom to experience as the freedom to use our minds, but as the willingness to allow our minds their freedom.

The unbidden expresses us, it manifests us. It realizes or actualizes us. It gives emotionally and cognitively tangible form to what we are. For my purposes, then, the unbidden lies at the heart of therapeutic action, at once both the heart of the process of change and the index we consult to assess it.

Unbidden experience is not arcane. It is not a rare event, and it is not necessarily powerful or dramatically enlightening (although the clinical example I will offer later on happens to be both). Unbidden experience appears routinely. In this sense, creativity is rampant in our lives. It happens in the office all day long, to therapists just as often as to patients. A patient looks up at me and I have the sudden perception that she is quite sad: that is an unbidden experience. Or a tone in her voice alerts me to a note of regret that I have missed until then: *that* is an unbidden experience. A flash of her eye awakens my awareness of her irritation at me: unbidden again. Something she says makes me understand that her worry that I will think she is self-indulgent is her mother talking: once again, unbidden. None of these things comes about because I try or decide in any consciously purposeful way to have the experience, and all these thoughts are novel. They just happen. As a matter of fact, you can see that unbidden experience is more the rule than the exception, the result of what, 20-some years ago, I (Stern, 1990) called the process of courting surprise. The freedom to experience is a deeper-than-conscious willingness to let go and allow the unbidden to come into being.

The interpersonal field

I may have made it sound as if I believe that this kind of experiencing goes on in the confines of one person's subjectivity, as if all this spontaneous unfolding comes about like a spring bubbling up out of the earth. But that metaphor is terribly incomplete. Let me explain.

What I have just described as the freedom to experience is the process by which unformulated experience is articulated or formulated (Stern, 1997, 2010a). I have not yet made the crucial point that, even when the process of formulation unfolds without inhibition, disruption, or detour, its course is charted in the same moment that it takes place, and its final shape therefore comes into being only as it arrives in our minds. Prior to that moment, what will become formulated experience is only possibility. Experience, that is, does not preexist its formulation; it is not predetermined, but emergent; it is not the revelation of something that is already "there" in the mind, but a process, an activity.[1] In fact, if we were to insist on precise expression, we would refer not to experience but to *experiencing*. We can never be certain of what our next experience will be.

What, then, determines which possibility, among the several or many that constitute any moment's "wiggle room," will come into being in the unbidden formulations of any given moment?

Reality does constrain the possibilities. If we claim validity for experience, we are not free to articulate the unformulated in any way we please. We create the articulated meanings that arrive unbidden in our minds from among the potential meanings offered by unformulated experience; and all of this meaning making generally goes on outside awareness. Ideally, the resulting unbidden experience fits the purposes that animated it in the first place, while simultaneously respecting reality's constraints.

How should we think about these purposes—the ones that select formulation from the unformulated possibilities offered by reality, the ones that animate the unbidden? Here we reach the interpersonal, relational, or intersubjective dimension of the experience. My position has always been that the experience that can be formulated within the analytic dyad is a function of the nature of the relatedness between the two people (Stern, 1983, 1997, 2010a). The possibilities for the changing contents of consciousness, in other words, are determined by the equally mercurial nature of the *interpersonal field*, a concept that Harry Stack Sullivan began to formulate in the 1920s (Sullivan, 1940, 1953; Murphy and Cattell, 1952) and that was then developed in an explicitly psychoanalytic direction by many others (e.g., Wolstein, 1959, 1964; Levenson, 1972, 1983, 1991; Ehrenberg, 1992; Stern, 1997, 2010a; Bromberg, 1998, 2006, 2011a; Fiscalini, 2004).[2] Stephen Mitchell's (1988) *relational matrix* and Jay Greenberg's (1995) *interactive matrix* belong to the same theoretical tradition.

The field is a jointly created configuration of relatedness, a social medium that is the result of the conscious and unconscious involvement and intersection of two subjectivities.³ The participants in the field may or may not be aware of the field's influences on them, depending at least partly on the consequences that would ensue from that awareness. The field is more like concepts of the analytic or intersubjective third (see Ogden's [1994a] and Benjamin's [2004] conceptions, which overlap but are distinctly different), or what Gerson (2004) calls the relational unconscious, than a mere context or surround. We might say that the field is that configuration of influences that continuously gives clinical process its particular, changing shape and nature.

The fact that the field links two subjectivities, however, does not mean that it is a simple additive combination of influences. Instead, it is a unique creation, a new and ceaselessly changing *gestalt* that expresses and represents the present, shifting states of relatedness between patient and analyst. The field is not synonymous with transference–countertransference. If the idea of transference–countertransference remains meaningful (if, that is, it has not become so diluted that it refers tothe entire analytic relationship), it must refer to patterns of relatedness modeled on the nature of experience with significant people from the past. The interpersonal field is broader than that. It includes the influences on each participant of the entire nexus of affects, motives and intentions, thoughts, proto-thoughts, meaningful behaviors, metaphors, and phantasies that come into being when two people are involved with one another.⁴

Freedom in the interpersonal field is defined by the degree of latitude patient and analyst have to relate to one another without the kinds of constraints introduced by unconscious defensive purposes. In the language of relational dissociation theory, the most potent and limiting of these constraints appear in the field as enactments, jointly constructed by patient and analyst. These enactments are defensive operations that prevent the eruption of dissociated "not-me" experience into the consciousness of at least one member of the pair, thereby protecting the stability of the self, or identity. That is, the exclusion of not-me from awareness preserves one's sense of who one is (Bromberg, 1998, 2006, 2011a; Stern, 2004, 2010a) by restricting what parts of subjectivity can become known, formulated, unbidden experience.⁵ Enactments are the attribution of one's dissociated parts to the other, who one then treats as the alien, dissociated part of oneself. Enactment can therefore be described as "the interpersonalization of dissociation" (Stern, 2004, 2010a), a rigidity in the field, an impasse or "deadlock" (Stern, 2003), a single-mindedness that allows no alternatives. In the Barangers' (1961–62/2008, 2009) neo-Kleinian theory of the "bipersonal psychotherapeutic relationship," or in their later, more felicitous term, "intersubjective field" (W. Baranger, 1979), similar, jointly constructed constraints or frozen parts of the field are referred to as "bastions" or "bulwarks" (depending on the translator). Ferro (2006b) describes bulwarks as "nuclei of resistance" or "the couple's blind spots" (p. 998). In both the dissociation model and Bionian field theory, rigidities in the field lead to stereotyped interactions that can be destructive constraints on the freedom to create the future;[7] and from both perspectives, the more relaxed the field is, the more the minds of each participant are free to create unbidden experience.

How the field is composed in any particular moment encourages some unbidden articulations of experience and discourages others (Stern, 1997, 2010a). In turn, we can say that the composition of the field is created by the interaction of the self-states of its participants, and is therefore in continuous flux. As self-states shift in the minds of each participant, as they routinely do, in responsive reciprocity with the self-states of the other participant (e.g., Bromberg, 1998, 2006, 2011a), the field changes.

But the interpersonal field remains a concept, not an experience. In more experience-near terms, changes in the field are changes in the possibilities for relatedness—i.e., changes in the kinds of relatedness that are facilitated and inhibited. We rarely "know" the field. For the most part, the field comes to our attention only through what we *sense* or *feel* of its influences. To explicitly reflect on the field usually requires a conscious effort, one that few people besides psychotherapists, with their professional interests, have a reason to expend; and there are many circumstances, or aspects of the field, that do not even allow the possibility of such reflection. On the phenomenological level, as the nature of the field shifts, but generally without attracting our conscious attention, different kinds of relatedness feel most obvious or natural to the participants. Patient and analyst fall most easily into, and out of, certain relational patterns. These events are unnoticed, unremarkable—in a word, "natural." As one kind of relatedness becomes natural (say, to take a simple example, friendliness), other kinds of relatedness (say, irritability) fall into the background and feel less comfortable, easy, or natural to create in this environment, or are even actively avoided, sometimes with unconscious purpose (i.e., unconscious defensive purpose).

From this perspective follow two further points: First, if we take seriously the facilitating and inhibiting influences of the field on the contents of individual minds, we also must take the position that the freedom to allow the greatest range of unbidden experience rests on the degree of flexibility and freedom of the field. Second, the degree of the field's flexibility is defined by the range of relatedness available to the participants. We can summarize these points in terms that express what I am trying to say in this article: the freedom to experience—that is, our access to the widest range of unbidden experience—rests on what we might call *relational freedom*, a topic to which I will turn momentarily.

And so my answer to the question of why the metaphor of the spring bubbling up from the earth is incomplete is that this metaphor might give the impression that the "ground" from which the "spring" emerges is solid and unmoving. But I am taking the position that unbidden experience emerges from the possibilities allowed and prohibited by the interpersonal field, which is in constant flux. And so, while each person's unbidden experience can indeed be conceived as a continuous stream, as William James (1890) may have been the first to note, what the stream grows from is something much more complex than the earth. It is hard even to imagine the kind of mobile geometry that might represent the process, although the emergent processes of nonlinear dynamic systems offer interesting possibilities.

Let me review what I have said to this point. Therapeutic action depends on our freedom to allow ourselves novel, unbidden experience. But the particular novel formulation that appears in our mind is just one of the possibilities that can be created from any moment's unformulated experience. We therefore need to conceptualize the process by which that particular formulation becomes the one that arrives in consciousness. That process, I have claimed, depends on the conscious and unconscious events of the interpersonal field. Therapeutic action has to do with the creation and emergence of unbidden formulations of experience from the nexus of influences that is the interpersonal field.

Now let me add the third and final piece of the puzzle, and, for my purposes in this chapter, the most significant part of what I want to say.

Relational freedom

If the interpersonal field is the gateway into consciousness, facilitating some formulations of experience while preventing others, then whatever

...vs the most freedom in the field is also what will allow each ...ant in the relationship to best take advantage of whatever personal ...eedom he or she brings to the encounter—or creates there. And therefore, we can conclude that whatever we can do to make it possible for the analytic relationship to evolve freely, without constraint, inhibition, or constriction, is the best way we have to encourage the freedom to experience. Relational freedom makes the freedom to experience possible, and therefore underpins therapeutic action.

In practice, of course, psychoanalysts also think of this idea the other way around: that is, we think of new understanding as the means by which we accomplish new relational effects. In fact, this is the more traditional conception: increased understanding dissolves the rigidities of the transference–countertransference and in that way becomes the source of greater relational freedom.

The truth is that all psychoanalysts approach the problems of therapeutic goals and therapeutic action from both of these directions. It would be impossible not to. Sometimes we work toward greater freedom to experience, hoping that such an outcome will free relatedness; at other times, we work toward a greater freedom in relation to the other, hoping that this outcome will free our capacity for unbidden experience. To the extent that our various theoretical commitments differ on this point, the differences are not absolute; they are, rather, differences of emphasis. In the interpersonal/relational perspective, the emphasis falls on the mutative effects of freeing clinical relatedness, while more traditional approaches tend to conceptualize the interpretive understanding of transference. The emphasis in this article on the creation of relational freedom rather than on the conventional pursuit of interpretive understanding should not obscure the recognition that analysts of all persuasions work and think in both ways.

And so my primary interest falls on this question: How can we encourage relational freedom? The dilemma here is that, to be able to answer the question about what is transpiring in the interpersonal field at any particular time, one would need to know precisely what one does not and cannot know in that moment. Our reflective grasp of relatedness is always at least one step behind the relatedness itself. That is doubly true for any problematic aspects of the relatedness, the parts that represent patterns of unconscious involvement between analyst and patient. That is, what one would need to be able to formulate, if one were to be able to observe whatever is problematic and having a constricting effect on the therapeutic relatedness, is always unformulated, and therefore invisible, until the moment in which it resolves—until the very growth in question has become possible. And by that time, the reason the solution is visible is that it has already taken place.

I have written elsewhere (Stern, 2004, 2009a, 2009b, 2010a; and see also Bromberg, 1998, 2006, 2011a, who is the source of this idea) that enactments resolve not through insight, but via new perceptions of the other and oneself, new perceptions that come about unpredictably. The best one can do to influence problematic aspects of relatedness is to be sensitive to the kinds of affective "snags" and "chafings," ranging from feeling vaguely uncomfortable to actively unpleasant, that signal the presence of dissociated enactments (Stern, 2004). One stops and attends to such experiences, asking oneself what can be learned about what lies behind them.

Enactments comprise a subcategory of the broader class of field rigidities that inhibit the freedom to experience. Enactments, that is, are extreme examples of these inhibitions; but in any analyst's daily work, there are many, many other, milder constrictions in the field, and they need to be relaxed, too. Since dissociative enactments are one kind of field constriction, we can use what we know about them to think more broadly about encouraging relational freedom.

Our goal in relaxing milder constrictions of the field is the same in kind as our goal in working with dissociative enactment: we want to do whatever is possible to become aware of, and then loosen, constricted interaction, thereby promoting therapeutic action by unlocking the capacity of relatedness to serve as the crucible for the unbidden. But because these events—this relaxation of relatedness—are an *emergent* quality of the relatedness itself, it is impossible to specify in advance a technique to accomplish it. Events arise from within the analytic relationship in a way that simply cannot be predicted. And so we can almost never describe exactly what needs to be done to expand relational freedom. Such episodes can be encouraged by our openness to the unexpected (an openness that is always and necessarily only partial), but only that much is possible. There can be no prescriptive theory of technique (cf. Tublin, 2011). We do our best to court surprise. We attend to affective snags and chafing, and we allow ourselves to feel the clinical relatedness so deeply that its subtle possibilities for growth affect us in ways that we do not necessarily even formulate in so many words. Our affective involvement and thoughtful study of our own experience are all we can contribute.

Sometimes the process of expanding relational freedom takes place as the result of interpretation; but more often in my experience—in the illustration I am about to offer, yes, but also in most instances in my own work in which relational freedom has expanded—the change is better described as a relational effect, a kind of groping, by one or both participants in the treatment, toward affectively charged meaning, meaning that may or may not eventually be expressed in words. It often *appears* that verbal interpretation is the source of therapeutic action, because when new understandings do come about verbally, the words are often surprising, gripping, powerful. And sometimes verbal interpretation *is* mutative, of course, as I have already made a point of saying. But I believe that, usually, the key event has already taken place by the time a new verbal understanding appears, even when the verbal understanding in question is unbidden. The key event that so often precedes verbal understanding is the appearance of new relational freedom. It is this relational freedom, a loosening or relaxing of the interpersonal field, that creates the possibility of new experience, including new verbal understanding, that each member of the relationship can have in the other's presence (Stern, 2009b, 2010a). As relational freedom expands, the field changes and new, unbidden meanings appear spontaneously, the way water rushes in to fill an empty space.

The new experiences that patient and analyst can have in one another's presence when relational freedom expands are not limited to experiences that correspond to, or represent, this new interpersonal opening. The unbidden experience that opens from new relational freedom, in other words, is not limited to the aspects of transference–countertransference that composed the previous constriction. The novel experience that becomes explicitly available may be fantasy or memory not obviously related to the new relational freedom; or it may be some kind of insight about other, seemingly irrelevant matters, such as the sudden appearance in the mind of one of the partners of an understanding of some aspect of his own or the other's character; the novel experience may even be (as in the clinical illustration to which I will turn in a moment) a new observation or grasp of some part of the patient's history or current life outside the treatment. The relaxation of a constriction in the field, we can say, "unlocks" the potential in certain other experiences that, while they must be in some way connected to the constriction, are not necessarily linked to it in ways that are immediately obvious.

In general, as the possibilities of relatedness expand, we become more and more able to allow our minds their full measure of creative invention and expression; we tolerate and even enjoy thinking and feeling with relative freedom, even when that freedom brings a certain amount of discomfort. The greater the degree of relational freedom, the less the interaction is guided or interrupted by the kinds of derailments, distortions, or distractions that take place when unconscious defensive needs, in order to manage affective discomfort, force relatedness into certain themes, or down certain pathways. Instead, we create a relatively welcoming attitude toward our own capacity to feel, think, and innovate, allowing our conscious experience to shape itself in whatever way best serves our deepest nondefensive intentions at the moment. By "deepest nondefensive intentions," an ambiguous phrase at best, I mean intentions that are integrative or synthetic, and sometimes articulating or differentiating. I mean the constructive, what Freud meant by Eros.

I do not mean to suggest, though, that relational freedom is a concrete goal, as if it were a position that is possible to reach. I mean, instead, to present clinical relatedness as a continuous amalgam, or dialectic, of freedom and constriction, so that our work is organized by the ongoing challenge to identify constriction and create freedom. Each change in the field, including each successful creation of new relational freedom, leads to new possibilities for both freedom *and* constriction. The challenge of creating relational freedom lasts as long as the treatment endures.

How does the idea of relational freedom relate to the traditional ways of representing freedom in discussions of technique, i.e., the patient's free association (Freud, 1913) and the analyst's evenly hovering attention?

Free association and evenly hovering attention are matters of individual intention and decision. Analyst and patient quite knowingly, and separately, take on these attitudes, functions, and ways of conduct. Bollas (2001) calls them "the *Freudian pair*" (p. 93; italics from the original). Of course, neither free association nor evenly hovering attention can be adopted in any absolute sense. Each is always compromised by unconscious factors—analyst and patient can do no more than try to fulfill the intentions described by these terms. Nevertheless, even in the presence of these compromises, free association and evenly hovering attention are understood to be consciously chosen. In this frame of reference, even if analyst and patient must maintain the greatest respect for the encroachments of the unconscious, some part of freedom can be made to happen.

Relational freedom, on the other hand, is not a set of intentions, but a welcome but unpredictable outcome, and so it cannot be adopted or "taken on" by choice at all, either separately or jointly. When it comes about, it occurs as a joint, nonconscious creation of analyst and patient. Relational freedom, like (say) Benjamin's (1990, 2004) "intersubjectivity," is a mutually created attribute of the analytic relatedness that, while it can be hoped for, cannot be intentionally selected or chosen, by either participant, in any meaningful sense. It must, instead, grow spontaneously from activities that the analytic pair engages in at least partly in the hope of provoking it. Unconscious encroachment has the same degree of salience it has in the classical view, but in the relational scheme the location of its primary influence has shifted from the single mind to the dyad: the unconscious of both the patient and the analyst, both that unconscious that encroaches and that other unconscious that expands creatively into new experience, expresses itself in a joint creation—the field. And therefore we cannot say that relational freedom is chosen in any sense at all; we must say instead that it emerges. In relational terms, no part of freedom can be made to happen.[8]

There are myriad discussions of the subject of freedom in the psychoanalytic literature, but I must be content for the time being to examine only the questions I have raised about free association and evenly hovering attention. I particularly regret not being able to carry out a comparison between my views and those presented by Symington (1983) in his classic article on the analyst's "act of freedom" as agent of therapeutic change.

One last point before going on to my clinical illustration, a point that I cannot overemphasize: relational freedom is created and reflected as much in the experience of the analyst as the patient. From a relational psychoanalytic perspective it is axiomatic that patient and analyst are each routinely and continuously involved with one another, both consciously and unconsciously.

Clinical illustration

When he started treatment, my patient, William, was a talented and successful 50-year-old corporate lawyer who had just married for the first time a few years earlier, and now had three young daughters. He felt lucky to have met his wife, Jan. He felt close and intimate with her, and he was wildly in love with his children. He had always wanted a family of his own but had worried, as he got older, that he would never have one. Earlier in his career he had worked for a large law firm in Manhattan, and he had worked the usual horrendous hours demanded by such jobs. He had enough anxiety about romantic relationships in those days to have used the excuse provided by his work hours to avoid an active social life with women and instead to have spent most of his few free evenings either alone at home or watching sports with male friends at bars. He met Jan, who was 15 years younger than he was, while collaborating on a case with another firm, and it was then that he began to feel willing, and eventually eager, to confront his inhibitions. He felt for the first time that he just could not bear to limit himself to professional success, and that perhaps he really could have a family. After much soul searching of this kind (and prior to entering treatment), he managed to find a corporate job in a boutique firm, small but wealthy. While offering him a lower income than he had made as a partner in his previous firm, the new firm allowed him enough time to develop his life with the woman who would eventually become his wife. The relative freedom of his new job also allowed him to pursue a four-time-a-week analysis, which Jan encouraged him to begin, and that he himself came to feel that he needed because of longstanding anxieties, including, but not limited to, his previous avoidance of romantic relationships; and a strong degree of self-criticism that sometimes descended into agitated depression. He already took antidepressants, but once he began his analysis he nurtured the hope that treatment would eventually help him do without them.

William grew up in the suburbs of New York City with his parents and two sisters. He was the oldest of the three siblings and always did well in school. From early in his life it was taken for granted, both by others and by himself, that he would do well; and he did, all the way along. He earned high grades and was popular, well liked, and athletic.

During his second year of college, he had what he considered to be the formative experience of his life, a terrible automobile accident. He suffered broken bones, internal injuries, and disfigurement that required extensive (and successful) plastic surgery. He lost consciousness, and it was not clear for some time after the accident how much brain damage he had sustained and how well he would recover from it. It was not even clear for a considerable period whether he would survive. Treatment went on for months, during which time he had many surgeries and was often in severe pain and in and out of critical condition. He spent much time in the Intensive Care

Unit. Thin to begin with, he lost more weight. Eventually he spent time in a rehabilitation facility and recovered remarkably well, both physically and cognitively, although he does have medical sequelae to this day.

But I am primarily concerned here with the psychological trauma. William certainly recognized that he had been emotionally traumatized by these terrible events, but he also knew that, despite trying to be open to their impact on him, he had always maintained a certain distance from them. The trauma of his accident and the awful aspects of his treatment were important to him, and he often looked for the impact of these things in other, later happenings in his life. As I said, he thought of the accident as the single most important event of his life. But his explorations and associations about it, at least when he spoke of them to me, were never as powerful as one might think they would have been; and he was a little melancholy about this inability to feel the depths of his trauma in the relatedness between him and those with whom he was close, including me. As important as this piece of his life was, he just could not feel it as deeply as he longed to, or share it with the fullness that he could sometimes imagine but could not create. He had a sense of loss about this. It was not until after the session I will recount that either he or I really formulated the fact that, despite the presence of caring people around him, he had always lacked a witness for these experiences; but in retrospect, after that session, we agreed that on an implicit level he had always missed having the sense that someone was there, during those events, who really grasped how he felt about what had happened to him. That is where we were at the time of the incident I am going to describe.

One of the sources of William's self-criticism was his sense that, despite backing off from his professional commitments to the degree he had, he was still too involved in his work life, and that his family suffered as a result. He had made a lot of money as a partner in his previous firm, and so he did not really need the income he made now. But he had not felt ready to give up a work life yet, and as long as he did continue working, his self-regard required him to do it responsibly. And so he was well aware that he had made choices that kept him from being with his family as much as he could have been if that had been his only priority. He sometimes felt, guiltily, that his family should be his sole consideration. But his worries went further: he could become quite upset, even frightened, that his willingness to spend time working, away from them, would alienate his wife and children; he worried that he would cease being important to them. And yet he was not willing to give up his work, either.

It may not surprise you to find out that, despite these worries, William is as involved a father as I have known. His relationship with his wife and children, although it has its difficulties (and I will detail those in a moment) is warm and intimate.

And so William's worry about becoming unimportant to his family was unnecessary, at least as far as reality was concerned. Jan did not resent his work, although she was often impatient and sometimes quite angry about William's need for ceaseless reassurance of her love for him. It was also obvious that William's children felt proud of their father's success, secure in their attachment to him, and quite happy to see him off to work in the morning. No, the problem was William's self-criticism—and the nature of his relatedness to his parents.

William worried that he would reproduce his parents' narcissistic relationship with him, in which a great deal of the interaction between them and him was intended to demonstrate his parents' love and generosity. That would have been difficult enough for William; but the more significant purpose of these expressions of affection and concern from William's parents was to harvest appreciation and gratitude, so that William's father and mother could feel affirmed in their role as parents. There were endless presents for the grandchildren, for instance, for which not only the grandchildren, but also William and his wife, were expected to be impressed and grateful. Never mind that the gifts were never matched to what the children really wanted. The gifts and the children's wants were so poorly matched, in fact, that the children seemed to take it for granted that the presents were nothing more than reasons that they needed to say thank you. On one hand, William resented and battled the narcissism in his parents, while on the other he unconsciously identified with this way of being. As a result, in his relationship with his wife and children, William tried to avoid a narcissistic investment in his own life that would compromise his relationship to them and, simultaneously and unwittingly, sometimes put his wife and children in the same emotional position that his parents had put him—which is to say, a position in which William needed his wife and kids to appreciate him for his generosity and goodness and felt frustrated and resentful if that response was not forthcoming. When he saw all this clearly, especially his resentment, he felt guilty and ashamed. William was quite authentically warm and generous, while also angling for his family's affirmation in ways that he disapproved of whenever he understood himself to be acting on these motives. He was anxious when he worried about his selfishness, and he was resentful when he felt his family withheld the affirmation he needed.

The analytic relatedness, of course, was partly shaped around these same themes. William worried that when he had to change the time of a session or was late in arriving, I would resent him for his selfish preoccupation with himself and his own needs. And he sometimes barely suppressed his irritation with me when I behaved in a way that he could tell had something to do with my own needs and not only with his. It goes without saying that I found myself being able to understand my own behavior, at times, as the reciprocal roles in these two kinds of interaction. William and I had a good collaboration about these parts of what went on between us; we noted and spoke about them frequently.

One day William arrived for his session in a state of extreme upset. He had had a particularly bad time the evening before with his wife. It was one of those times when he needed her reassurance, and when she became, as she sometimes did at these moments, more and more irritated and withholding. William was in and out of touch with what he was doing, pressuring her in his subtle way, which he acknowledged could be manipulative, playing on her guilt. He sympathized with the way his wife felt; but he also needed the reassurance and felt angry that she would not give it to him. He just couldn't stop trying to elicit it, all the time feeling more and more miserable, desperate, and alternately angry at her and hating himself. His unhappiness was palpable, and I felt badly for him. I am fond of William, and I felt keenly that, despite being able to understand his wife's feelings, there was a way in which William really couldn't help the way he behaved and felt.

As he was talking to me (he was on the couch), I was also having another reaction, one fairly unusual for me. I was thinking that perhaps I would have liked William to feel that he could call me during this awful time the evening before. I guessed that he would not have felt comfortable doing that, for several reasons. He would have worried that he would burden me, and he would have doubted the justification for interrupting my evening. Under many circumstances, I might have agreed with him.

The people with whom I work seldom call me, and I only infrequently encourage them to do so. I usually do so only when I know they are in a terrible reality that may collapse. I have often encouraged people to call me after surgery or a crucial diagnosis, or asked them to allow me to check in with them after such events; I have told people to feel free to call if a friend or relative took a turn for the worse or died before I saw them next, as has sometimes appeared likely; I have certainly told people to call me if they were suicidal; and so on. But I cannot remember an occasion on which I have encouraged patients to call me because they felt unhappy, especially if the unhappiness had to do with a problem with unconscious roots that was a focus of the treatment. That is what I meant just above when I said that, under many circumstances, I might not encourage a patient to call me. I want to be reliable and available, but I don't necessarily want to encourage the perception that contact with me outside the session solves problems (see Balint, 1968, on malignant regression).

And so, as William talked to me, I mused about why I was having the thought that maybe he should have called me. Why did this particular incident call out this response in me? But I made no headway. The minutes ticked by. William talked to me, and I listened. I felt that my opportunity to speak my piece was draining away. Soon, I could sense, the moment would be gone, and it would no longer be possible for me to tell him that he should have called me. But what was I doing by saying this? I could not tell. Finally, the last moment came, the moment after which I knew the opportunity would have passed.

I still felt like speaking, and so I did, without knowing exactly why, but feeling that my impulse was, at the very least, not merely narcissistic. I felt that I was speaking up for William. I felt that saying something at this moment was in William's interest, although I could not really give a strong argument to support that conclusion. I said simply, "Maybe you should have called me."

William was suddenly quiet. Although he is deeply emotional, he does not cry easily. Actually, I think that, up to that time, he had not cried with me at all. After a few moments of silence, a tear rolled down the side of his face. I was deeply moved. He didn't respond verbally, but it wasn't necessary. I felt content to sit quietly. The silence continued for a couple of minutes. William then began to talk again, telling me about how the prior evening had eventually ended in a kind of rapprochement with his wife that had made him feel a little better.

Then he began to tell me about the next morning—that is, the morning of this same day, just a few hours before the session we were having right then. William and his wife often took their children to school together. That morning, the five of them came downstairs in their apartment building together, and William's wife and daughters continued out the door and down the street, while William took care of some business about a package with the doorman. When William finished and walked out the door and on to the sidewalk, he saw his wife and daughters walking down the street, their backs to him, perhaps 50 yards ahead. He was struck with a sudden, intense melancholy, seeing them together like that. They seemed to be natural in one another's company, and here he was, alone and apart from them, looking at them walking away from him.

I felt William's wistful sense of being left behind, and I found myself thinking about the months after the auto accident all those years ago, and about his surgeries and recuperation, first in the hospital and then at the rehabilitation facility. For some reason, I imagined what it would have been like for him at the end of each day, when friends and family would leave him alone in his room. I imagined that, as they left, he was sometimes in pain and frightened about the future. I had no idea then, nor do I now, why this was my association, but the thought was unbidden and very clear. I had no idea if my thought bore any relation to his experience all those years ago, but I did know that I wanted to tell him about it. I said, "I don't know exactly why, but when I think of you looking down the street like that, after Jan and the kids, I think of you in the hospital after the accident and what it could have felt like to you whenever your friends and family left you there at the end of the day, when they went home for the night. I thought that being left alone like that could have been pretty terrible, especially when you didn't really know whether you were going to be OK, and that maybe that feeling is something that's been missing from our talking about that time in your life. Maybe being left behind with that pain and fear was pretty awful."

William responded by bursting into tears. He sobbed on and off for the remainder of the session. We said very little about content, except to agree on two things: William's feelings of being left alone and behind were indeed crucial, but had never before really been formulated in just that way; and the episode that had taken place earlier in the session, when I suggested that maybe William should have called me the night before, had somehow made possible what happened later in the session. In this case, the loosening between us seems to have begun with me and not with him. I am not sure why that was, although I have some thoughts about it that I will describe in a moment. Nor do I know, for that matter, whether, if we followed the sequence backward in time, we might find some way in which it appeared that it was not me but William who initiated the process. I suspect, actually, that trying to establish which participant sets off such sequences is an exercise in futility. Sometimes it appears that one participant initiates the sequence, sometimes it appears to be the other; but it is hard to imagine that the relation between the appearance of priority and its reality is anything other than complex and ambiguous.

In any case, when I told William that maybe he should have called me the night before, something released or relaxed in me. Something in me opened to him. I felt in that moment an unalloyed sense of wanting to be there for William, uncomplicated by any reservation. I had felt the depth of his need, and in that simple suggestion that maybe he should have called me I had responded to that need with a depth that (I felt) matched his own. I have mentioned that, despite the fact that William frequently had company during the recuperation that followed the accident, he had not really had a witnessing presence during that terrible time (see Stern, 2009a, 2009b, 2010a, 2012). Something changed in that respect during this session, and the change continued over time in William's life, both with me and with others. After this session, he found himself able to talk about his accident and his recuperation with his wife and close friends in ways that he could not before—and of course that difference in the way he could talk about it reflected a difference in the way he experienced it. In finding our way to the possibility of knowing this part of his experience together, William and I brought a new intensity and depth of feeling to the way he occupied this part of his life.

These events between William and me are an example of what I mean by an expansion of relational freedom. Perhaps now it is clear why I have also said that such an expansion is not usually accomplished by interpretation, and often not by any kind of verbal understanding at all. Relational freedom is usually something we grope toward. It is sometimes the result of one person serving as witness for the other. The outcome is that the way is opened to unbidden experience of other kinds, as the way was opened for me, in this instance, to imagine something entirely new and unbidden about William's experience after his accident. Note that, as I have already claimed, the new unbidden experience that came about as a consequence of the relaxation of the clinical process cannot be described (at least not without an effort of imagination—see the paragraph that immediately follows this one) as the unbidden symbolization of the transference–countertransference exchange most relevant to the appearance of the new relational freedom. What came to light was something else, something that no doubt bears some meaningful relation to the relaxation of clinical process that provoked it, but that cannot be reduced to its representation.

But let me also acknowledge what might be the point of view of those many analysts, probably the majority, for whom the concept of interpretation is central to therapeutic action, and will remain so. I suspect that most of these analysts, to the extent that they disagree with me, do not differ so much over what I did with William, but rather over how I understand what I did. They will perhaps argue that when I said, "Maybe you should have called me," my intervention can actually be understood as an interpretation, or, as one commentator put it, at least "interpretation adjacent." Their point, that is, might be that what I said can be read to imply something about the nature of the transference–countertransference, something perhaps like, "Maybe your history with your parents, and the worries you can't help having about my emotional responsiveness as a result, leaves you in a position in which you don't turn to me for help, comfort, or reassurance as much as you might otherwise want to do."

But that kind of interpretive statement is not what I thought I was doing in the moment. In fact, in order to understand what I did as an interpretation, I had to feel my way into it on the basis of my imagination of the perspective held by colleagues who hold views different than my own. I also think there is something to be said for reserving the concept of interpretation for interventions that are expressly interpretive in form and intention—and mine was neither. In any case, I do want to acknowledge the possibility of looking at what I did as an interpretation, because I want to avoid the implication, which might be drawn mistakenly by some readers if I don't make this point explicit, that I think of interpretation in simplistic, caricatured terms, as if I believe it to be an intellectualized, impersonal, emotionally removed form of intervention made "from above" by the analyst.

Constriction, relaxation, and relational freedom

To this point, I have addressed the expansion of relational freedom between William and me primarily as a matter of growth. That, I believe, is one good way to understand what took place: there is a perspective from which it seems reasonable to say that freedom found its way, without much controversy or conflict, into aspects of our relatedness in which it had been absent.

But these events can also be understood as the relaxation of constrictions in the relatedness between us. Before I end, I want to tell you something about the obstacles to relational freedom between William and me—the nature of the constrictions that may have been inhibiting the range of our relatedness, and what I think may have happened to relax them.[9]

When patient and therapist first meet one another, they have not yet created patterns of relatedness between them. That fact leads to a surprising possibility: patient and analyst may be more free to formulate certain observations of one another at the inception of their relationship than they will be once they have established a relational history between them. That is not to say that a relational history is anything less than central to the possibility of favorable treatment outcomes. We all know, whatever the details of our particular theories, that the creation of patterns of relatedness, and then the use and description of these patterns, lies at the heart of therapeutic action. But as patient and therapist get to know one another and these patterns begin to be established, it becomes more and more likely that the relatedness between the two people is structured in ways that become habitual. The two participants establish mutually interlocking ways of being; they "get used to" one another. These habitual patterns of relatedness tend to be conservative; they preserve the status quo; they are safe.

Some part of the atmosphere of safety in any treatment is authentically secure, of course—by which I mean that this part of the atmosphere of safety rests on each partner's well-earned confidence in the other's sensitivity and emotional responsiveness. (It goes without saying that the patient's sense of safety is more important than the analyst's; but the analyst's confidence in the stability of the patient's connection to him or her is also important, and gets too little attention.) This authentic kind of safety not only does not inhibit new experience, it facilitates it.

But the atmosphere of safety also has a dark side: it is defined partly by patterns of relatedness that represent the mutually constructed *avoidance* of aspects of relatedness that we (unconsciously) fear would be unacceptably uncomfortable if we experienced them more openly or directly. As these patterns are constructed over time, the range of the unbidden experience that each participant can have in the presence of the other can actually become narrower. Unexpected moments become less frequent, replaced by a (frequently comforting) sense of familiarity. Harry Stack Sullivan (1956) described selective inattention, the process that mediates this kind of relatedness, as "so suave that we are not warned that we have not heard the important thing in the story that it has just been dropped out" (p. 52), a description that conveys the feeling of naturalness that, for both parties, eventually slips into the atmosphere in a way that inhibits new experience and discourages surprise.

The constrictions of relatedness that are hidden by seamless patterns of interaction—that is, the sources of discomfort that seamless patterns of relatedness are unconsciously created to obscure—constitute knots that must be relaxed if relational freedom is to expand. As I have said throughout these remarks, successfully relaxing these constrictions, and thereby shifting the parameters of the interpersonal field in a way that frees the minds of both analyst and patient, is one of the most important ways we have to open the analytic relationship to the wider and deeper range of unbidden experience that is the hallmark of successful psychoanalytic treatment.

In retrospect, I can speculate about the patterns of relatedness that were functioning to constrict the experience that was possible between William and me. Given what I have told you already, you can no doubt imagine easily enough that William worried that his need of me would be burdensome. I believe that he often did his best, from one moment to the next, and without awareness, to give me the sense that he wanted or needed very little from the relatedness between us. And yet, of course, he did; that is, he wanted something important from me and he conveyed to me that he did, although in ways that usually allowed him to keep from himself the significance of what he was doing. I have already mentioned that sometimes he was mildly annoyed with me when he sensed my own interests, even if the evidence was as minor as my wish to share with him a funny moment.

Looking back in time, it seems likely to me that, feeling William's worry about burdening me or being disappointed in me, I responded with a certain caution, hoping (in a way that I did not formulate) to avoid the outcomes that would have let him down, annoyed him, or shamed him by making him feel like a burden to me. This was all quite subtle, if I am right to construct our history this way; and it resulted in a certain tightness or awkwardness (though "awkwardness" feels like too strong a word) around my nurture and concern for William. That tightness, in turn, would have made William feel just a bit tighter about these things himself, resulting in a kind of subtly inhibited quality in the atmosphere. The possibility of William's shame was, I believe, ever present. All of this (again, if I am right) was obscured by a seamless quality in our dealings with one another, a quality that, by allowing us to keep these issues blunted or dampened, protected both of us from direct exposure to our subtle awkwardness with one another.

When I think back on it I feel that, for a few weeks prior to the episode I have recounted, I had a certain anticipatory awareness of all of this, a kind of orienting toward it, the way a flower turns to the sun. Without having found any words to describe it, or even explicitly noticing it—and certainly without having explicitly reflected on it—I was sensing certain affective snags and chafings related to the tightness I have described. In a less than conscious way, I was playing with these snags, noting them and giving them increasingly free rein to gambol about in my mind. I think I worked myself into a slightly different relation to these aspects of our relationship, so that when I spoke to William about calling me on the phone, I spoke from a state in which I was more relaxed about these issues between us than I had been. I think the impact of my less inhibited state registered on William. I think he might have felt, rightly, that when I spoke I was just giving voice to a spontaneous thought. He could have taken this impression from my tone of voice or my relaxed informality. The very spontaneity of the remark, in fact, probably contributed to the way it moved William. He could tell, I speculate, that what I said came from my wish to comfort him and not from a technical prescription—although it would be precisely my contention that the point here is that these two kinds of response can be, and in this case were, indistinguishable. But of course, like me, William put none of these events or understandings into words prior to our later discussion of them.

As a consequence of this expansion of relational freedom and the changes in the interpersonal field that fell into place as a result, we each became spontaneously capable, in the presence of the other, of unbidden experience we had not been capable of having before. I had the urge to tell him he should have called me, and he could be moved by it; and then, later on, I had the unbidden thought about his abandonment in the hospital; and again he could respond to it and allow himself the spontaneous experience of being witnessed. William's response to me was just as much the result of a new relational freedom as my responses were: that is, the fact that I could offer William an experience of witnessing did not necessarily mean that he would be able to accept it.

Or am I imagining this whole preparatory history? Maybe the episodes in that session happened pretty much the way they felt in the moments in which they came together: all at once, without anything like gradual development. Maybe events reached a tipping point and then just toppled over into change, as we might characterize the events in the language of nonlinear dynamic systems theory.

In either case, though, whether we are using a linear or a nonlinear model of change, I am comfortable with the conclusion that all the events I have described had to happen by themselves. They had to be unbidden. William and I could not have *made* them happen, although it is certainly fair to say that we *wanted* them to happen. Or at least he and I would agree that we *would* have wanted them to happen, if, prior to their occurrence, we could have imagined them explicitly enough to make wanting them possible. This was especially true of my part of the relatedness, since I can't imagine that I would have spoken as I did to William about calling me without the hope, even if it was implicit, that what I said would somehow be useful to him. Why else would anyone say such a thing? I did not formulate what I was about to say in so many words; but it seems to me, looking back at it, that I wanted to convey that I cared about how William felt, and also that I wanted him to be able to feel whatever he would feel in response to knowing this.

If someone had stopped me in that moment, asked me to spell out my motive for wanting to tell William that maybe he should have called me, and given me a few seconds to think, I suppose that I could have offered some sort of coherent explanation. But I certainly wasn't able to think that clearly before I spoke. I *couldn't* have, not in that moment, not the way it unfolded. As I have said, even before we take account of our unconscious involvement with our patients, which of course complicates matters even further, our thoughts lag behind our conduct. Our capacity for reflection is always at least a step behind our participation; and that means that we psychotherapists often must make our decisions without knowing exactly what we are doing. In such moments of choice, which are so frequent that we cease even recognizing them, our experience is not formulated and cannot be, at least not in time to serve as the basis for our judgment about what to do next. We depend on our own analyses and the rest of our training, and on our clinical experience, all of which are in our bones. But in the end, even though our participation is educated, we are really just doing our best to find a response that is adequate to our clinical and human purposes. We are feeling our way. We are courting surprise. This particular moment with William did surprise me. And the relatedness between us then opened in a way that I could not have predicted.

Notes

1 Making this point always requires adding a proviso. It is not as if the mind is empty of content until the process of formulation creates it. But the content that preexists formulation remains to be given an explicit shape, and can take on any one of a number of such shapes that exist within the constraints that limit the valid possibilities for articulation in any particular instance. Regarding reality and its constraints, see the text, just below.

2 If we do not restrict attention to the formulations of the interpersonal school, many other writers could be added to this list, notably relational analysts (e.g., Aron, Benjamin, Davies, Hoffman, Ogden), a number of whom are also identified with interpersonal psychoanalysis and are therefore not cited here but in the text. Other contributors are object relations theorists and other Middle School writers (Fairbairn, Winnicott, Guntrip, Balint, and so on); self psychologists and intersubjectivists (Stolorow, Lachmann, and their colleagues); students of development (Beatrice Beebe; Daniel Stern, including the work of the Boston Change Process Study Group); and neo-Kleinians and Bionians (see footnote 4). Contributors to field thinking also include Freudian writers such as James McLaughlin and Hans Loewald. The significance of Loewald's work in this regard is not often recognized, but note Mitchell's (2000) observation: "Perhaps *the* central feature of Loewald's revisions of Freudian theory is his shifting the locus of experience, the point of origination, from the individual to the field within which the individual comes into consciousness. . . . In the beginning, Loewald says over and over again, is not the impulse: in the beginning is the field in which all individuals are embedded" (p. 35).

3 By specifying both conscious and unconscious involvement, I mean to emphasize that the interpersonal field should not be understood to exclude object relations. This point has often been misunderstood, and as a consequence the interpersonal field has been mischaracterized in sociological terms. In interpersonal psychoanalysis, social phenomena and the unconscious mind have always been understood to be reciprocal and interpenetrating. Neither is meaningful without the other, and each is the context in which the other gains its significance. Interpersonal relations are simultaneously provocations or reasons for internal, individual, unconscious events and reflections of those same events. See, for instance, Sullivan (1940, 1953); Levenson (1972, 1983, 1991); Bromberg (1998, 2006, 2011a).

4 The conception of the field described in this paragraph is influenced not only by interpersonal and relational writers, but also by neo-Kleinian and Bionian theorists of the field (Baranger and Baranger, 1961–62/2008, 2009; Chianese, 2007; Civitarese, 2008, 2012; Ferro, 2002b, 2006a, 2007, 2009; Ferro and Basile, 2009a; Brown, 2011b). Racker (1968) might also be included in this group. This is not the place to compare the understandings of the field held by interpersonal/relational and neo-Kleinian/Bionian analysts. Chapters 3 and 4 take up those comparisons.

5 For a related but different relational view of dissociation and enactment, see Davies (1996, 1997, 1998, 1999, 2004).

6 There is a significant degree of overlap here with the concept of projective identification, at least when projective identification is used defensively. But there are differences, too. For a comparison, see Stern (2010a, pp. 17–18).

7 But it is also true that, precisely because enactments (and bastions and nuclei of resistance) inhibit the free unfolding of the future, their resolution is one of the most important influences liberating the future to unfold more freely than the past did. This point is made explicitly in both literatures (e.g., Stern, 2004; Ferro, 2006b).

8 Although a discussion of Hoffman's (2006) relational critique of free association and evenly hovering attention would take me too far afield here, I subscribe to Hoffman's argument that accepting free association and evenly hovering attention as the basic functions of our work implies the denial of three things: the patient's agency, the patient's

and the analyst's interpersonal influence, and the patient's share of responsibility for co-constructing the analytic relationship. In fact, one might say that the concept of relational freedom is one way to imagine living in a psychoanalytic world in which these denials do not exist, and in which, therefore, free association and evenly hovering attention are not the key concepts that they remain for most analysts today.
9 Samuel Gerson (1996, 2004) has explored a similar area of clinical work under the rubric of "intersubjective resistance."

Chapter 6

Witnessing across time
Accessing the present from the past and the past from the present

Trauma and witnessing

Over the last several decades, after a long history of virtually ignoring the role of "real" experience[1] in the development of personality, many psychoanalysts have become so familiar with the impact of trauma on memory that we take the basic facts for granted. We know that the past can be frozen in our minds, its affective aspects especially inaccessible, and that under such conditions this experience cannot serve as the inexhaustible resource we otherwise depend on it to be in the course of our day-to-day creation of meaning. In one way or another, the past is foreclosed for so many of those who suffer trauma. In some cases the entire memory is inaccessible. More frequently, though, the memory is present but affectively drained, i.e., de-animated or denatured in such a way that it has meaning only as fact, not as living experience.

One of the psychoanalytic bodies of work that makes most sense of the effect of trauma on memory is Arnold Modell's (1990, 2003, 2005, 2009, 2011), influenced by Modell's reading of neuroscientist Gerald Edelman (1987, 1990) on neural networks and cognitive processing, and cognitive linguist George Lakoff and philosopher Mark Johnson (Lakoff and Johnson, 1999, 2003) on the central role of metaphor in cognition. For Modell, the past participates in the creation of present experience by means of the creation of metaphor. That is, in the present we are reminded of something about the past. We have the sense that our experience of the present is in some way *like* our experience of some aspect of the past. In this way, a memory becomes a metaphor for some aspect of the present. What Modell calls an "emotional category" is formed—things feel as if they belong together.

Let us say I am walking down the street with a close friend who, in the course of conversation, says something that reminds me of a certain turn of phrase commonly used by my beloved, deceased grandfather. I may or may not be explicitly aware of the correspondence, but it is there in my mind. If there is a feeling-connection between the two episodes—that is, if I am feeling warmly about my friend—some of the feeling of my relationship with my grandfather may begin to participate in the way the relationship and the afternoon feel, and the day is enriched. As a result, perhaps I see something new about my friend, some experience that had always been there in a potential way, but that I had never formulated. I may consciously think of my grandfather during these events. But I may not—I believe that such events often take place outside awareness, leaving us with only an affective resonance that nevertheless colors our conscious experience in highly significant ways.

In this way, a link between past and present comes about, and the past becomes an unconscious resource for the creation of present meaning. The past lends something to the present; and the present, by being linked to the past, keeps alive the continuous, unconscious growth and development of our histories. Modell (2009) characterizes metaphor as "the currency of the emotional mind" (p. 6). Elsewhere he (Modell, 2009, 2011) suggests that "metaphor and metonymy are the primary and crucial cognitive tools of unconscious thought" (2011, p. 126), and he makes the proposal, quite welcome as far as I am concerned, that "we are more liable to find common ground with neighboring fields if we take the position that the unconscious mind [is] the area within which meaning is processed as metaphor" (p. 126). A similar sensibility runs through the work of Loewald (see especially Loewald, 1960), for whom the concept of transference has several meanings, one of which is the transfer of the intensity and emotional power of the unconscious and the past to the preconscious and the present.

With Modell's orientation to metaphor in mind, let me return for a moment to that walk with my friend. It is not necessarily only that my sense of my friend has been enriched by my memory of my grandfather. The reciprocal may also be true: my memory of my grandfather may now be just a little different than it was before, enriched by this moment with my friend. Along with Modell and Loewald, I believe that, in such a case, it should hardly be said that my experience of my friend is distorting my memory of my grandfather; rather, this present-day experience is helping me to sense some subtle aspect of my grandfather, unformulated for me

until now, that, as a result of my experience in the present, may be n
fully realized, via metaphorical experience linking past and present, in t.
growing sense of who my grandfather was. That is, we can imagine metaphor enriching not just the present, but the past as well. In this way the life
of the mind remains alive and in flux. But note that this process requires
both the past and the present to be somewhat plastic.²

Trauma, on the other hand, as Modell (2003) writes, "freezes" the past and thereby deprives it of the plasticity it needs if it is to connect to the present. Memories of trauma are very often rigid, unmentalized, concrete. They are things-in-themselves or singularities—in Bion's terms, beta-elements. Because such memories often can be only what they have been, and nothing more or less, they tend to be neither adaptable nor generative, qualities they would need to have if they are to be useful in creating new experience. In other words, the past experience of trauma often just cannot be contextualized in the present.

In these instances the past is, as Modell (1990) says, timeless in the sense that it exists beyond the *experience* of time, beyond *kairos*, the Greek term Modell uses for human cyclical, nonlinear time, the kind of time that can turn back on itself in ways that allow meanings to change and grow—the form of time, for instance, in which events that come later can change the meaning of what took place earlier, the way that the birthdate of a famous person accrues meaning, retrospectively, because of accomplishments carried out many years after the day that this person entered the world. *Kairos* contrasts with *chronos*, or time understood scientifically or objectively. This kind of time lies outside the realm of human experience; it cannot turn back on itself and does not allow the future to affect the past. Rather, it leads inexorably from birth to death; it is linear, irrevocable, and without human meaning.³ In the passage that follows, Frank Kermode (1967) specifically addresses the way that fictional devices convert *chronos* to *kairos*. But we can broaden Kermode's frame of reference about this temporal conversion without violating his meaning. We can say, that is, that not only the techniques of fiction, but *all* human meaning-making activities

> have to defeat the tendency of the interval between *tick* and *tock* to empty itself; to maintain within that interval following *tick* a lively expectation of *tock*, and a sense that however remote *tock* may be, all that happens happens as if *tock* were certainly following. All such plotting presupposes and requires that an end will bestow upon the

whole duration and meaning. To put it another way, the interval must be purged of simple chronicity, of the emptiness of *tock-tick*, human uninteresting successiveness. It is required to be a significant season, *kairos* poised between beginning and end. . . . [T]hat which was conceived of as simply successive becomes charged with past and future: what was *chronos* becomes *kairos*.

(p. 46)

Unless meaning is embedded in *kairos*—that is, unless experience can move freely between the past, present, and future—new meaning cannot come into being. New meaning just cannot root in the inexorable *tick-tock* of *chronos*—objective time, "humanly uninteresting successiveness." We need *kairos* if new meanings are to grow. We need *kairos* if life is to feel vital. In *kairos*, we circle back on our histories in ways that are routinely nonlinear and cyclic, and sometimes also capacious, endless, and oceanic. It is precisely this embeddedness in the fertile ground of *kairos* that trauma steals from us.

In Modell's understanding of Freud, if the past is to live in the present, it must be linked with contemporary perception; that is, memory must be connected to life outside the mind, to the external world, to today.[4] To use the word Modell most often chooses for this function, if memory is to be a living presence, it must be continuously *retranscribed*. In using this word, Modell is invoking Freud's (e.g., 1895, 1900, 1909, 1918, 1950) *Nachträglichkeit*, a theory of temporality more implicit in Freud's work than clearly spelled out in any one place, and limited in its application to certain special circumstances.[5] In views of *Nachträglichkeit* that have developed more recently, our grasp and use of the past changes, retrospectively, as we encounter new experiences in the present that give the past meanings it did not have before. Faimberg (2005a, 2005b, 2007), for instance, proposes a broadening of the concept in a way that explains the retroactive assignment of new meanings of many kinds, usually via interpretation. *Nachträglichkeit*, or the retranscription of memory, in other words, by reaching back into the past and potentiating previously unimagined aspects of old meanings, is an important part of what allows the past to contribute to a new experience of the present.

Retranscription of memory, though, as I have already implied, is precisely what frequently does not and cannot happen to the memory of trauma. In traumatic memory, the reach of old experience across time (*kairos*) to new circumstances cannot take place, and so the creation and use of emotional categories, and the metaphors that arise as a result of that stimulation of meaning, are prevented. For this reason, trauma often cannot be cognized, fully known, or fully felt. Trauma, even if we remember it, is "humanly uninteresting successiveness." We cannot *think* with it. Reis (1995), citing Modell among others, and arguing that time, and particularly the concept of *Nachträglichkeit,* is essential to the understanding of traumatic memory disruption, agrees, writing that "it is the disruption of the experience of time that goes to the heart of the dissociative disturbances of subjectivity" (p. 219).

Returning to my example of my friend and my memory of my grandfather: no matter how lovely the day was with my friend, walking down the street, those hours would not have developed some of the emotional nuance, the glow that they had, if they had not connected (beyond awareness) with my representation of my grandfather; and my image of my grandfather would have remained as it was before, important to me but not further elaborated, if I had not been able to retranscribe them within this present moment with my friend.

Building on Modell's work, I (Stern, 2009a) have argued elsewhere that it is clinically profitable for us to look at the process of metaphor formation through the lens of what I have called witnessing. This is not a new idea. In the psychoanalytic literature, Dori Laub (1991, 1992a, 1992b, 2005; Laub and Auerhahn, 1989), Sophia Richman (2006), Chana Ullman (2006), Bruce Reis (2009), and Samuel Gerson (2009), to cite only a few, have drawn our attention to the role of witnessing in creating the possibility for affectively charged memories of trauma. Some of these writers have gone further, arguing that witnessing is a routine component of therapeutic action, especially in cases of trauma. Warren Poland (2000) has taken yet another step, bringing the concept of witnessing into our general understanding of psychoanalytic treatment.

Most of those who have discussed witnessing in the psychoanalytic literature, including Poland, have meant the term to apply to an interaction between two real people—in Poland's case, the patient and the analyst. While accepting that an important part of the activity of witnessing goes on between patient and analyst, I (Stern, 2009a, 2009b, 2010a), along with others (e.g., Laub, 1991), have expanded the application of the term into the inner life. I have argued that we need a witness if we are to grasp, know, and feel what we have experienced, especially trauma; and I have argued that this witness may be internal and, in that sense, imaginary.

Someone else, even if that someone is another part of ourselves, must know what we have gone through, must be able to feel it *with* us. We must be *recognized by an other* (Benjamin, 1988, 1995, 1998), even if that other is now part of us. We need what I have called a "partner in thought." I accept Modell's contention that the use of memory in the creation of metaphor is a continuous, although largely unnoticed, process in experiencing. My suggestion, in the recent sources to which I just referred, was that this continuous creation of metaphor requires an equally continuous process of witnessing. I emphasized in those articles that the internal witness grows from what was originally an internalization of presences that, much earlier in life, existed only outside us. I refer readers to the earlier accounts for a description of the development of the imaginary witnessing presence as an internalization of early relationships with "real," external others. In my frame of reference, witnessing, like the use of memory in the creation of metaphor, is a feature of ongoing experiencing.

In the terms of a recent contribution by Poland (2011), we could say that self-analysis, on which Poland argues clinical psychoanalysis rests, is an internal conversation between parts of oneself. Parts of oneself, as Poland also seems to accept, often begin as representations of others, or as it often seems to me, representations of our *involvements* with others: "others can be felt as both deeply internal and clearly external" (p. 989). Internal conversation, then, or self-analysis, because it requires the recognition of one part of oneself by another, can be understood to presuppose the process of internal or imaginary witnessing, or even to be equivalent to it.

It is via witnessing that we come to know experience as our own. As we listen to ourselves (in imagination) through the ears of the other, and see ourselves (in imagination) through the eyes of the other, we hear and see ourselves in a way we simply cannot manage in isolation. I have suggested (Stern, 2009b) that this is one of the primary uses of clinical psychoanalysis: psychoanalysts listen to patients in the way that allows patients to listen to themselves. In such listening, links between the past and the present are forged, and metaphor comes into being. Modell tells us that metaphor allows the creation of new meanings in the interaction of the past and the present; and, in turn, I propose, witnessing allows the creation of metaphor.

One last point of emphasis before I move on to illustrations. Perhaps I repeat myself, but the point is important enough to me to be worth the risk: witnessing is a relational process; it goes on in an interpersonal field, between two subjectivities. But these subjectivities, although their origins lie in relationships with the earliest caretakers, may not always rate human beings, especially later in life. Witnesses are not ne real people; they can be imaginary. In fact, they are more often imaginary than "real." One part of us witnesses another part (Stern, 2009b). We can make the point in the language of contemporary theory of the multiple self: from within one self-state we witness the experience created within another (e.g., Davies, 1996, 1998, 1999, 2001, 2004, 2005; Pizer, 1996, 1998; Bromberg, 1998, 2006, 2011a; Howell, 2006; Stern, 2010a). Dori Laub (1991), in relation to the role of witnessing in memories of the Holocaust, has said that one of what he calls the three levels of witnessing is "the level of being a witness to oneself in the experience" (p. 75). I will return to Laub's work later on.

You can see immediately some of the theoretical possibilities here: dissociation, being the sequestering of self-states from one another, prevents imaginary witnessing within the personality—what Laub calls being a witness to oneself. The dissociation of two states of being from one another, that is—which simply means that these two states cannot be experienced simultaneously—makes it impossible for either state to serve as a witness for the other. The absence of such internal witnessing then prevents the creation of metaphor, because the elements that must combine to make the metaphor—memory and the experience of the present—cannot coexist. We are left with a new avenue of approach to the common observation, with which I began, that dissociation prevents the creative use of traumatic experience (Stern, 2009b).

Now, in opening these remarks I also pointed out that psychoanalysts have become familiar with the effects of trauma on memory. But we are used to thinking of those effects as working from the past to the present, as if it were always the case that trauma is in the past. But what if the trauma takes place in the present? Are there instances in which the disruption of memory occurs in the other direction—from the present to the past? I will offer several illustrations of that kind, examples in which the memory or the affective resonance of the more distant past is inhibited, dampened, or damaged in some other way by traumatic events in the present or recent past. The first of these illustrations is fictional, another is from the work of a colleague, and a third comes from my own clinical experience with a Vietnam veteran 35 years ago. After recounting these stories, I return to the question of memory and witnessing, with a new point to make about the relation between them.

Michael

Michael and Dukie were two teenage African-American characters on *The Wire*, a five-year-long dramatic series that, as far as I am concerned, is, hands-down, the best programming ever made for American television. The series revolves around the illegal drug trade in Baltimore, and it shows that, for African-American kids in the poorest sections, the drug trade is really the only way available to make any kind of success of yourself. By the time the series ends, Michael and Dukie are maybe 17 years old, have both grown up in the housing projects, and have been friends for much of their lives. Dukie is a sweet, bright, depressed, and hapless boy whose family is so lost to drugs that they sell absolutely anything they can get their hands on, including Dukie's clothes. In fact, Dukie is pretty much limited to the one change of clothing he has on at any particular time; and so at least part of the reason that Dukie is shunned and bullied is that he smells bad. We know from a previous episode in the series, years earlier, that Michael once saved Dukie from a humiliating beating by a gang of younger kids in the street, and then bought Dukie an ice cream. That day it became unmistakable to Michael that Dukie needed to be taken care of, and Michael more or less took on the job. Dukie came to live with Michael and became responsible for the care and the homework of Michael's beloved little brother, seven- or eight-year old Bug. That is Dukie's job. There are no parents left in Michael's house; the father has been murdered over his pedophilia and the mother has been lost to drugs. In the meantime, Michael, who was recognized at a young age by some of the neighborhood thugs as the most competent and intelligent of the kids in his age group, is recruited at the age of about 15 to be trained as an enforcer and assassin for the 20-something young man who runs the local drug trade. Michael's education in killing is carried out by the two people who are the current assassins, one a man in his 20s and the other a teenaged girl. These two turn out to like Michael, and they befriend him. Michael is an apt pupil who progresses in his studies. In a matter of months he begins to carry out executions.

Eventually, when Michael is 16 or 17, he is mistakenly blamed for being a snitch and is himself targeted for execution; but he figures out that he has been accused, and he kills the assassin sent to murder him, who it turns out was the teenaged girl who had been one of those who had taught him the business of execution. It is now too dangerous for Dukie and Bug to have anything to do with Michael, and so Michael moves Bug to the house of an aunt, who has agreed to take him.

We arrive now at one of the final episodes of the series. Michael and Dukie are sitting in a car on a darkened Baltimore street just after having dropped Bug off at the aunt's house. The mood is dark and sad. It is clear that life will never again be what it was when the three boys lived together. We know without having to be told that Michael will be hunted by the drug lord until he is killed; and we suspect, correctly it turns out, that the fact that Dukie is about to be dropped off in front of a place where a man is shooting up heroin in plain sight means that, without the family of Michael and Bug, and having nowhere to go, Dukie will follow the rest of his family into addiction and despair.

Dukie is trying to figure out how to say goodbye to Michael. Suddenly he seems to think of something: he smiles broadly, and he animatedly reminds Michael of that day several years earlier when Michael saved him in the street and bought him an ice cream. That life is gone, and the audience knows it as well as the characters do. But Dukie is happy at the memory. He is really happy. He says excitedly to Michael, "Do you remember that?"

Michael puts his hands on the top of the steering wheel, and bends over it, closing his eyes. "No," he says very softly. "I don't." It is a shocking moment, and it stays with me as if it actually happened.

Menachem

I think, too, of another story, but a true one: Dori Laub's (1991, 1992b) recounting of the early years of Menachem S., a five-year-old boy who lived with his parents in the Krakow ghetto at the time of the Holocaust. A rumor went around the ghetto that the children were to be rounded up and exterminated. The parents of the little boy talked in the evenings about how they might smuggle out their son, and of the fate that awaited him if they could not. He was supposed to be asleep as they talked, but he heard. One night, somehow, the guards were distracted and Menachem was sent out the gates of the ghetto by himself into the streets, with nothing more than a shawl his mother managed to wrap around him at the last minute, an address written on a scrap of paper, and a passport picture of her as a student, which she told him to look at whenever he felt the need to do so. She and the boy's father promised Menachem that they would find him when the war ended.

The address turned out to be what Laub describes as a whorehouse, and Menachem was welcomed there. He thought of it as a hospital.

Soon, though, it became too dangerous for him to stay, and he spent the remainder of the war on the streets, often with gangs of other homeless children. Off and on, but always temporarily, he lived in the homes of sympathetic families who found him on the street. In one of these homes the mother, who Laub suspects knew that Menachem was Jewish, told Menachem that he could pray to whomever he wanted; and Menachem chose to pray to the picture of his mother, saying "Mother, let this war be over and come and take me back as you promised." Laub tells us, "Mother indeed had promised to come and take him back after the war, and not for a moment did he doubt that promise" (Laub, 1991, p. 86). "In my interpretation," Laub continues,

> what this young vagabond was doing with the photograph of his mother was, precisely, creating his first witness, and the creation of that witness was what enabled him to survive his years on the streets of Krakow. This story exemplifies the process whereby survival takes place through the creative act of establishing and maintaining an internal witness who substitutes for the lack of witnessing in real life.
>
> (p. 86)

It is miraculous that Menachem survived, and nearly beyond imagination that his parents actually did find him after the war. Somehow, though, this is what happened. But Menachem had lived through the war by talking and praying to his photograph of his mother as a healthy young woman. When eventually she and his father, who also survived, did locate him, they had been sent to concentration camps, and were sick, emaciated, and haggard, his mother's teeth loose in her gums. No doubt her spirit was at least as badly wounded as her body. Laub (1992b) tells us that the mother who found Menachem "was not identical to herself" (p. 91). One wishes, of course, that Menachem was now delivered from terror; but the arrival of his parents was instead the event that finally pushed him over the edge, and he fell apart. Laub writes, "I read this story to mean that in regaining his real mother, he inevitably loses the internal witness he had found in her image" (p. 88).

These two stories are united by more than their pathos. Notice that in both of them, something from the past that *has* been accessible becomes *in*accessible, seemingly as a result of the intervention of trauma. How can we understand this phenomenon? What does it have in common with the way we are used to looking at traumatic experience? Take Menachem first, because his case is in some ways simpler. Once he was deprived of his illusion, the veil fell from his eyes and the recent past fell into place, appearing suddenly in all its brutality. He no longer had effective, or *affective*, access to what we imagine was the sweetness and gentleness of his early years with his mother.

Now consider Michael. His life has become horrendous. We are not meant to believe that he was especially well suited for his job as assassin, except for the fact that he was unusually emotionally capable and intelligent in a general sort of way. We are certainly not meant to believe that Michael is bad. He is no psychopath. He is portrayed, actually, as sweet and generous, which makes his transformation all the more heartbreaking. His metamorphosis into a killer costs him dearly, despite the fact that by accepting it he has found his way to money and, more significantly, prestige. We are free to condemn him, and we do; but we are also touched by the plight of this sweet child-man, as we are touched by the vicious child soldiers of Sierra Leone and Burma, and by returning veterans of combat anywhere, many of whom have killed their equally young enemies.

Darryl

My next story is about one of those young soldiers. I once saw in psychotherapy an African-American man who had been a high school football star, a running back, and who came back from Vietnam with paranoid schizophrenia and a left leg amputated above the knee.[6] He must have been a powerful runner, because even when I knew him, two years after his return from combat, his thighs were of prodigious size. He was 21 or 22 years old, poorly educated, not very bright, and had always lived in the ghetto. His prospects were not good. His medication helped with the hallucinations and delusions, but he was nevertheless often terrorized by his demons, with whom he was in fairly continuous and literal communication. I will call this man Darryl. He was in treatment with me 35 years ago at an inner-city Veterans Affairs (VA) hospital, usually twice a week, sometimes three times a week. (It was more possible then than now to see people frequently; we did it whenever we could and it generally helped.) I don't know what happened to Darryl after I left the VA. I wish I did. His family told me that he had been mild-mannered in high school, which did not surprise me, because he was actually quite connected and sweet with me, even while he was crazed and terror-stricken. Darryl told me that when he got to Vietnam he took very well to killing—perhaps (I thought) because of the paranoia of his incipient psychosis. He liked sniping from a perch in a tree, and he reported being very good at it. It was strange: I knew these things, and Darryl and I couldn't have been a lot more different than we were, but we became very fond of one another. We didn't talk about that, but we both knew.

In Vietnam, Darryl became frightened of the military compound and refused to live there with the other soldiers, insisting instead on billeting in a hut in the South Vietnamese village outside the gates of the compound. For some reason, the people of the village accepted him, even though he had by then had his psychotic break. He had a girlfriend in the village and he slept in her hut. He did forage for extra food for the villagers, both inside the compound and in the forest, where he hunted. Maybe that was part of the reason they accepted him. Perhaps they also thought Darryl would protect them from the North Vietnamese guerillas who were always somewhere in the vicinity. If that's what they thought, they were probably right, although the necessity never arose. In any case, Darryl told me that whenever his unit was ordered to go out on patrol he got wind of the plan and would show up at the gates of the compound as the unit was moving out. He always wanted to be point man, the guy in the front of the unit who looked out for the enemy and therefore took the greatest risk. I knew from other ex-soldiers at the VA and elsewhere, who had explained the danger to me, that the members of Darryl's platoon were no doubt happy to oblige him.

One day, on point, he got shot and lost his leg, and he was shipped home, feeling that his life was over. He had hoped to be a professional football player. When I met him, he was so afraid of the army and its representative, the VA hospital, that he couldn't get himself to drive to the hospital for his appointments with me (yes, he drove), although he wanted to attend his sessions.

For some reason, his feeling about the army didn't infect his relationship with me. So we had an agreement. He would drive as close to the hospital as he could get, and if he couldn't make it, he would stop the car at the time of his session and call me from a pay phone on the street. Many of our sessions were on pay phones.

Darryl's biggest current difficulty was probably the problem he was for others. He kept a number of guns, mostly rifles, which his wife told me he was in the habit of discharging through the ceiling of the family apartment whenever he was frustrated, which was frequently. He lived in a small and crowded apartment in public housing, with his wife and their several little children, whom he had fathered in quick succession when he returned from Vietnam; and so the idea of Darryl discharging his weapons terrified me even more than it might have otherwise. So far he had not hurt anyone, although as far as I could see it was only luck that he hadn't shot someone in the upstairs apartment. I explained to Darryl, with my heart in my mouth, that I didn't want to call the police, but that I would have to, if he kept shooting. I wasn't so much afraid of Darryl's rage, which I thought he would keep in check with me, but I was actually quite worried that I would damage our relationship. But I didn't. Darryl agreed to stop shooting, and his wife corroborated that he had. I counted it as a major success that by the end of my year in that VA, he took his guns to the police department and surrendered them.

I have told you about Darryl because his time in Vietnam seemed to have obliterated his emotional access to certain aspects of his childhood. He remembered the factual content of many events of his early life. But he came from a warm, related family and he just could not seem to feel that warmth any more. He knew it well enough to explain it to me in way that convinced me it was true, and his family provided independent confirmation by their very presence; but he did not feel it. He was distant from this loving atmosphere in a way that drained it of reality for him. The years prior to Vietnam did not feel to him as if they belonged to the same life he was leading at the time I knew him. What felt most real to him was life in the Vietnamese village, and the sniping, and being on point. (I note, just in passing, because I don't have the luxury of exploring this aspect of the case in the present context, that despite the fact that his explicit emotional memory of his early life was blunted, it was preserved and reflected in the connectedness of his relationship with me. Nor do I have time to address the strangeness of this connectedness in a clinical picture like Darryl's. But it is not the only time I have experienced that.)

I began this chapter by reviewing what we all know: when the past was traumatic, it sometimes cannot be accessed from the present, especially its affective aspects. On the basis of the stories of Michael, Menachem, and now Darryl, I add to that point this proposal: when the *present or the recent past* is traumatic and the more distant past had significant nurturing and loving qualities, those good parts of the distant past may not be emotionally accessible from the present. I am suggesting that trauma may make it difficult to access the goodness of the past for either of two reasons: because the past *was* traumatic *then*, or because the present *is* traumatic *now* (or recently). The retranscription of memory, in other words, needs to be able to proceed in both directions, not only from the past to the present. There must be a point of attachment to the past from the present *and* to the present from the past. *Kairos* must be free to fold back on itself toward either end of its axis. Ghislaine Boulanger (2007) has recognized the dissociation of the past from the present as a central part of adult-onset trauma. When people are "wounded by reality," as she puts it in the title of her book, they often express the impact of the trauma by saying that they feel they have died. This metaphor conveys as powerfully as any metaphor could the disjunction of the lives before and after the trauma. (See also the powerful testimony provided by Leed [1979] of World War I soldiers, who say exactly the same thing.) Like Michael, Menachem, and Darryl, the old lives of some of those who have suffered adult-onset trauma are gone, leaving them without the same *kind* of memories they had before—leaving them without a past that feels real.[7]

Retrospective derealization

If two parts of ourselves separated in time are to know one another, one part in the past and one in the present, each part must feel like "me." That is, in the terms I introduced earlier, if metaphor is to come about, each of these parts must be capable of serving as witness to the other. There are two prerequisites for this kind of internal or imaginary witnessing: (1) past and present self-states must each be capable of full-bodied, consciously felt affective experience; and (2) this affective experience in each part must be tolerable as a consciously felt and known experience by the other part. The contribution of memory to the present, and the contribution of the present to reorganization of the past, requires a bridge of affect across time, a kind of call and response from both directions: we must be able to contextualize, feel, sense, and know the past from within the present, and we must simultaneously be able to create that same kind of grasp of the present from within our experience of the past.

We are familiar with the contention that the parts of ourselves that are dissociated for unconscious defensive reasons—that is, "not-me" (Sullivan,

1953; Bromberg, 1998, 2006, 2011a; Stern, 2003, 2004, 2009b, 2010a) — are associated with traumatic events in the past, and especially with disequilibrating *patterns* of relatedness. When the past is traumatic, being forced to experience it, or being forced into allowing it to shape the present, can disregulate us, disequilibrate our sense of ourselves, rob us of our continuity of being and the feeling, which we need to maintain at all times, that we are familiar to ourselves, that we know who we are (Bromberg, 1998, 2006, 2011a). After trauma, we can say, our capacity to create experience is at least partially *derealized*, by which I do not mean that it is drained of reality so much as that it is drained of vitality. Derealization is much more frequently a question of actualization, in other words, than of reality testing. Very simply, posttraumatic experience—especially experience directly related to the trauma, but spreading out from those associative links as well—is likely to be less fully realized than it would have been if the trauma had not occurred.

We know these effects of trauma that took place in the past. But perhaps we need to broaden our view. Perhaps the distant past can be unbearable, and thus unknowable or unfeelable, for the same kinds of reasons that trauma of the past prevents the realization of the future. Perhaps, as Boulanger (2007) tells us, when the present or recent past is dark and full of pain and terror, it hurts too much to know the goodness of the more distant past; or it becomes impossible to believe in that goodness; or the sense of that goodness actually dies. Sam Gerson (2009) offers us the profound speculation that such a thing happened in the case of Primo Levi, the writer who survived his internment in a Nazi concentration camp and then, after the war, offered some of the most harrowing testimony to what happened there. I, for one, feel more able than I was before to understand and accept Levi's suicide, so many years after the war, through Gerson's eyes.

If such a thing happens, if the long-ago past loses its vitality and goodness because of events that took place more recently, we lose the capacity to hear the past through our ears in the present, and we lose our capacity to hear the present through the ears of a "me" in the past. Perhaps the past, that is, when it is too emotionally discrepant from the life we lead now, can feel as if it simply no longer belongs to the world within which we live. If we adopt the term *prospective derealization* to refer to the conventional understanding of trauma—that is, the derealizing effect of trauma in the past on experience in the present—then we might refer to the effect on our experience of the *past* of more recent trauma as *retrospective derealization*.

Perhaps the worlds of *now* and *then* can shatter in such a way that, like Humpty Dumpty, they cannot be put together again. Perhaps, as Gerson (2009) suggests, Freud overestimated the possibilities of mourning and, instead, as Gerson quotes a character from a novel by Martin Amis, "The truth . . . is that nobody ever gets over anything." Perhaps from either direction, the past and the present can be, to use Leed's (1979) precisely descriptive word, incommensurable.[8]

Are there people for whom a past of goodness is irretrievably lost, as the metaphor of Humpty Dumpty would suggest? I certainly would not want to claim to know that the possibility of goodness can always be retrieved. I know what all of us know about the extremity of pain and trauma that it is possible to suffer in this world; but I have been spared the despair suffered by many others less fortunate than me. And so it is probably realistic for me to say only that I nurture the hope that love and goodness are seldom or even never completely irretrievable, even when life is as bleak and brutish as it was for those I have written about. Experiences like the one I had with Darryl, the Vietnam veteran, despite the bleakness of his life, seem to me a justification of that hope. The story of Menachem, which I continue momentarily, is another example.

But before I turn back to Menachem, let me say a bit more about Sam Gerson's (2009) work on the "dead third." Gerson's view is a perspective that, while it does have basic therapeutic implications for victims of trauma, does not necessarily depend on hope at all, but on the acceptance of its absence. Or perhaps Gerson would prefer to say that the acceptance that hope has vanished is, at least to begin with, the closest thing to hope that we can offer certain victims of severe trauma, such as genocide. Gerson describes the results of genocide as "the presence of absence," by which he means that all that can be felt or known is the "not-there-ness" of what had been present. There is no presence. The third, the witness that, had it survived, might have made it possible to remember what had been real and feel what has been lost, is itself dead. Gerson cites the absence of a culturally located witnessing presence for the victims of the Holocaust. We remain shocked by, among many other things, the absence during the Nazi years in Europe (and in most of the rest of the world, too, for that matter) of a broad social recognition of the horrors of the Third Reich, a recognition that would have made it possible for the atrocities of the Reich to have been witnessed—for the victims to have felt that someone knew and cared. The victims of the Holocaust, if the third had survived inside the Reich, could at least have imagined their treatment through the lens of what should have been a culturally sanctioned condemnation and horror. But there was so little of this attitude that, for Gerson, the third actually died, and all that could be experienced to be real was its absence. Gerson is convincing and moving in his understanding that, for victims of genocide, having a witness to this presence of absence—a witness to the very absence left by the death of the third—can be the only form of human interchange that remains restorative.

I am not going to address exactly how we embed whatever hope we have for the retrieval of some aspect of goodness in our clinical technique or theories of therapeutic action. I have addressed questions of technique and therapeutic action elsewhere (Stern, 1997, 2010a), with many clinical illustrations, and each time I have addressed these matters, my answer has depended not on any particular conception of what to do with our patients, not on a prescription for conduct, but on a way of understanding the unformulated aspects of clinical process and an attitude about how to work with them. Just as in therapeutic work with trauma that took place in childhood, or at least long ago, working with retrospective derealization—trauma in the present that robs us of the goodness of the past—requires that we conceptualize how the special qualities of analytic relatedness somehow make possible a new, affectively vital interpenetration of past and present. We must especially understand how analytic relatedness makes it possible for dissociated experience, which is unformulated, to be articulated (or transformed into alpha elements, in the Bionian frame of reference) in a way that makes it possible to *think* it. The outcome of this kind of clinical work is a renewed, revitalized, or even newly created capacity for the patient and therapist to witness one another—and, for that matter, to witness themselves.

It turns out that Menachem, the little boy who fell apart when he finally saw his mother after the war, grew up to be a high-ranking officer in the Israeli military. The reason Laub knew Menachem and the story of his childhood in Krakow was that, as an adult, Menachem spent a sabbatical year at Yale, during which he contributed his memories to the Video Archive for Holocaust Testimonies, located at Yale and co-directed by Laub. Laub's seminal work on the significance of witnessing, and about the "restoration" that can occur when one is witnessed, grew from Laub's experience of directing the Archive, experience from which he (Laub, 1991) concluded that the Holocaust destroyed the very possibility of witnessing: "the very imagination of the *Other* was no longer possible. There was no longer an other to whom one could say 'Thou' in the hope of being heard, of being recognized as a subject, of being answered." And "when one cannot turn to a 'you' one cannot say 'thou' even to oneself. The Holocaust created in this way a world in which one *could not bear witness to oneself*" (p. 80; italics from the original.) (Here we see Laub's work link with Gerson's understanding of the presence of absence, a commonality also noted by Gerson.)

Menachem grew up believing he was invulnerable. In battle, he walked through hails of bullets believing that he could not be hit by them, and he rescued other soldiers under circumstances that seemed to everyone present to spell virtually certain death. He lived through it all, though, without even being injured, and he considered himself not at all brave, merely unkillable. Laub (1991) sees this as the "denial of the child victim in himself" (p. 87). In my vocabulary, I would say that any sense of helplessness or vulnerability was "not-me" for Menachem, the kind of unbearable or intolerable experience that would make him unrecognizable to himself, and that was therefore dissociated.

Laub's invitation to Menachem to contribute his testimony to the Archive provoked a crisis, because Menachem had never told the story of his childhood to anyone besides his wife. One evening, she tried to convince him to tell the story, thinking it might help him with his anxiety and his lifelong nightmares of being on a conveyor belt moving toward rolling presses that will inexorably crush him. In the repetitive dream, Menachem is helpless and terrorized, knowing he will die horribly.

That night, after talking with his wife and deciding that it might indeed be a good thing to offer his testimony, Menachem had the nightmare once again. But this time it was different:

> *For the first time in my life, I stopped the conveyor belt. I woke up, still feeling anxious, but the anxiety was turning into a wonderful sense of fulfillment and satisfaction. I got up; for the first time I wasn't disoriented. I knew where I was; I knew what happened . . . I feel strongly that it has to do with the fact that I decided to open up.*
>
> (p. 88; italics from the original)

Laub comments that, "it is this very commitment to truth, in a dialogic context and with an authentic listener, which . . . makes the resumption of life . . . at all possible" (p. 89). He ends this powerful article with these words:

> It is the realization that the lost ones are not coming back; the realization that what life is all about is precisely living with an unfulfilled hope; only this time with the sense that you are not alone any longer—that someone can be there as your companion—knowing you, living with you through the unfulfilled hope, someone saying, "I'll be with you in the very process of your losing me. I am your witness."
>
> (p. 89)

This is witnessing in the literal sense: one person tells his story to another. Literal witnessing does go on in psychoanalysis and psychotherapy, of course; in fact, as I have already said, one of the points I (Stern, 2009b) have made in writing about the ubiquity of witnessing in clinical work is that analysts listen to patients in the way that allows patients to listen to themselves. But much of the witnessing I have referred to here, in this essay, and much of the witnessing that goes on in clinical work, is more accurately described as implicit—what I have called imaginary, or internal, witnessing. This is certainly the case in witnessing from one self-state to another across time.

Like most psychoanalysts and psychoanalytic psychotherapists, I could tell many stories that substantiate, within the broader frame of reference of psychoanalytic treatment, the conclusions Laub offers regarding the restorative effects of Holocaust witnessing; and these restorative psychotherapeutic effects, in my experience, are the outcome of both literal and implicit witnessing. I am going to have to try to be content, though, with allowing Laub's work to speak for me on this subject here at the end of these remarks. I will offer just one thought about the nature of psychotherapeutic help of this kind. In fact, this thought is a claim I have already made: witnessing in psychotherapy and psychoanalysis allows past and present to link through metaphor, via affect categories, as Modell (1990, 2003) has described. In this way, dissociation is breached, trauma thaws and can finally be dreamed and thought, and traumatic experience returns to *kairos*, liberating the interchange of meaning across time.

I have one last thing to say about Menachem. We know that his early, apparently secure childhood succumbed to the retrospective derealization that took place when he fell apart after the war, at the time that he first saw his mother. But by the time he grew up and met Laub, something more and different had happened. Because he was now an adult, looking backward in time, his experience in the streets of Krakow had become a trauma of the more conventional sort—that is, a trauma from the distant past. Inevitably, trauma of the present becomes trauma of the past, so that the effects of the trauma reach from the time of the traumatic experience not only into the past, as in the retrospective derealization suffered by Michael, Menachem, and Darryl, but also into the future and the succession of present moments that the future becomes as it arrives in the here and now. I believe that Menachem's healing had to do not only with the witnessing of his past trauma from a self-state in the present; I believe his healing also had to do with the reawakening of his capacity to witness his long-ago, traumatic *present*—the present in which he fell apart just after the war—from within the warm and protected self-state of his secure childhood with his mother. I believe we can learn something about the healing of the retrospective derealization that took place in Menachem's childhood, in other words, from the restoration provided by Menachem's willingness to allow himself a witness all those years later.

I want to be as clear as I can here, because these different perspectives in time, looking forward from the past and backward from the future, can be difficult to keep straight. Menachem's healing was due not only to the thawing of his frozen past, as we are used to conceptualizing trauma of long ago. That factor is there, true enough. We can see that it is: from Menachem's perspective in the present, his decision to allow himself a witness did indeed thaw the past. But Menachem's healing was also due, I think, to the way his decision to tell his story allowed the little boy who *was* Menachem in the streets of Krakow—and who, in some part of his being, remained a little boy even at the time of his Holocaust testimony so many years later—to restore some of the goodness and safety that was offered to him by that photograph of his beloved, protective mother. Menachem's decision, as an adult, to tell his story freed him to bring to bear some of that early childhood goodness on *the very time from which it disappeared*—that time in the whorehouse and the streets of Krakow which was a present moment long ago. The goodness of Menachem's image of his mother could not vanquish the evil—not then and not now—but Menachem's new willingness to link past and present perhaps restored the power of some part of that maternal goodness to once again coexist with the sense of helplessness and despair of the little boy's life alone in the streets. The witnessing that at least partly healed Menachem, in other words, linked parts of himself across time, and in both directions.

Notes

1 I use the word "real" to differentiate this experience from other experience that is more internally generated. But of course there is no single version of experience that can actually be described as the "real" one, which leads me to use quotation marks around the word "real" in the text.
2 Although Freud described a different kind of plasticity of present and past than I am presenting here, in his work on screen memories he was the first in psychoanalysis to write about the reciprocal effects of past and present on one another. He (Freud, 1899) first suggested that early memories were sometimes used as screens for later events. Soon thereafter he (Freud, 1901) presented the idea used more commonly ever since—that later events are used as screens for earlier memories.
3 Along with Modell, Daniel Stern (2004) has brought the concepts of *kairos* and *chronos* into the psychoanalytic literature on the processes of experiencing.
4 This is a perspective that, under the rubric of dissociation and enactment, Philip Bromberg (1998, 2006, 2011a) and I (Stern, 2003, 2004, 2010a) have also considered.

   I will describe some of my own work on witnessing below, but it would take me too far afield here to outline the close connection between the ideas all three of us have proposed about the significance of perception, as opposed to verbal insight, in therapeutic action. I will continue to develop what I have to say about perception in these remarks on the basis of Modell's thinking.

   In considering the contribution of the past to the present, especially the affective contribution of the past to present experiencing, I am also reminded once again of Loewald's (1960, 1978) seminal work on the subject.
5 The concept of *Nachträglichkeit* was given a new explicitness and brought to significance by Lacan (2004), who assigned it a fairly limited meaning. LaPlanche and Pontalis (Laplanche, 1976, 1999; Laplanche and Pontalis, 1968, 1974) are primarily responsible for giving the concept greater prominence and a broader frame of reference.

   Those who have written about *Nachträglichkeit*, incidentally, while they do not necessarily use the words *kairos* and *chronos*, often do employ the conceptions of time that correspond to these two words. Birksted-Breen (2003), for instance, argues that "developmental" or "progressive" time (the linear time of most developmental theories) and "reverberation" or "retrospective" time (the time of retranscription) inherently go together and, in fact, are requisites for one another. Dahl (2010) finds in Freud a similar distinction between two "time vectors" in *Nachträglichkeit*. One of these is "a causal process operating in the forward direction of time against the background of a factual reality," while the second is "a backward movement that permits an understanding of unconscious scenes and fantasies taking place at a primary-process level" (p. 727).
6 Because it was impossible to request permission to use this material, I have disguised Darryl and his story in a way that makes them unrecognizable.
7 Of course, trauma does not always result in reduced vitality and decreased capacity to witness one's own experience across time. The capacity in the aftermath of trauma to maintain one's vitality and meaning-making ability is part of what is described as "coping," "resilience," or "self-righting" (e.g., Schneider, 2003; Cyrulnik, 2005; DiAmbrosio, 2006; Parens *et al.*, 2009). The *Psychoanalytic Review* has published a collection of articles that directly address the resilience of those who, like Menachem, survived the Holocaust and other violent ethnic/religious trauma (Berk, 1998; Fogelman, 1998;

Hogman, 1998; Kalayjian and Shahinian, 1998; Nagata and Takeshita, 1998; Rousseau et al., 1998; Sigal, 1998). Valent's (1998) contribution to this collection is specifically concerned with the resilience of certain child survivors of the Holocaust. While Anna Ornstein (e.g., 1985, 1994) does not necessarily use the word "resilience," she has contributed work on the response to trauma, especially the Holocaust, that is forged in the same spirit.

8 Once again Freud was the first to discuss reciprocal modifications in experience across time—modification of the present by the past and the past by the present—in both his description of *Nachträglichkeit* (see footnote 5) and the concept of screen memories (see footnote 2).

Chapter 7

Unconscious phantasy and unconscious relatedness

Comparing contemporary Freudian and interpersonal/relational approaches to clinical practice

I am pleased about the mutual respect and interest implied by the meeting for which the original version of this chapter was written, an interest in comparing contemporary Freudian and interpersonal/relational ways of thinking about and conducting our work.[1] I am also grateful for the clinical material, supplied by a graduate of the New York Psychoanalytic Institute, that served as the springboard for discussion on the panel I was on, one of the two panels that took place that day. Four of us, two interpersonal/relational analysts and two Freudians, were charged with discussing this material, each from their own perspective. In offering this written version of the remarks I made, I am pursuing the same intentions I had at the conference, which were these: I differed with the presenter of that material about the nature of psychoanalytic work and theory, but I did not wish what I said to be understood as a criticism of either the presenter's work or his theoretical orientation. I wanted my presentation to be understood as an attempt to delineate the differences between us. Mutual respect, if it is to be authentic and not just an effort to paper over disagreements, requires such delineation. In keeping with that goal, I did my best to represent each of our two points of view in a way that I hoped adherents of each perspective would recognize as their own. I may have failed to accomplish that goal in one spot or another in these remarks; but if I have, the fault lies in my knowledge and means of expression, not in a rhetorical intention.

When I read the clinical material the first time, I recognized it as the work of an experienced analyst. I sensed in it continuity, coherence of purpose, and clinical confidence. I found I trusted the work of this analyst. I trusted his sense of purpose, and I trusted the connection that he had with his patient. I believed that good things would happen, and had happened, in this treatment.

But I also felt that there was something missing. It took me several readings to figure out what it was, because the material had a certain seamlessness, a quality that all experience created from a coherent perspective has. That is what a theoretical perspective is, after all: it is what we use to mold the world into one shape or another. And that is why, despite the fact that what I said that day arose in my mind as my reaction to the clinical material, I did not address the material in line-by-line detail.

Before I had read the clinical transcript, I imagined that I might be able to compare my perspective and the presenter's by reviewing what I would have done differently than he did at various choice points. But eventually I changed my mind. Our theories wield greater influence on all of us than a nudge toward different answers to the same questions. The most profound significance of a theory, and perhaps the least visible, lies in how it shapes the questions themselves, how it shapes what we actually see—that is, how it influences us to create the data in the first place.

And so I concluded that the data offered by the presenter that day had been shaped in the image contributed by his theory, as the data of my work are shaped in the image of mine. For that reason, I ended up feeling that I could not really use his material to talk about where, in his transcript, I would have done something differently than he did.

The observation I made about the presenter's material, after going through it two or three times, was that he told us nothing about *his* experience while in the room with his patient. I tried to imagine some other reason for this absence than the analyst's sense that such data were not immediately relevant. The only thing I could imagine was that perhaps he presented the material this way in order to give us an account of his work that could be defended as unvarnished, an account embellished as little as possible by anything that would smack of skew or spin. Yet that way of understanding the construction of the transcript merely made the absence of the analyst's own experience more notable, since the implication, if he left out his subjectivity because it did not seem to him to be as basic to the clinical process as the patient's subjectivity, is that the analyst's experience is auxiliary, not part of the heart of the matter, as it is for me.

Now, this hardly means that the presenter did not use his own experience in his work with his patient. In fact, his responsiveness and connectedness to his patient in the material he presented showed us that he *did* use his own experience. It seemed to me, then, that the most important meaning of the absence of any report about what was going on with him was that his theoretical model did not encourage him to *think about* or *present* his own experience as a central part of the treatment. As Argyris and Schön (1976) said, now many years ago, our "espoused theories" are not always the same as our "theories-in-use," so that we often take wise actions for reasons we do not think to specify.

The presenting analyst focused on two things: (1) his impressionistic reactions of the patient—i.e., not his own feelings and reactions, but his observations of hers; (2) what he thought the meanings of his patient's utterances were. Using these two sources of information, the presenter then tried to tell the patient about the unconscious meanings embedded in what she said to him. In other words, this analyst worked a vein that should not surprise us a bit: he interpreted. He interpreted content, and he interpreted resistance; but he interpreted.

Like most interpersonal and relational analysts, though, I seldom, if ever, think of what I do with patients as interpretation, even when what I am doing may look like interpretation to those for whom the concept is central to clinical practice. But if not interpretation, then what? What is it that I do instead? In this chapter I do intend to say something about this in the abstract, but I also want to illustrate what I mean. I present a clinical vignette, one from an earlier paper of mine (Stern, 2009a; see also Stern, 2010a, Chapter 6), and then say something about the processes I believe the illustration demonstrates. My vignette is written like a story; it is not verbatim clinical process, as the presenter's material was. The story format works well for my purpose, because interpersonal and relational analysts are convinced that our own experience is just as important as the patient's in understanding what happens in the treatment; and therefore a story of the intertwining of two people's subjectivities works as clinical narrative for us. For interpersonal and relational analysts, as I emphasize throughout this book, what transpires is a ceaselessly changing, emergent field, a field continuously in the process of being created by the interaction of both partners' conscious and unconscious influences on one another.

I hasten to add, however, that when I say this, I certainly do *not* mean to suggest that the interpersonal or relational analyst's experience is *nothing but* countertransference. Just like our Freudian colleagues, we are professionals offering a service to our patients, and so of course much of our experience in our consulting rooms consists of weighing our options in our attempts to judge what will best serve those professional purposes.

But we do place particular emphasis on our experience of the ongoing relatedness. And so when I tell a patient about my impression of an unconscious meaning he is conveying, the way I see it is that I am not *only* telling the patient something—that is, I am not interpreting; I am participating in the life of the field between us, and I am doing so in ways that it is simply impossible for me to fully understand as I am carrying them out. That is the reason I don't use the word "interpretation" to describe what I do—that word lays too much emphasis on what I can know about the patient's mind and my own, and too little emphasis on my inevitable unconscious affective and interactive (enactive) participation in the treatment.

Now that I have made this point, though, let me try to avoid throwing out the baby with the bath water: the fact that I do not use the concept of interpretation does not mean that I'm not interested in *understanding*. I am. But as I have written elsewhere (Stern, 2009b, 2013c, Chapter 5 of the present book) I see the possibility of new understanding as the outcome of a new relational freedom between the patient and me, a freedom to feel, see, and say differently than before. The shifts that lead to new episodes of freedom absorb my clinical interest more than my intention to make and convey objective observations.

I hope that the following illustration demonstrates my contention that my own unconscious affects and reactions are playing a mutual part, with the patient's, in creating the clinical process between us. The episode in my vignette is dramatic, although drama is no more characteristic of my everyday work than it is of anyone else's. But dramatic or not, I do routinely base my work in the belief that the interaction of the patient's unconscious influence and my own is continuous. It is not always verbalized, though, nor need it be. You will notice that, while most of what happens in this vignette transpires without explicit discussion of the nature of the conscious or unconscious relatedness between the patient and me, relational considerations are nevertheless the source of all the events I describe.

Clinical illustration

I began working with this person just two or three months prior to the events I will recount. She was an unusually attractive, charming, socially adept, intelligent, and well-educated woman who, despite always having assumed that she would marry and have children, could not seem to make relationships take that direction. Now approaching the age of 40, she was worried about her future. To begin with, I was baffled at her lack of success, and despite myself, I began to wonder if perhaps her problem was that her positive attributes threatened most of the men she met. (I did not yet understand that she threatened me.) But this explanation did not seem to me to be a very good one, because it seemed unlikely that she could have threatened *all* the men she met. And besides, that interpretation would ignore whatever her own contribution might be. At this point, though, I could do no more than refer to "her contribution" in the abstract. I was struggling with the thoroughly nonrational perception that she was flawless. I knew better, of course. I was even able to note her apparent lack of psychological mindedness as an illustration; but, unsurprisingly, I could not convince myself: the perception that dogged me was a feeling, not a reasonable observation. I did not yet see that her perfection was itself the point: she was like the perfect princess who lived at the top of the glass mountain. Like the suitors who tried to ride their horses up the mountain to reach the princess, I could find no point of purchase, no way to talk to her that would create some kind of sense of relatedness with her. It was easy for me to feel inadequate in her presence.

I was reduced to hashing and rehashing with her the end of the relationship that had finally brought her into treatment. She was in genuine pain about this, and she appreciated my suggestion that her pain was less about the man himself than about her worry that her hopes for the future were dimming fast. But this idea was hardly sufficient to carry the treatment. I could sense that, unless I found a way to help her deepen the work—which is to say, unless I found a way into a discussion of the less-than-perfect parts of her experience, but without shaming her about them—the treatment was going to end shortly. She would feel better, at least temporarily; and if I had nothing more to offer, she would leave.

I had ceased anticipating this patient's visits with pleasure soon after we had started meeting, and at this juncture, maybe three months in, I was becoming quite familiar with the feeling that I was not a very competent analyst for her. My rehashing of her recent relationship seemed vapid, superficial, and intellectualized to me; and while it was not difficult for me to connect my feelings of inadequacy with her impenetrability, I also imagined, with moderate discomfort, that she agreed with my assessment of my efforts.

Actually, it is not true to say that I could observe nothing beyond this woman's perfection. I have mentioned being impressed with her impenetrability and her lack of psychological mindedness. I had also noticed the defensive quality of her continuous, brittle good cheer. She could cry about her pain, and she could be angry, but only if some objective situation in the outside world merited it. I had the sense that sadness or anger under any other circumstances would feel unjustifiable to her, and would probably represent a weakness in her eyes. It would shame her.

She could not be vulnerable to me, in other words, and I felt sure that I was not the only one with whom she felt this way. As a matter of fact, I imagined that this might be exactly the problem she was encountering in maintaining a romantic relationship. I could not just offer the patient that observation, though, not unless I had something to say that would help her make use of it in a way that did not potentiate the shame I could sense in the wings.

Time was running out. This was not a person who could discuss her frustration with the treatment or with me in a productive way. To do so would seem unacceptably hostile to her, rather like criticizing her marvelous parents (one of many attitudes that had made it difficult to get the treatment moving). Or rather, even if she *were* able and willing to talk about her frustration, it would do her no good unless I could say something that would give that frustration a different or broader meaning than it had now, something that would bring some life into the work for her. If I could not do that, then talking about her frustration would simply be a prelude to her departure.

And so one day, with the time left in the treatment swiftly draining away, I took a deep breath and stumbled into an attempt to say something authentic to this woman about my reaction to her presentation of herself. I did not know where I was going, or exactly what I would say when I got there. I talked to her for a couple of minutes about feeling that there must be parts of her that she was not pleased about, that maybe she didn't even like, because everyone has parts like that. Yet (I told her), I didn't seem to be able to get to know her that way. I told her that I felt she was having a very hard time being vulnerable with me, letting me really know her. I told her that, while vulnerability could be uncomfortable for anyone, I thought it must be particularly uncomfortable for her. I could see, I said, that unless we were able to move what we were doing in the direction of me getting to know her in a way that would no doubt make her feel vulnerable, the treatment was going to end, because she was going to cease seeing any value in it. I told her I knew how frustrated she must be with what we were doing, and, like me, how little she must be able to figure out how to make things different between us.

These thoughts did not come smoothly, nor did I express them that way. I struggled with them. And of course I was watching her reaction. She seemed interested in what I had to say about vulnerability, and she agreed outright with my estimation of her frustration. These things were good; but still I could not see how I was going to identify something in her experience, something that she could see at least as well as I could, that would open what we were doing into a psychoanalytic treatment.

At some moment, as I was talking, she appeared to me to change. It was quite subtle. She seemed softer and more open. That description, though, "softer and more open," was not available to me in the moment, only later on, when I thought back on it. In fact, I was not even aware of the presence of my new perception of her, and of the softer feeling in me that went with it, until, in retrospect, I tried to understand what had happened in the moments before I finally found myself able to say what occurred to me next, which was something new about her experience, something that I thought she would recognize and that might just help us into a more analytic kind of relatedness. The thought formed itself as I was speaking. I am quite sure that its possibility was created by the prior subtle change in my perception of her, which was, in turn, created by some change in her own affective state. As I spoke, I think that my novel perception was also helped along by my patient's facial expressions, through which she expressed a frank, friendly, and inquisitive interest in what I was saying.

But I am describing these moments with more precision than I experienced at the time. The truth is that I surprised myself—I didn't know what was coming until I was in the process of uttering it. I said, "I think you must be lonely. I think you must always have been lonely." Seeing her shock and recognition, and the tears welling in her eyes, I was encouraged to continue: "I wonder if you have ever felt really known by anyone."

She wept, but this was not the hard crying that had accompanied her angry descriptions of the way her boyfriend had treated her. She hid her face in her hands. After a minute or two of silence she looked up at me and said simply and sadly, "I *am* lonely. I've always been lonely." After another silence, she confirmed that, indeed, she had never felt that anyone had known her.

The session ended. It was obvious to both of us that we had started to do something quite different. As she walked in the door for her next session, she said as she sat down and smiled at me, "Now we have something to talk about." It was unnecessary to say it.

Discussion

With this material in mind, let me make a couple of final points. First, a note about the experience of analysts of different stripes: I believe that Freudian analysts have frequent experiences with their patients of the personally resonant sort that I have recounted just now with my patient. And I have had, with my patient, the same kind of interpretive opportunities that those analysts take advantage of in their work. The difference between their clinical selves and mine, then, is not at all that they are cool, detached, and rational and that I am hot, involved, and impetuous. The real difference between us is that we locate therapeutic action in different parts of clinical experience. These divergent beliefs about how treatment works then shape our sense of the nature of clinical process, both what it is and what it should be. Let me say just a few words about that.

I have the impression that most, maybe even all, Freudian analysts would be likely to agree with the proposition that their aim is to understand the patient's inner world. More specifically, most would say that their work derives from, or revolves around, the concept of unconscious phantasy. Now, fantasy, conscious or unconscious, is symbolic in nature. And that point, in turn, is the reason that the primary defense in Freudian psychoanalysis has always been repression. Repression, because it requires the recognition of the experience that is to be ejected from awareness and maintained in an unconscious state, requires the capacity for thought; and thought, of course, requires symbolization.

The patient's trouble, then, from this perspective, is that his mind contains unconscious symbolized meanings to which he has no access, but which influence his living in profound ways. In the patient's life, certainly including the sessions of a psychoanalytic treatment, these unconscious symbolized meanings are expressed in disguised fashion. It is the analyst's job to observe those disguised meanings, untangle them from current external circumstances, and trace them back to the unconscious fantasies from which they issue, a process which, when successful, illuminates the patient's motivations in a way that will make it possible for the patient to live differently.

The mind, in this case, is *inside* the person. It is an internal matter. And so if you intend to treat it, you need to understand analytic interventions as conduct that originates, or comes from, *outside* of the patient and that affects, or influences, the *inside* of the patient. That influence of the outside on the inside, if it is to protect the patient's autonomy, should not be direct influence, but a new understanding of the inside. The analyst, therefore, tries to do his best to transmit understanding directly, or to facilitate its awakening in the patient's mind, usually by the analysis of resistance. The analyst, that is, does his work by interpreting.

I really should qualify what I just said about the role of the symbolic for Freudians: as a group, that is, they do not work *only* with the symbolic form of unconscious experience; they study unmentalized or nonsymbolic experience, as well. I am thinking here of the work of a number of analysts, not all of whom would identify themselves as Freudian, but all of whom have been influential in Freudian circles (e.g., Segal, 1957; Bion, 1962a, 1962b, 1963; Winnicott, 1971; Green, 1975; Lacan, 1977; Modell, 1984; Bucci, 1997; Lecours and Bouchard, 1997; Fonagy *et al.*, 2002; Boston Change Process Study Group, 2008). But it does seem reasonable to say that Freudian analysts *emphasize* the symbolic, in the form of unconscious fantasies.

Most relational and interpersonal analysts, however, do not. Let me use the same construction: I think it is reasonable to say that the interpersonal/relational emphasis is on the *un*symbolized. I hope that I am correct in believing that I speak for most of my interpersonal and relational colleagues when I say that unconscious experience is potential experience, experience that can be shaped and symbolized if the relevant dynamic factors, internal and interpersonal, allow that outcome. My own particular name for unconscious experience, which is intended to convey its vague and unsymbolized nature, is unformulated experience (Stern, 1983, 1997, 2010a). I should add here, since I am often asked this question, that unformulated experience is not simply anything one wishes it to be. The formulated shapes it can take are constrained, both by reality and by the mind itself. This is not a relativistic view.

Now, if unconscious experience is unformulated experience, then repression, too, must be reconsidered, because only symbolized experience has the degree of organization that allows us to imagine that it can be purposefully (and unconsciously, of course) ejected from consciousness. You can throw a rock or a snowball, that is, but not a handful of rain. And so, in most interpersonal and relational schemes, dissociation replaces repression. In dissociation, one's openness to the experience one might formulate, an openness I usually refer to as curiosity, is curtailed, and the result is that the experience of oneself that one finds intolerable is not created at all. It remains nascent or potential—in a word, unformulated.[2]

What, then, determines which possibilities enter awareness? What determines which unformulated experience is formulated, and which shapes that unformulated experience takes? For me and most other interpersonal and relational analysts, in a way that I hope I have illustrated in my vignette, it is clinical process, the conscious and unconscious relatedness between patient and analyst, that determines the formulation of the contents of consciousness, in both the analyst's mind and the patient's (Stern, 1997, 2009b, 2013c, Chapter 5 of the present book).[3]

Notes

1 An earlier version of this chapter was presented at "Minding the Gap: Freudian and relational/interpersonal psychoanalysts in dialogue," New York Psychoanalytic Institute, February, 2009.
2 I hasten to add, since I am so often asked about this matter, that I have addressed the question of how one can avoid the awareness of experience that has not yet been formulated. How, that is, can one know what not to formulate without formulating it first? For my attempts to grapple with this question, see Stern, 1997, Chapters 6 and 7.
3 I have offered elsewhere (Stern, 1989, 1990, 1991, 1997, 2002, 2003, 2004, 2009b, 2010a, Chapter 5 of the present book) detailed description of the processes by which unconscious relatedness mediates the contents of consciousness.

Chapter 8

Implicit theories of technique and the values that inspire them

> [T]he psychoanalyst can be regarded as an instrument, a sort of probe into the psychoanalytic situation, that organizes the experience the analyst has in interaction with his patients through the formation of unconscious theoretical structures... It is my firm conviction that the investigation of the implicit, private theories of clinical psychoanalysts opens a major new door in psychoanalytic research.
>
> (Sandler, 1983, p. 37)

I have written many times about my view of technique (e.g., Stern, 1997, 2010a). Those discussions of technique came up naturally in the course of writing about my *conception* of treatment, including my understanding of therapeutic action, subjects that have everything to do with what kind of technique I practice and advocate. I have never actually sat down to write about technique apart from its role as an expression of my understanding of the aims, goals, and means of psychoanalysis, and in fact it makes little sense to me to consider the question of technique apart from those broader questions.

To those who feel that any discipline should be defined by a single set of techniques that every practitioner applies in a prescribed way, our field must appear to be a hopeless jumble. It does not appear that way to me. In this chapter, I want to contribute to the justification of what can seem (to the jaundiced) to be an endless accretion of mutually exclusive theories of technique in our field. To those skeptical of multiple theories, the intention behind each new idea seems to be the defeat and retirement of those that have come before it. What we are left with, from such a perspective, is nothing but an embarrassing squabble.

I could not feel more strongly than I do that this is a serious misconception. It is certainly true that we psychoanalysts have not always tolerated the differences between us very well, especially differences in our theories of technique. But that era has largely ended, and conversation between us is now as common as intolerance and cold silence used to be. Disagreement is sharp at times, but that's fine. At least our differences no longer routinely inspire the contempt of one group for another and/or the wholesale dismissal by the powerful of the views of those who are less powerful. It's no longer even self-evident which group is the most powerful.

Psychoanalysis—the field that is home to us all, not just one school of thought or another—needs not only to defend itself more effectively, but to assert itself with greater confidence. There is no shortage of intelligent people, including influential psychoanalysts (e.g., Brenner, 2000; Rangell, 2002, 2006, 2008; Green, 2005), who shake their heads ruefully over the fact of multiple psychoanalytic techniques, as if multiple ways of practicing psychoanalysis and psychoanalytic psychotherapy signify a deplorable fracturing of something that should be a unity. In a representative passage, Rangell (2002), the psychoanalytic writer who may have been the most frequent critic of multiple theories, writes,

> At the end of its first century, the theory of psychoanalysis is in a state of disarray. A person considering psychoanalysis is confronted by half a dozen alternative schools, frequently dismissive of each other, each claiming theories superior or superordinate to the others. In addition, disciplines outside psychoanalysis offer competing approaches. Today potential patients face a confusing array from which to choose a helping professional. Little wonder that the public has difficulty feeling confidence in analysis.
> (p. 1109)

But there is another view. There exist perspectives from which there is nothing at all the matter with a field harboring multiple, conflicting theories. In an important recent article, Foehl (2010) offers a compelling way of understanding the inevitability of this state of affairs. He argues that, while mainstream theory in the past attempted to portray the *causes of experience*, contemporary thinking focuses on the nature of *experience itself*. This is an observation with which I not only agree; it is an impression of the current state of psychoanalysis that I hope my work has participated in creating.

It is Foehl's contention that this focus on clinical process is responsible for our multiple, often conflicting ways of understanding psychoanalytic work. Experience can be reduced to a set of inevitable, predictable outcomes only if you posit that it (experience) is the product of a set of knowable causes, causes that are defined to be more fundamental than experience itself. But once you focus on *experience* as the object of interest and not simply as the product of a cause, you can no longer so easily perform the same reduction. Experience becomes the point, no longer merely a predetermined outcome, and so it cannot so easily be characterized in terms other than those that actually constitute it. Under these conditions, no single theory can explain everything—and, in fact, explanation is no longer necessarily even the point.[1]

I am in full agreement with Foehl when he urges psychoanalysts to accept what he calls *epistemological pluralism*. As a matter of fact, from the kind of hermeneutic perspective I have long embraced (and that I introduce momentarily), as long as the practitioners of conflicting theories are conducting what Gadamer (2004) calls genuine conversation with one another, the existence of multiple conceptions of practice is a sign of a field's vigor.

And so I focus in this chapter on how we might think about our multiple theories without mortification. I take the position that the existence of multiple theories of technique is inevitable, and therefore unworthy of vilification. But I also add fuel to the fire, because I claim that multiplicity is only the beginning of the controversial issues I believe we should include in any general consideration of our theory of technique. Even more troubling to some will be what seems to me the inescapable conclusion that we also seem to be continuously guided by *implicit* theories of technique. How should we think about these problems?

The ideas that lie at the heart of my answers to this question have to do with the necessity for us to recognize the foundational role of moral values in our notions of how to practice, and a hermeneutic ideal for our theory of technique. I first make the case for implicit theories of technique, then suggest that our explicit theories emerge from these implicit notions. Finally, I argue that implicit theories, in turn, arise from value positions that we often hold with only minimal explicit reflection, or with none at all. Values that may be relatively unexamined, then, underlie all technical theories, implicit and explicit alike. Because the formative influence of values on our theories of technique is inevitable, it is unworthy of criticism. It merely requires our acknowledgment, and the deployment of our curiosity about the relevant value positions.

But before I reach those arguments, I offer a very brief overview of certain philosophical issues that are relevant to what I want to say. I will not return to epistemology after this sortie, but I will rely upon what I am about to tell you for the remainder of my remarks.

Philosophical issues

Our culture's dominant philosophical paradigm, reflected in the folk psychology we all live with every day, leads us to believe that reality is singular and unitary. Facts are givens in this scheme, and interpretation is limited to the meanings we assign to those facts. The data, that is, have an existence that is independent from their interpretation. From this perspective, if we can establish "the facts" defining a problem, a single set of best practices should be specifiable as the solution for that problem, or at least the best approach to it. This position is often known as technical rationality.

Technical rationality is so deeply embedded in our minds that it can seem self-evident, simply the "natural" way of the world (and medical insurance companies), so that when we think in a way that contradicts it, we can feel at risk; and if we stray from these guiding principles, we sometimes feel vulnerable enough that when someone authoritative tells us to return to the fold, we can be intimidated into doing it without a great deal of thought. When Adolf Grünbaum (1984, 1993) published his critique of the scientific status of psychoanalysis, for instance, too many psychoanalysts took for granted that the question was only whether psychoanalysis met Grünbaum's criteria. Too few realized that Grünbaum was, in fact, taking an epistemological position simply by *adopting* his criteria. Grünbaum himself did not draw attention to this point, which is entirely consistent with his position that there is only one right way to adjudicate psychoanalytic claims: the logic of positivism. To the extent that psychoanalysis is composed of scientific hypotheses testable by traditional, objectivist methods, he was right. His position is, in that sense, defensible.

But many of us, maybe even most of us, no longer agree that psychoanalysis should be conceived in the terms of positivism. There exist other defensible conceptions of psychoanalysis that differ in significant respects with Grünbaum's view and with his assumptions. I (Stern, 1997, 2010a) claim, for instance, along with many other like-minded psychoanalytic writers,[2] that psychoanalytic techniques are ways of creating and assigning meanings, and that such techniques should be judged by their utility in furthering the aims and goals that inspired them. This way of thinking is inspired by hermeneutics and pragmatism rather than objectivism and positivism. Psychoanalytic interpretive schemes should not be judged by whether or not they can be confirmed objectively, in some denatured, quantitative, empirical context, by application of the scientific method. The question is not whether oedipal or selfobject transferences "really" exist, for instance (i.e., whether they exist in a decontextualized world, like a cell on a slide), but whether working according to techniques inspired by these conceptions of transference actualizes the purposes behind the conceptions, and whether we accept these particular purposes. Each school of thought in our field is based in a certain set of value positions, and the actualization of these value positions in the analyst's conduct is that school's theory of technique. More about this point later.

My own view is hermeneutic and constructivist, meaning that there are multiple valid versions of reality (see especially Gadamer, 2004).[3] But that does not mean that truth can be whatever we claim it to be. Hermeneutics is not relativistic. In the hermeneutic view, reality is "there" and must be respected. But it cannot be perceived in an unmediated way. Instead, reality is revealed only via the constraints that it imposes on our interpretations. Reality, that is, determines the range of valid interpretations in any particular instance. *Any phenomenon can become meaningful only within reality's constraints.* If we shape an interpretation that falls outside these constraints, we are either lying or demonstrating poor judgment (*in extremis*, crazy). As they define the range within which interpretation can be valid, these constraints simultaneously exclude from consideration a much wider array of (invalid) interpretive possibilities. (I am using the word "interpretation" now in its general sense as a kind of understanding, not in its more specific psychoanalytic meaning.) To return to my example: both oedipal and selfobject transferences are valid conceptions. Which one we use depends on the broader psychoanalytic purposes we embrace.

Let me take a simpler example of multiple interpretive possibilities. When we see a tear on someone's cheek, we consider that this person may be sad, highly amused and laughing "until he cries," frustrated to the point of tears, in physical pain, or allergic. We do not imagine any number of other interpretations, most of which seem absurd: greed, having eaten too much, sexual excitement, and so on. If we do see a tear at a time when one of these other activities is uppermost (sexual arousal, for example, during which it is not unheard of for tears to be shed), the event is anomalous and requires explanation. In fact, under most circumstances, we seldom even stop and think about everyday interpretive processes; thoughts, feelings, perceptions just "appear" in our minds, having been selected from the array of possibilities by our (usually nonconscious) participation in the context at hand.

Which valid interpretation we create on any particular occasion depends, speaking most broadly, on the era and the culture in which the interpretation is made. That is, the widest possible range of valid interpretation can be defined as the limits of meaningfulness specific to our time and place. This point is what led me to claim, just above, that we do not, and cannot, grasp reality in an unmediated way. Culture mediates the relationship between reality and individual human beings. This is the doctrine of historicity, and philosophical hermeneutics is rooted in it.

But it is when we consider what goes on *within* these broad historico/cultural trends that we reach the level of everyday experience, and of the kinds of meanings and understandings that are constructed in the practice and theories of psychoanalysis. Within the broad cultural limits on meaningfulness, it follows that an individual's interpretations, selected in a particular moment, must depend on some other factor. That factor, we can say, is the context of the moment in which the interpretation is made, especially the interpersonal and intrapsychic context (Stern, 1997, 2010a). That is, the meaning we assign to our experience from one moment to the next depends on the nature of the current interpersonal field.[4]

The constraints on our understanding, and thus the range of interpretive validity, vary from wide to narrow in any particular instance, depending upon the phenomenon in question. Some unformulated experience can be articulated in many ways without violating the limits of validity, while other aspects of what is unformulated can be articulated only within very narrow bounds. There is not much interpretive wiggle room when it comes to identifying an airplane visually, for instance (what else could it be?), or in concluding that the object on which my computer sits is a table; but under some circumstances a *sound* that might be made by an invisible airplane might be indistinguishable from the sound of a lawnmower, a car, a train, thunder, and so on. At such a moment, we cannot settle on an interpretation without grasping a more complete context. Or think about the affective impact of a piece of music. We might go so far as to say that the ascription of joy to a dirge is such a strange interpretation that it violates certain constraints. But without violating any interpretive constraints, we would accept that Stravinksy's *Rite of Spring* inspires a range of emotional accompaniments that runs the gamut from love and communion with the piece to contempt for what some would call its schmaltz.

There is one last, crucial point underpinning philosophical hermeneutics: the idea that we are continuously interpreting leads to the conclusion that *experience itself is an interpretation,* every moment of it. We create experience; we construct it. We do not merely lend meaning to some kind of mythical and empirically verifiable stuff that the world deposits in our minds. Facts are *not* simply facts. The contents of our minds, even our sensations and perceptions, are themselves interpretations of a world that, inner and outer alike, is inherently ambiguous. In objectivist schemes, as I said above, data exist prior to and independently of their interpretation. From a constructivist vantage point, on the other hand, the data are inevitably *constituted* by interpretive acts. It is impossible for data to precede interpretation, because it is interpretation that creates them. We always measure for reasons, and those reasons define what phenomena will count as data. In human experience there can be no such thing as an objective bottom line.

Our attempts to understand our patients and ourselves in the course of psychoanalytic work are complex analogues of the simple examples I have offered (e.g., the airplane and the modernist symphony). We must create myriad experiences and then often combine them into larger wholes. One of the ways we do that is by constructing theories, which can be thought about as interpretive tools. Some psychoanalytic ideas contribute to the shape of our experience or our observations (conceptual theories); others organize our ways of going about our work (theories of technique). Because they are interpretive schemes, the question about any psychoanalytic theory, from a hermeneutic or constructivist perspective, is not simply whether it is right or wrong, but instead whether it accomplishes the purposes for which it was devised while respecting reality's constraints.

Multiple, implicit theories of technique

Virtually no one today can support either the hard-line position that there exists an objectively shaped set of rules about how to practice proper psychoanalysis or the "from-the-gut" position that one simply does what feels right. I feel sure that there is universal agreement that we need some conception of what we are doing; and from the other end of the issue, given the increasingly widespread appreciation of the formative, unconscious influence of clinical process on both participants, more analysts than ever before accept that analysts are not even consistently *capable* of practicing within the dictates of a single, model technique. That is, we no longer believe that it is feasible or reasonable for analysts to work as if it is possible for them to plan the nature of their impact on their patients. The two extreme positions—i.e., for and against formal theories of technique—have ceased having a significant influence on contemporary discussion (and the "from-the-gut" position probably never did), their use today limited to creating bloated targets out of ideas that conflict with one's own.

The more reasonable position is to imagine a continuum, perhaps anchored by the two extreme views, but composed more by trends or tendencies: on the one hand, a tendency to support a model technique or some of its axioms; on the other, a tendency in the direction of an acceptance of spontaneous give-and-take.

Putting the question in this looser form, by seeming to remove its sharpest edges, may appear to encourage us to avoid bombast and other kinds of rhetoric. I have just finished claiming, after all, that the positions with the sharpest edges have little influence. But despite what may seem to be the improved capacity of a looser approach to represent the positions of real, working psychoanalysts, I think that a conceptual relaxation of this sort, fuzzy around the edges, actually does not help us at all. In my view it hinders us, in fact, because it results in confusion. I think it confuses the nature of both the question and its answer. You can't "tend toward" a theory of technique. You either believe that theory of technique is necessary, or you don't. (I am not considering here the position that we tack back and forth between the application of technique and personal participation, a position identified by Hoffman [1998] as the dialectic of ritual and spontaneity.)

I believe that each of us *must* hold some theory (or, as we shall see, *theories*) of technique. It seems to me that it is impossible not to, because in our offices we are doing one particular thing and not another. Each of us is a psychoanalyst of one kind or another; we are not grocers, anesthesiologists, or plumbers. The fact that we identify ourselves in this way means that each of us believes that he or she does something that qualifies as psychoanalysis and/or psychoanalytic psychotherapy. In our attempt to fulfill the aims of the kind of practice that is ours, we necessarily operate on the basis of some set of principles that define that activity, however unarticulated those principles may be. Our possession of *some* theory of technique is therefore simply unavoidable, no matter how little enamored we may believe we are with such ideas. The question is not, then, *whether* we have conceptions of how we practice what we do for a living; the question is only whether we *know* about them. And I mean "know" in a very particular way: verbal-reflective knowing. There are other forms of knowing, after all. Psychoanalysts at work are often "drawn" or "pulled" toward some course of action in a way analogous to the movement of iron filings toward a magnet. At other times, it feels less as if we are pulled or drawn and more as if we are actively groping toward a course of action we feel (or hope) that we will recognize when we manage to embody it. Groping and being pulled are probably reflections of certain kinds of nonverbal or nonsymbolic knowing; but neither of these kinds of knowing is the verbal-reflective mode that we identify as the way we know explicit theories of technique.

All of us use explicit theories, of course. We learn them in our training and from the literature. Sometimes we use them one at a time; other times we use several of them in conjunction with one another. And it goes without saying that we often use explicit theories with full awareness of exactly what we are doing. But I think it is also fair to say that our use of explicit theories is often preconscious. It seems uncontroversial to claim that, often enough, we are *not* fully aware of using ideas that we originally learned explicitly (see also Canestri, 2006b). At such moments, we may have a sense of what we want to do, but we have not considered exactly why we want to do it; but if someone were to ask us to explain ourselves we would be able, after a bit of thought, to specify the explicit theory that is the source of this sense-of-what-to-do. If someone were to ask me why I was silent with a patient on one occasion but not on another, for instance, I might think for a moment and then answer that when I stayed silent it was because I felt (without having formulated this view at the time) that the patient's silence was a thoughtful one. This answer would be a way of citing the view that it is best not to interrupt a thoughtful silence, a view that I was taught explicitly over and over again. I might go on to say that on the other occasion—that is, when I broke the silence by speaking to the patient—it was because I believed that the patient was experiencing the kind of defensive block in his thinking that I thought (again, without having explicitly formulated the thought) that I might be able to help to resolve. This intervention, too, was based in an aspect of technique I originally learned explicitly. Yet neither rationale was necessarily formulated until I was asked about my conduct with a patient; and both have become so much a part of the way I work that I probably use them in this unformulated way very often. Preconscious application of theories we originally learned explicitly becomes more likely after we have had such long acquaintance and familiarity with them that they get into our bones. They eventually come to influence us on a nonconscious level.

But I want to suggest something beyond this, something more than the point that we make preconscious use of theories we originally learned explicitly. I want to suggest another whole category of technical theories, a category beyond those theories we explicitly recognize, a category of theory and clinical thinking that we may actually be surprised to realize that we use. This is the kind of theory rooted in nonverbal or nonsymbolic knowing—what I have elsewhere referred to as unformulated experience (Stern, 1997, 2010a)—the kind of theory that leads us to grope or allow ourselves to be pulled, the kind of theory that exists only *implicitly*.[5] Despite the fact that this other, nonexplicit kind of technical theory has never been articulated, we use it more or less continuously. It seems to me, as a matter of fact, that whether or not we think about it, virtually all psychoanalysts understand the analytic process and the nature of our participation in it, including but not limited to our interventions, in ways that exceed or differ from our explicitly formulated theories. I believe that one of the most important functions of clinical supervision is to help in the articulation of some of our supervisees' unformulated notions about how treatment works and what they believe they do to encourage mutative events. The more such formulation is encouraged in supervision, the more supervisees are liable to recognize the opportunity to carry it on later, after supervision has ended. In this instance, as is so often the case, the freedom to think is an important route to clinical discipline.[6]

I would not want to deny for a moment, of course, that we absorb directly from the literature and our teachers many of the ideas about technique that influence us most. Rather, I am arguing that each psychoanalyst *also* works according to his or her own ideas of technique, often or even usually implicit, developed in the course of clinical experience, sometimes co-created with the patient in the moment of their use. In fact, while I hardly wish to minimize the impact of explicit theories, I believe that they *all* begin as implicit or unformulated ways of grasping and influencing clinical process. These implicit theories are the products of personal experience—clinical experience most significantly, but other experience as well.

As an illustration and an exercise of imagination, consider Harry Stack Sullivan's development of "the detailed inquiry," the name Sullivan (1954) gave to the way he worked. The principle here is that one listens for gaps and absences in the patient's material and then inquires about them:

> [T]he psychiatrist listens to all statements with a certain critical interest, asking, "Could that mean anything except what first occurs to me?" He questions (at least to himself) much of what he hears, not on the assumption that the patient is a liar, or doesn't know how to express himself, or anything like that, but always with the simple query in mind, "Now could this mean something that would not immediately occur to me? Do I know what he means by that?"
>
> (p. 19)

By the time Sullivan wrote this passage, he had been seeing patients for many years. One imagines that he could not have formulated the thought as a fledgling psychotherapist. It required experience. Yet on some level, we can also guess that Sullivan was always attuned to the issues of difficulties in communication. He was a pragmatic psychiatrist who, somewhere along the line, became painfully aware of how frequently people did not effectively convey meanings to one another, either because the transmitted meanings were private (private, that is, even to themselves—"parataxic" or "autistic," in Sullivan's argot) or because the meanings were inadvertently assimilated to equally private, parataxic meaning schemes in the mind of the person on the receiving end. This broad idea about the nature of communication no doubt percolated for years before Sullivan could voice it in language. And during all the years before Sullivan could do that, I imagine him groping his way toward the kind of conduct in interviews with patients that would satisfy what became his sensitive grasp of communicative inefficiency. Eventually, having enacted this groping over and over again, I imagine him beginning to give articulate shape to the path he had so often traversed "by feel." I imagine glimmers of what became his principles of detailed inquiry being formulated in his mind, until he could finally write the passage I have quoted.

Of course, Sullivan is hardly unique in this respect. I could have picked a specific statement of technique from any writer to make this point. Atwood and Stolorow (1994) have made a convincing case that one's own implicit, unformulated grasp of living is the source of *all* the theories that have been articulated in writing by their authors and recognized as contributions to the body of psychoanalytic knowledge.[7] Our explicit theories of technique are certainly not exceptions to that rule. In an earlier, classic contribution to the problem of relating theory and practice (and the same paper from which I have drawn my epigram), Joseph Sandler (1983) offers a very similar perspective:

> With increasing clinical experience the analyst, as he grows more competent, will preconsciously (descriptively speaking, unconsciously) construct a whole variety of theoretical segments which relate directly to his clinical work. They are the products of unconscious thinking, are very much partial theories, models or schemata, which have the quality of being available in reserve, so to speak, to be called upon whenever necessary. That they may contradict one another is no problem. They co-exist happily as long as they are unconscious. They do not appear in consciousness unless they are consonant with what I have called official or public theory, and can be described in suitable words. Such partial structures may in fact represent better (i.e., more useful and appropriate) theories than the official ones, and it is likely that many valuable additions to psychoanalytic theory have come about because conditions have arisen that have allowed preconscious part-theories to come together and emerge in a plausible and psychoanalytically socially acceptable way.
>
> (p. 37)

In the paper from which this passage is drawn, Sandler discusses all kinds of psychoanalytic theory, offering as examples of implicit theories certain ideas concerning drives and motives, conflict, and object relationships and transference. More recently Canestri (2006a, 2006b; Canestri *et al.*, 2006; see also Jiménez, 2009) focuses more narrowly on implicit psychoanalytic theories of technique, arguing not only that they exist, but also (and echoing both Sandler, and Atwood and Stolorow) that as they are formulated, they become the sources of our explicit theories of practice.[8]

As I have promised, I will turn soon to the role of values in technical theory. At this juncture, let me merely expand upon one crucial point about those matters, a point that I briefly mentioned in beginning. I suspect that we can agree that our values are highly significant in shaping our conduct and our experience of living. We live according to our conscious and unconscious beliefs and assumptions about what matters most in life. These beliefs and assumptions differ greatly from one individual to another, and from one group to another.

Now consider how many of our decisions come about without careful, conscious thought on our parts (or without any at all), and what that implies about how often our foundational values go unexamined. If even the parts of life that we play some role in consciously choosing are deeply affected by values we have often never really thought through, then how much more must the part of life that we grasp in only an unformulated way be shaped by unexamined value positions? Now remember the claim I have just made, the point that our explicit theories of technique emerge from parts of life that have existed up to that moment only as unformulated experience. Must it not be virtually certain that our explicit theories of technique are inspired, and even shaped, by our deepest, and often unarticulated, feelings and thoughts about what is most important in living? Theories about how to do psychoanalysis, in other words, not only our implicit theories but our explicit ones as well, are not the idealized, rational products of detached, objective minds; they are instead the rather direct expressions of our values, many of which are both unarticulated and very close to our hearts.

Implicit theories and technical rationality

Clinical psychoanalysts learn what to do by reflecting on their experience of what is happening in the situation at hand; and they learn about their experience of the situation at hand by trying to reflect on what they are doing. One simply cannot know in advance how to handle situations that arise spontaneously. In any and all professional fields (e.g., medicine, engineering, law, psychotherapy) each professional's daily work is a succession of happenings that, while bearing enough similarities to situations that have arisen in the past to make the professional's explicitly held theories useful, also often constitute unique moments demanding unique solutions (Schön, 1983, 1987).

And so while we can say that it is generally desirable to reflect on our implicit theories, we must also admit, it seems to me, that no matter how successful we are in such reflection, we will forever hold multiple, implicit theories of technique, because we will forever need to invent new ones as we face the situations that demand them. I am currently working with a man, for instance, with whom I have found my way, via experience that was implicit for a long time, to the (recent) explicit conclusion that, if I am to help him, I must do no more than listen to his highly creative and sometimes bizarre experience and dreams, imagining for myself my own version of them. It is better if I do not try to make sense of these experiences in any other terms than the ones in which he conveys them, although I can work at finding our way more deeply into them. (This is a variety of the active groping I have already referred to.) I have some ideas about why it is necessary to conduct myself this way with this man.

With the very next patient, I am just as convinced that I must more often try to say what I think his experience *means*. And when I ask myself, I notice that, just as in the case of the patient who came before, I do have ideas about why I believe that this way of proceeding helps him. These conclusions, too, grew from implicit versions of themselves: I found myself drawn to (pulled toward) behaving in certain ways over and over again, and eventually I thought about these things in words.

I don't believe there is anything unusual about the sequence of events in either of these cases; multiple, implicit theories of technique are par for the course across any analyst's workday.

To reject our continuous creation of implicit theories, or to view them as unfortunate signs of ignorance, would be to accept that our ideal should be the development of universally applicable principles—principles adequate to every situation, principles that we could be confidently use in a predictive fashion: when x happens, you take y action. To reject our implicit theories of technique, that is, would be to accept the doctrine of technical rationality that I introduced earlier in discussing Adolf Grünbaum (see also Hoffman, 2009).[9] All psychoanalysts know that their moment-to-moment decisions about what to do in their offices cannot be reduced in that way without suffering a catastrophic loss of meaning. And so, while it is desirable to reflect on our work, to continuously convert our implicit theories to explicitly held ideas, we must accept that some part of our work will always need to be guided by the kind of tacit knowing and tacit principles described by Polanyi (1958).[10]

The appearance of new explicit theories of technique

We need new, explicitly formulated theories of technique if psychoanalysis is to continue to develop. But when I refer to the continuing development of our field, I do not mean that psychoanalysis will necessarily become something better than it has been, or more accurate or useful, or even that our efforts are leading us to a closer approximation of the truth. Such things may happen. But even if they don't, psychoanalysis will certainly have to become something *different* than it has been, over and over again, because we psychoanalysts serve people who live in particular social worlds, and those worlds change. It has been argued repeatedly during the last few decades that the relatively new influences in our field—self psychology, for instance, or interpersonal/relational psychoanalysis—should not necessarily be viewed as claims to better versions of underlying, universal truths about human nature, as if new theories could aspire to nothing more than improving their aim on the same targets. But if not a closer approximation of truth, then what might new theories be instead?

New theories might be seen as responses to changes in our social worlds, changes that in turn then exert an influence on the shape of individual experience. It may be that there are more patients today who can be helped by these newer theories of technique than there were in times past, and that the newer theories were, in that important sense, called into being by our need for them.

We may take less for granted than we once did, for instance, that rampant individualism is a primary value. Has the relatively recent, widespread acceptance that interdependence is a thorough and inescapable part of life begun to play a new role in the development of the mind? Perhaps this new value is reflected in our culture's enthusiastic embrace of the significance of mother–infant interaction research in the study of psychological development, and in new views of the mutuality of relationships between adults. Perhaps we can even see this new value in the increasing recognition that each city, state, and country has no choice but to depend on all the others in the effort to preserve the earth's capacity to sustain life. We know that influential writers help to shape their times, but we also know that writers are shaped by the times in which they live. It is in latter sense that it is probably no accident that Winnicott, Sullivan, and Fairbairn came along when they did. This impression is actually underlined by the fact that, despite the significant overlaps in their views, Winnicott and

Fairbairn never indicated that they even knew Sullivan existed, nor did Sullivan ever seem to have read Winnicott or Fairbairn. That is, none of these writers seems to have influenced the others. And yet all three, writing at the same time, were harbingers of what seems to have become our field's recognition of interdependence.

Other social changes, perhaps related, have arrived at about the same time that we started to recognize mutuality and interdependence. We know with certainty that our confidence and trust in authority have waned over the last five decades. We know that people's formative experiences with authorities outside their families (e.g., teachers, religious leaders, politicians, and professionals such as doctors and lawyers) have altered substantially. Two or three generations ago, psychoanalytic patients frequently wanted or needed their analysts to know the truth about their minds. Today, while there are those for whom the analyst's exercise of traditional authority remains reassuring, most patients seem much less frequently to want their analysts or therapists to be omniscient.

No doubt families themselves have also been affected. Have they been affected in a way that has changed the nature of relationships between parents and children? Perhaps they have; perhaps parent–child relationships in the West, or at least the ideal of parent–child relationships, has changed in the direction of less authoritarianism and greater mutuality.

Self psychology, interpersonal psychoanalysis, and relational psychoanalysis are all constructed in ways that may be unconsciously responsive to the recognition of a change in our ideals and values in the direction of greater interdependence and mutuality and away from heroic individualism and automatic trust in authority. The significance of individual unconscious phantasy as the template of experience has given way in these theories to a close examination of the affective details of mutual clinical process (e.g., Bromberg, 2011b; see also Chapter 7); and the analyst's authority to know the patient's mind has been drastically reduced by the recognition that the analyst is always unconsciously involved (read: interdependent) with the patient in ways he or she cannot know (e.g., Hoffman, 1996; Mitchell, 1997). I am suggesting, in other words, that the clinical practices of self psychology and interpersonal/relational psychoanalysis may be the explicit expressions of implicit theories developed over several generations by analysts responding to the changing conditions of human living in our part of the world, and to the changing personalities that began to arise as a result of these conditions.

I began this section with the claim that we continuously need new explicit theories of technique. One justification for this claim is what I have just said about the possible responsiveness of theories of technique to social change. But let me go a step further: We do not only respond to change; we also participate in creating it. The more we manage to convert our implicit clinical purposes into explicit theories of technique, the more effectively we can think about and evaluate whether we are serving the purposes we most value.

We need new, explicit theories for more than their own sake, though, and for more, even, than the actualization of our values. Imagine explicit theory as a kind of core or foundation around which implicit theory grows, the way that new, living coral builds on the structure left behind by older generations. As new theories of technique are explicitly articulated, our clinical perceptions are broadened and deepened, and our implicit theories are therefore able to reach farther. Explicit and implicit theories bear a generative, dialectical relation to one another. Without new varieties of each, innovations of the other kind would never arise, and the process of thinking in psychoanalysis would grind to a halt.

Values and the evaluation of technical theory

One crucial lesson suggested by accepting the necessity for, and even the desirability of, multiple theories of technique is that, while we can certainly extol the virtues of practicing in one way rather than another, we cannot validly claim superiority across the board for any one theory. We can claim only that a single theory is the superior way to study certain phenomena and/or to create a particular state of affairs or address a particular kind of circumstance. That is, the utility or effectiveness of a technique cannot be addressed apart from its goals. A technique is useful or effective, in other words, in accomplishing *what*? Every theory has a particular context of application within which it is intended to be effective.[11]

And so, as in my earlier example of different conceptions of transference, the question about most concepts is not necessarily whether they are supportable, or central to psychoanalysis. Take the concept of drive, for instance. Without a doubt, the concept of drive is both supportable *and* central—but only within a certain view of the world. The question is whether making drive a centerpiece of our thinking leads us to intervene and understand in the clinical situation in ways that have consequences we believe are desirable enough to encourage. And then there are the costs. What parts of life does conceiving drive as central make *less* apparent in daily clinical practice? Do we lose something we value by thinking this way? Or do we gain something that we value more than whatever it is that we lose?

In this way, an appreciation of the significance of the context of application makes the task of evaluating theories of technique and therapeutic action much more complicated than it once seemed. But that task also becomes more realistically possible. It has been several decades since we could be satisfied simply to pit each theory of technique against every other one, and all on a level playing field. That is one of the reasons why, incidentally, the empirical scientific method of testing one theory of technique against another, using measures that are generally selected without regard to the values underlying them (or rather, selected as if values are immaterial), has very limited application here. We cannot argue issues of general effectiveness and accuracy in evaluating theories of technique; today we know enough to see that we must first formulate the context of application, the range of circumstances within which it is meaningful to ask about a technical theory's effectiveness, and we must then compare that context of application to the way the world looks from other psychoanalytic perspectives, asking ourselves about what working from within each of these perspectives might accomplish. What matters most to us, in other words, and what theory of technique does the best job of making that happen? In this sense, psychoanalysis and psychotherapy can be described as the clinical practice of ethics.

Sometimes the context of application for a theory, or some portion of that context, is easy to specify. That is true of theories of technique devised for work with a particular group of patients, for instance. But quite often, even in the case of theories such as these, other aspects of the context of application are much harder to pin down. The goals of a theory of technique are an outgrowth of the values that have informed its construction; and that means that establishing the context for evaluating a theory of technique requires identifying the values that shaped its goals. Even if a theory of technique is intended to apply specifically to borderline patients, for example, that theory of how to work with these people must be based in certain positions about what is most important about borderline problems. Those positions, in turn, grow from the writer's sense of what borderline patients are missing in life, or what problems they are creating for themselves and others; and that leads inexorably back to what the author believes is most important in life. Empirical research is just as thoroughly value-laden as clinical writing, although the culture of science can make it harder to acknowledge these influences. A fact, that is, to repeat myself, is very seldom *only* a fact. It is a *selected* fact at the very least, a fact selected by values; and it is very possibly a fact *shaped* by values.

The same goes for more specific psychoanalytic ideas about amelioration, i.e., theory of technique itself. Whenever we intervene, for instance (or when we don't), we are emphasizing some possibilities and not others; and while some of these choices are made on grounds that we may be able to believe are more a matter of pragmatism or empiricism than anything else, most of them are thoroughly infused with value positions. And so when we believe that the values underlying two theories are different from one another, we must be ready to give up our wish to compare the ideas on the same scale, and must turn instead to the moral, political, and personal issues that underlie their differences of intention. Which set of consequences do we believe is most desirable?

As an example consider self psychology, which one cannot compare to contemporary ego psychology without first identifying the differences in the goals of these two ways of conducting psychoanalysis.[12] In one case, the ultimate value is the integrity and stability of the self; in the other it is the effectiveness of the ego in its dealings with drives, affects, self-punitive trends in the personality, and the external world. Self psychology grows from the value of secure, realistic self-regard, and it emphasizes the significance of whole persons (selfobjects) in the attainment and maintenance of that goal. Contemporary ego psychology's primary value, on the other hand, is the mature functioning of the personality, and so that theory emphasizes the role of other people less as particular, whole persons than as contributors, via the nature of their interaction, to the growth or deterioration of ego functioning in the patient. The values of these two theories often overlap, and neither theory ignores the goals of its competitor. But to argue the superiority of one theory or the other, one must come to terms with the fact that each theory begins with a vision of what is most important in human living, and its practitioners promote that vision by practicing according to their theory of technique.

All of this adds up to the conclusion that we can certainly continue comparing theories of technique in a world in which multiple theories are accepted as a fact of life. There is no need to fear relativism. But because our theories have different goals, and are shaped by different values, we must recognize that they are, to some degree, apples and oranges. We should recognize that fact by querying ourselves about the value positions that lie hidden in our ideas, values representing our visions of the good life on the one hand, and of what is bad, hurtful, or evil, on the other—our vision, in other words, of the nature of human being (see, for example, Cushman, 1995; Hoffman, 1998; Richardson and Zeddies, 2004). Thinking through the values we are advocating by embracing a particular theory of technique puts us in the best position to argue that theory's superiority.

Notes

1 The kind of thinking that Foehl is writing about, and that I advocate as well, is consistent with understanding the mind—and psychotherapy and psychoanalysis, for that matter—as emergent (in the third-person sense [see Chapter 1], a dynamic system in which perturbations from outside interact with the current state of the system to produce nonlinear effects (e.g., Galatzer-Levy, 1995, 2002, 2004, 2009a, 2009b; Seligman, 2005).

2 The hermeneutic and postmodern critique in psychoanalysis is by now well known and established. The following is a partial list of the writings that awakened that perspective in our field. This selection has been made from those writings that concerned general issues of psychoanalysis and epistemology. If I had included the writings of those who have brought this sensibility to particular areas, especially those who introduced feminism, gender theory, and queer theory to our literature, the list would have been several times longer (Klein, 1976; Loch, 1977; Steele, 1979; McLaughlin, 1981; Spence, 1982; Hoffman, 1983, 1998; Schafer, 1983, 1992; Stern, 1983, 1985, 1992; Protter, 1985, 1988; Sass, 1988; Flax, 1990, 1993; Cushman, 1991, 1995, 2005, 2007; Phillips, 1991; Cooper, 1993; Mitchell, 1993, 1997; Spezzano, 1993; Gill, 1995; Aron, 1996; Pizer, 1998; Fairfield *et al.*, 2002).

3 Hermeneutics is the study of the nature of understanding, i.e., what is it to understand? The heart of philosophical or ontological hermeneutics, which is identified with Heidegger, Gadamer, Charles Taylor, and others, is that all experience is created by a process of interpretation (see the text). We are not generally aware, moment to moment, of the extent of this interpretive process, though, so that we tend to accept our experience as given.

4 This point has been taken by some (e.g., Busch, 2001) to mean that relational and interpersonal theories do away with the individual mind. Any such contention represents a serious misunderstanding. Relational and interpersonal theories do take account of the interaction of minds, and are based in the position that such interaction is continuous. But that is not at all the same thing as suggesting that only interaction exists. No theory of psychoanalysis can do without the individual mind.

5 Of course, not every instance of groping or being pulled toward a course of action is the outcome of the kind of intuition we want to depend on in a straightforward way. The sense of groping and being pulled, after all, are also part of the experience analysts have in unconscious enactments (e.g., Stern, 2010a). As a matter of fact, identifying the nature of the pull on the analyst or the direction of his groping is at least as crucially important in working with enactments as it is in our attempts to reflect on our implicit theories. Although I am not going take on the task of distinguishing these two types of pulling and groping from one another, I will make one small foray in that direction: in unconscious enactments, the pulling frequently has an urgent or peremptory quality,

and the groping often feels compulsive (I must find a way to ...). In their intuitive forms, on the other hand, one feels curious and interested in the senses we have of groping or being pulled, but not controlled by them.

6 There are times when it is better not to formulate our implicit theories of technique. The determination of whether or not to formulate any experience depends on the degree to which the experience is "ready" to be articulated. We make such judgments more or less continuously in our work with patients, in our own exploration of countertransference, and in our relations with our implicit theories of technique. If there is any sense of "forcing" an explicit formulation, then the experience has not yet "percolated" enough to be given shape (Stern, 1997, Chapters 2–4). (I leave aside for the moment the consideration of unconscious defensive processes, which often enough provide other, dynamic reasons why unformulated experience is not "ready" to be articulated.) If the experience is not yet ready to be formulated, trying to cram it into language results in a desiccated or intellectualized meaning. The French novelist Nathalie Sarraute writes, "Scarcely does this formless thing, all timid and trembling, try to show its face, than all powerful language, always ready to intervene so as to establish order—its own order—jumps on it and crushes it" (quoted by Shattuck, 1984, p. 1).

7 Atwood and Stolorow (1994) conclude not only that explicit theory is the outcome of the formulation of implicit theory, but also, in agreement with the argument I will make as this chapter goes on, that the diverse theories in psychoanalysis "consist not in alternate theoretical models that can be tested against one another in a meaningful way but rather in competing ideological and conceptual orientations to the problem of what it means to be human" (p. 4).

8 Canestri (2006a) writes, "Some of the 'implicit' concepts or models that the analyst uses or creates in clinical practice have, over time, acquired theoretical status and have been integrated into official theories. Many of the concepts elaborated by Bion, Winnicott, Kohut, etc., followed this path. Sometimes it has been possible to trace their origins in clinical practice through the narratives of the protagonists—for example, Ferenczi's Clinical Diary, Bion (1992), and so forth" (p. 1).

9 The work of Donald Schön (1983, 1987) focuses on the necessity of continuous creation of technique—what he thinks about as reflection in practice—for professionals of any kind. What I call implicit theory Schön refers to as theories-in-use, theories-in-action, or theories-in-practice. Here is one of Schön's definitions of technical reationality, about which he is no more enthusiastic than I am.

> ... [I]nstrumental problem solving can be seen as a technical procedure to be measured by its effectiveness in achieving a pre-established objective.... [R]igorous practice can be seen as an application to instrumental problems of research-based theories and techniques whose objectivity and generality derive from the method of controlled experiment.... [A]ction [in this view] is only an implementation and test of technical decision.
>
> (p. 165)

10 For another expression of the view I am taking here, see Fonagy (2006).
11 A significant paper by Steven Tublin (2011), "Discipline and freedom in relational technique," may have influenced these passages and others in this chapter. At any rate, the views in Tublin's paper are thoroughly congruent with my own take on the issue of technique. Tublin makes the simple but profound point that theories of technique can no longer be descriptions of concrete analytic conduct, but should instead focus on the particular aims that the author of the theory believes are important to accomplish:

> I propose a far looser definition of technique, one that is tied explicitly to varying and at times incompatible notions of analytic *intent*. It is intent, not the objectivist-tainted

notion of correctness, that should guide the analyst's participation in the consulting room. An intent-driven conceptualization of technique, while limiting the analyst's moment-to-moment actions, would force the analyst to be explicit about how his communicative acts—his interpretations, questions, empathic expressions, as well as the various jokes, reminiscences, and lexical gestures that establish his unique presence—are meant to drive a therapeutic process.

(p. 537)

12 I limit myself to the contributions of Kohut, ignoring for the sake of simplicity the self psychology that has come after Kohut. For the same heuristic purpose, I employ a simple version of contemporary Freudian theory.

Chapter 9

Psychotherapy is an emergent process
Hermeneutics and quantitative psychotherapy research[1]

To the extent that most people in our country even know what psychoanalysts are (that is, as opposed to other professional groups, such as psychologists, psychiatrists, social workers, or the more generic category of psychotherapists) they are impatient with us. And to the degree that we resist the idea that quantitative empirical studies of the effectiveness of what we practice are necessary, some significant portion of the public thinks we are woolly headed at best, irresponsible at worst. We have all heard both characterizations of psychoanalysts. Of course, we also must contend with the medical insurance companies, which, because they exist for no other reason than to make money, are understandably reluctant to approve treatments any lengthier than they have to. Our lack of enthusiasm about quantitative research plays right into their hands. It's easy to imagine medical insurance executives grinning and rubbing their hands gleefully whenever we give them reason to believe that we shy away from measuring the success of our work in quantitative, "objective" terms.

We are all well aware that we live in a world in which, because of the economic factor introduced by insurance coverage, psychotherapy—psychoanalysis included—is classified as a medical procedure. As long as medical insurance covers psychotherapy, that classification is probably inevitable. We are all also aware that medical procedures are judged by empirical, quantitative measurements of their effectiveness. In the case of most other procedures than psychotherapy, that way of proceeding seems perfectly sensible, even to us. Our own attitudes in this regard tell us exactly how most people outside our field think about quantitative, "objective" measures of psychotherapy: it seems as obvious to them that such measures should be privileged in our field as it does to us that such measures should be privileged in the evaluation of medical procedures. The issues of epistemology to which I will turn below are no doubt unknown to most Americans; but if they did know about them, the questions I am going to take up would seem to almost everyone in our country to be hairsplitting distinctions, irrelevant and unworthy of serious consideration. If you want to be paid for your work, offer concrete, objective evidence that you do something worth paying for. Simple as that.

And so I think we must recognize that, as long as we accept insurance reimbursement for our work, or help to make it possible for our patients to be reimbursed, we are actively participating in a system that defines us in terms that demand quantitative measures of effectiveness.

This is a terrible quandary, and I have believed so for many years. On the one hand, I believe, along with Hoffman (2009), that psychotherapy of the sort I practice is not a scientific or medical procedure at all; it is something else, something more akin to the interpretive disciplines—the arts and humanities, and the social sciences conceived hermeneutically, the *Geisteswissenschaften*. Psychotherapy belongs to that realm of "practical knowledge" that philosopher Hilary Putnam (1978) describes (via Aristotle) as "ethics."

> I think that Aristotle was profoundly right in holding that ethics is concerned with how to live and with human happiness, and that he was also right in holding that this sort of *knowledge* ("practical knowledge") is different from theoretical knowledge. A view of knowledge that acknowledges that the sphere of knowledge is wider than the sphere of "science" seems to me to be a cultural necessity if we are to arrive at a sane and human view of ourselves *or* of science.
>
> (Putnam, 1978, p. 5)

That is, we must accept that the category of knowledge is broader than the category of science, and that there exist important questions that therefore should not be decided by scientific methods. Let me offer a comment in this direction by Hans-George Gadamer (1966), a hermeneutic philosopher who has influenced me greatly, and to whose work I will return later in this chapter.

> The genuine researcher is motivated by a desire for knowledge and by nothing else. And yet, over against the whole of our civilization that is founded on modern science, we must ask repeatedly if something has not been omitted. If the presuppositions of these possibilities for knowing and making remain half in the dark, cannot the result be that the hand applying this knowledge will be destructive?
>
> (p. 10)

On the other hand (referring back to the position that psychotherapy of the sort I practice is not a scientific or medical procedure at all), many of my patients, even most of them, profit from their work with me in a way that it is perfectly reasonable to call "getting better." By getting better, I mean that their lives improve in discernible ways. Sometimes, of course, even their health improves. And so, while I firmly believe that what I practice is not a medical or scientific procedure, it does frequently have salutary effects of the sort that those who think in terms of the medical model would happily describe as healthcare successes.[2]

Furthermore, despite having experienced years of ambivalence about it, I have always preferred to refer to the people with whom I work as "patients" than "clients." At least part of the reason for my ambivalence has been the worry that using that word, "patients," could give the impression to others that I see my work as medical in nature. Over the last two decades, though, I have come to accept my preference more comfortably, because I've come to see that the reason I use the word "patient" is that it expresses my belief that psychoanalysts need to have a certain physicianly attitude in their work, one that comprises a commitment to their patients' welfare and to behaving in whatever way seems to serve that welfare best. A client is simply a person who uses one's services; but a patient is someone you have a special responsibility to care for. Physicians are hardly the only people who take such an attitude in their work, but ever since Hippocrates, our idealization of the physician has been the Western model for this kind of professional care and concern.

Given the fact that I favor a physicianly attitude and that I claim that my "patients" often "get better," what exactly is my problem here? Why not simply play ball? Why not join in the "science game," as Hoffman (2009, p. 1058) tells us that Hans Strupp described it? Would it not perhaps be the most sensible course for us to heed Peter Fonagy's suggestion (quoted by Hoffman, 2009, p. 1057) that,

> It needs to be recognized that objections to research will not win the day. It is unlikely that the prevailing view that places controlled studies at the top of the hierarchy of evidence will change, no matter what the strength of opposing arguments. The complexity of the issues surrounding resource allocation, the drive to seek certainty and simplicity at the level of policy making, are such that alternative formulations will not be heard . . .

Fonagy is right, isn't he? Isn't this a losing battle? Am I not saying as much myself in recognizing that the insurance companies have us over a barrel?

Well, whether or not the most sensible course is capitulating to the privileging of quantitative research in the evaluation and study of psychotherapy really depends on how you understand "sense." Yes, that course would certainly be the least contentious one for us. But what would the cost be?

Symptom relief and other changes

The answer to that question is what Irwin Hoffman (2009) set out to write about in his paper, "Doublethinking our way to 'scientific' legitimacy: The desiccation of human experience." I want to offer my own take on the same problem. What I want to say begins with a reconsideration of what I have already said about my patients getting better. While I am pleased that they do, those effects are not what I set out to accomplish in the work. They are byproducts of what I think about as the outcomes I am actually trying to achieve. Don't get me wrong: I am hardly neutral about symptom relief. Actually, at a certain point in any treatment I would probably become pretty actively puzzled and disappointed if I *didn't* see symptom relief. I might even feel that such a treatment was unsuccessful. At the very least, in the case of a patient who is not doing better, I would have to ask myself how to explain it.

It is important, though, that I don't set out to create those effects. I don't aim at symptom relief. Mostly I am thinking about whatever the patient and I are actually talking about. Like all of us, I am having my own thoughts about that, watching what happens in my mind and my feelings, sometimes noticing myself linking it to historical matters in the patient's life or my own, noticing the place of the material in whatever is unfolding between the patient and me. I think of all these activities, along with others, as the deployment of curiosity, an active attitude of openness to whatever I can notice about the patient, myself, and what's transpiring between us. I am not thinking on the level of theory when I am with patients; but the theories that guide me, I believe, are so deeply embedded in my work that I am using them even when they have no conscious presence in my mind. The most important of the ideas about therapeutic action that orient me day to day have to do with curiosity, the expansion of the self, and freedom, both internal and relational. I work from the conviction that expanding self, curiosity, and freedom lead to relaxations in, and creative reformulations of, experience. These relaxations and reformulations are then, in their turn, reflected in, among other things, "getting-better" outcomes. That is a brief explanation of why, if symptom relief isn't forthcoming, I am disappointed and must query myself about it.

Even though I am willing to say that I expect to see symptom relief in a successful treatment, though, I am *not* willing to agree that symptom relief is any kind of adequate measure of my work. I think of psychoanalytic work as the investigation, deconstruction, and creation of meaning, especially those potential meanings that have existed heretofore outside the range of symbolization.

What matters to me most, and what counts most in my own evaluation of my work, are the same things that matter to virtually all of us: the moments in which something old is revealed, or something new comes about. These moments grow from events in clinical process, unexpected events that have much personal resonance for both the patient and me, and that grow in unique and surprising ways from the circumstances of that moment's relatedness, circumstances which are themselves also unique. Unlike behaviorally oriented clinicians, most psychoanalysts simply do not set out to create the changes that eventually come about.

From a psychoanalytic perspective, at least most of the time, it is not even practical to try to force change. That is, changing what it is that seems to make us unhappy is not a simple matter. One of Freud's great insights, of course, was that none of us is as singlemindedly committed to change as we may think we are. We humans are seldom, if ever, able simply to delete our problems at will, like a lizard leaving its tail behind; and that is why psychoanalysts are committed to the significance of unconscious process in all aspects of life. And so for reasons that have to do with both practicality and a commitment to a certain view of life, we do not practice an instrumental approach to psychotherapy. For many psychoanalysts, while it might be demonstrable that "x" percentage of our patients "get better," and that psychotherapy therefore "works" for them, it would miss the point to conclude on that basis that psychotherapy is effective.

Conversation with a researcher

I know how frustrating what I have just said must be for psychotherapy researchers, especially those who would like to offer support for psychoanalytic work. I suspect that they feel assailed on all sides: their interest in investigating psychoanalysis and psychoanalytic psychotherapy is no doubt derided as insufficiently rigorous by other empirical researchers, including other psychotherapy researchers; and psychoanalytic clinicians like me accuse them of supporting instrumental values. Psychotherapy researchers interested in psychoanalysis may actually feel quite nearly as embattled as psychoanalysts do. Of course, the difference is that our culture's most widespread notions of common sense and what counts as evidence, ideas so generally felt to be self-evident that they qualify to most people as parts of the "natural" world, are linked to the work of researchers, not clinicians.

We know the attitude taken by psychoanalytic researchers who conduct quantitative studies toward those of their empirically minded colleagues who are critical of their interest in psychoanalysis: they consider that such colleagues are throwing out the baby with the bath water. We psychoanalytic clinicians support them in this, of course. We also know their attitude toward us, their colleagues on the clinical side of things. They would say something like, "For heaven's sake! Why get precious about it? We get it: you don't want to privilege quantitative measures; you don't even feel that they represent what you do. But if we can use quantitative measures to show the kind of improvement that science needs to see in order to ratify your work, then why get your shorts in a bunch? Get over it. Just go along. And be grateful for it."

The problem is that to privilege quantitative measures as the criterion of successful treatment, or even as the medium of description of such treatments, is to accept that psychotherapy can be judged according to instrumental values, or maybe even that it should be. It is to accept that the purpose of psychotherapy is to make certain definable things happen. Why else use quantitative measures? A quantitative measure is employed only when you already know what you're looking for. You are trying to find instances of a category of phenomena that you have decided in advance is important. The hypothesis takes the form, "Psychoanalysis succeeds in creating, or changing, or increasing, or reducing 'x'."

To privilege measures or descriptions inspired by instrumental values, I believe, is to start down a very slippery slope. To accept that instrumentally inspired measures are valid descriptors of our work is to come perilously close to accepting an even larger conclusion: psychotherapy is an instrumental process. If psychoanalysis were defined instrumentally (and the case can certainly be made that manualized psychodynamic treatments are the evidence that it already is being defined that way), the slippery slope would be the least of our worries, because in that case we would already have fallen off the cliff. Psychoanalysis must not be defined as an instrumental activity.

"OK," says my interlocutor, patiently taking a deep breath and trying to accommodate me, "then we'll figure out how to measure the expansion of self, curiosity, and freedom, the very things you suggest are most important, and we'll determine our outcomes *that* way."

But I have to object to that procedure on the same grounds. By their very nature, events in which the self, curiosity, and/or freedom expands are unique occurrences, and unique occurrences arise from unique circumstances. They are emergent. (In the paper I have already mentioned, Hoffman [2009] refers to this phenomenon as "consequential uniqueness," which he, too, sees as emergent.) As soon as I accept an instrumental approach to "measuring" them, I've accepted that these events comprise a measurable category. That's not necessarily problematic in and of itself, except that I know it would not stop there. Would any psychotherapy researcher worth his or her salt be willing to conclude nothing more than that such events *happen*? No. The next step would be to determine the frequency of such happenings, what kinds of events precede them, what kinds follow them, which therapists are most successful in making them happen, and so on. All of these questions would be asked with the aim of predicting the events that index expansions of self, curiosity, and freedom. Prediction, in the realm of technical rationality (Argyris and Schön, 1976; Schön, 1983, 1987), is pursued with the eventual aim of influence and control: how do you *make* expansions of self, curiosity, and freedom happen? And of course, as soon as we accept the twin goals of prediction and control, we are rejecting the heart of the psychoanalytic approach to psychotherapy: the phenomenon of unique, unbidden, emergent events arising from unique circumstances. Hoffman (2009, p. 1054) made a similar point: technical rationality complements psychic determinism in such a way that both analyst and patient are effectively stripped of their freedom, of the possibility of creative agency.

My researcher tries yet another tack. "Well, then, why don't we just forget about outcomes for the time being and do process research instead? Why don't we try to identify and describe the processes that lead to the outcomes you feel are favorable?"

Once again I must demur. Descriptive process studies may appear to be less rooted in instrumental values and technical rationality than outcome studies are. But they are rooted just as deeply in that same soil. Granted, the point of process studies is not the evaluation of outcomes. But the question being posed in process studies is concerned with the clinical events, or characteristics of therapists, that are common in "successful" treatments. The researcher is still *looking for* something rather than taking the clinical attitude of waiting to find out what may emerge. And when relevant processes in "good" treatments seem to be identified, the implication will be drawn that the findings should encourage therapists to institute these processes in their work. Perhaps the finding will be used to create a "technique" that will be taught to students. The instrumental nature of such aims is unmistakable.

My conversational partner takes a different direction. "All right. Let's say that I accept your argument that quantitative measures are inspired by instrumental values, and even that privileging systematic empirical research with quantitative measures threatens to define psychotherapy and psychoanalysis in instrumental terms. What exactly is the harm in that?"

Ah, now, this is actually the heart of the matter! What exactly *is* the harm in that? This is Fonagy's point. What he suggests, along with many other psychotherapy researchers sympathetic to psychoanalysis and psychoanalytic psychotherapy, is that it's a lot worse to lose all credibility in the wider world than it is to give way to a position that is inevitably going to prevail, anyway.

Reflection-in-action

The problem is that accepting that psychotherapy can be defined in instrumental terms is not a simple compromise, or even a single battle in a wider war. It's not something I could decide to do, and then just go on as before. I can't pretend to believe it; I can't even agree to operate *as if* it's true while privately preserving my old views. The issue is too basic. It's not a detail, and it's not arcane. It's an epistemological issue—but an epistemological issue that matters in the real world. It has real, everyday, practical *bite*.

Can you imagine thinking of painting that way? Can you imagine classifying students' paintings according to how well they met an objectively measured outcome? Or by how well they mimicked the "technique" of a painter judged to be "successful?" Merleau-Ponty (1964), the philosopher, once described a film of Matisse being filmed in slow motion as he painted.

> The impression was prodigious, so much so that Matisse himself was moved, they say. That same brush which, seen with the naked eye, leaped from one act to another, was seen to meditate in a solemn and expanding time—in the imminence of a world's creation—to try ten possible movements, dance in front of the canvas, brush it lightly several times, and crash down finally like a lightning stroke upon the one line necessary.
>
> (p. 45)

The film, because it slowed the process, made it look as if Matisse "chose from among all possible lines that day." But he did not. "He did not have in his mind's eye all the gestures possible, and in making his choice he did not have to eliminate all but one" (p. 45). Instead,

> Matisse, set within a man's time and vision, looked at the still open whole of his work in progress and brought his brush toward the line which called for it in order that the painting might finally be that which is was in the process of becoming.
>
> (pp. 45–6)

We do not have to aggrandize ourselves into some version of Matisse to recognize that what Merleau-Ponty says here is true of any creative activity, psychotherapy included.

What shall we define as creative activity? My answer: any activity the details of which cannot be prescribed on the basis of knowing the nature of the activity. Following a recipe, then, is not a creative activity, while cooking according to one's judgment is. A creative activity is one that requires what Donald Schön (1983, 1987) called "reflection-in-action." Such an activity cannot be accomplished by applying a technique; it can be practiced only by reflecting on what is best under each new set of circumstances as those circumstances arise. (The cook adds spice according to the taste of the broth.) Psychotherapy is a prime example. Painting is, as well, of course. There are no rules for what Matisse did; each brush stroke was an emergent event that grew from the interaction of his developing intention with the canvas that he had changed by the brush stroke that came just before.

In the same way, I do not select the next thing I do with my patient on the basis of a conception of technique, even though it may be possible to describe whatever I choose to do in such terms (interpretation, silence, empathic reflection, confrontation, and so on); no, I select what I do next, just as Matisse selected the line that actualized his vision of the painting evolving in front of him, by feeling my way into a course of action that, on the basis of the situation as it has come together in this moment, I believe will contribute to opening the clinical material and freeing whatever constrictions bind the relatedness between the patient and me. The course of action I choose is a matter of judgment, and when I am lucky, of wisdom. It is not a matter of applying a conceptual template; it is much more like a kind of groping, a tropism awakened by my experience with the patient that allows me, when I am successful, to turn like a flower toward the sun. My groping and tropisms, and the choices to which they lead, are activities that depend on a lengthy and thorough education; but the form of these activities are specific to me and to the moment in which they come about, and for the most part, they are unbidden. They are the result of reflection, yes, reflection-in-action; but they are not the outcome of ratiocination, and whatever wisdom they embody is certainly not objectively verifiable. I can often explain to someone else why I did one thing or another, but I would always hesitate to claim that what I did would necessarily have been the right course for another analyst facing the same circumstances. What we do in our work is specific to all the unique circumstances of the moment, including, of course, the identities of the participants and all the history that has been contributed up until that moment by the fact that these particular two people have created it. And so, actually, if we are being precise, we must recognize that no two analysts can ever face the same circumstances.

Gadamer's hermeneutics

What is the alternative, then? If I propose not to privilege systematic empirical research, must I not also offer a different way of conceptualizing the issues? I believe I do have that responsibility, and I propose to satisfy it by presenting the hermeneutic alternative to objectivism.[3] I will focus on the work of the modern ontological hermeneutics of Hans-Georg Gadamer.

Gadamer (1960, 2004) believes that understanding requires what he calls "genuine conversation." By using that term, he means to refer to each partner's attempt to grasp the subject matter between them. One does not understand by understanding the other person per se, but by coming to a new view of what the other person is saying. There is no support in Gadamer's views, in other words, for a psychotherapy based on a direct, empathic grasp of the other's internal world. The personal origins of a meaning are not at issue in understanding it; only the subject matter itself is. In coming to this new understanding, of course, one does eventually understand something about the other, but this understanding is incidental, not primary.

To my ear, this way of grasping the process of understanding is quite consistent with the absence of intellectualization that serves psychoanalysis best: we have our best moments not when we figure out an explanation for what makes someone else tick (think of the myriad dynamic explanations commonly offered at case conference and you'll know what I mean), but when there occurs an episode of understanding, usually affect-laden, about whatever occupies the psychic space between the patient and ourselves.

The key to Gadamer's thought is his conception of preconception, or prejudice. But Gadamer's understanding of the nature of preconception is quite different than the understanding that we inherit from the Enlightenment. In that rationalist or objectivist frame of reference, preconception is prejudice defined as we usually define it: a bias that it is desirable to rid ourselves of; and to the extent that dialogue between people succeeds, it succeeds because it helps us "move beyond" our preconceptions.

In fact, Gadamer does use the word "prejudice" very frequently, along with "preconception," "bias," and "prejudgment." All these words are ways of referring to manifestations of what is Gadamer's single most basic and innovative idea: tradition. Prior to Gadamer, hermeneuticists such as Schleiermacher and Dilthey had claimed that understanding was a way of subtracting preconception (i.e., subtracting the traditions that the person trying to understand is embedded in), leaving only the truth, now unobscured by distorting effects. For Dilthey and Scheiermacher, understanding meant grasping the truth; and the truth had, in Cartesian fashion, an existence independent of the person trying to grasp it. In fact, to find the truth was to duplicate in one's own mind the exact thoughts and intentions created by the person who created the text or work of art in the first place. In this way of thinking, because their truth is eternal and unchanging, understanding is the natural state of affairs. If it were not for obstructions, prejudices, and preconceptions, truth would be plain to see.

There is an important corollary, especially important for the current discussion. If there exists a single truth behind the distortions and encrustations of tradition, then it follows that there should be methods to find it, or free it. There ought to be definable ways to illuminate the truth by cracking away whatever distorting effects are encrusted around it, obscuring it. This is the doctrine that subtends the most traditional model of science, which has long reigned as the most powerful method yet discovered to subtract noise and error and reveal truth. In the cases of rocks and comets and chemicals, it works well.

Actually, Gadamer (1976, 2004) makes a compelling case that, even in the natural sciences, our embeddedness in tradition precedes all other meanings, so that hermeneutic exploration should be the source of the questions put to natural science and should also be used to think through the implications of the methods used by natural science to answer these questions. An examination of this issue would take us too far afield here. Suffice it to say that if there exists reason to question the privileging of traditional science in matters concerning the nonhuman world, there is even more doubt about the privileging of science in matters of human meaning such as art, the humanities, the social sciences—and psychotherapy, especially the psychoanalytic kind.

Gadamer, taking issue with Cartesianism, insisted on an entirely new understanding of prejudice, preconception, and tradition. He devised the idea of "horizon" to represent the view of the world from within any given set of traditions, and he then argued that those traditions, and the horizons to which they give rise, are not simply error or bias, but what makes understanding possible in the first place. Prejudice, he claimed, is actually an important part of what *constitutes* understanding. There can be no "view from nowhere," as Thomas Nagel (1986) put it years later; there can only be a view from within a particular set of horizons. Gadamer (1966) writes, "Prejudices are biases of our openness to the world. They are simply conditions whereby we experience something—whereby what we encounter says something to us" (p. 9). Elsewhere Gadamer expresses the point this way: "It is not so much our judgments as it is our prejudgments that constitute our being" (translated and quoted by Linge, 1976, p. xvii, from Gadamer, 1960). In other words, we are not led astray by the traditions that do so much to shape our understanding; we are *made* of them.

Understanding comes about when the tradition that grounds us is allowed free play in our construction of meaning. Understanding, then, is not the *reproduction* of something that existed before; it is, rather, the *construction* of something new. We must be free to allow texts, works of art, and of course people, by their very existence, to question our preconceptions; and we must be free to use our preconceptions to question *them*. When there is a melding of what is to be understood and the tradition through which we try to understand it, Gadamer (2004) refers to our resulting new grasp as a "fusion of horizons." Understanding, then, is always *new* understanding. Something new always comes to be. The possibilities for understanding are ceaselessly in the process of being recreated. Nothing is ever exactly what it was before, because the role of tradition is not to force the world into its image, but to lend new meaning to what we encounter, just as what we encounter changes and continually enriches tradition. That is why a work of art, or a text, or a memory, or a moment that took place between a patient and you just now, can be experienced and understood in the present in ways that could not have been envisioned in the past. And to accept all this, we do not have to posit that potential meanings were already there "in" whatever we are trying to understand. The potential for new meaning is the continuous creation that results from the interaction of tradition with preexisting meaning. And so while it is true that we do sacrifice the original form of our prejudices in the course of new understanding, we do not actually move or see *beyond* them; we see *with* them, or *through* them, or *by means* of them.

Remember that, in the Cartesian way of thinking, because truth has an independent existence, understanding is the natural state of affairs, appearing as soon as prejudice is removed. But in Gadamer's frame of reference, *mis*understanding becomes the baseline condition, because understanding is always a creation, and requires the fusion of horizons. Prior to the fusion, we are liable to be puzzled, or to understand poorly or superficially—with or without knowing it, and with or without a genuine conversation with the other.

Think once again of Matisse, arm raised and hand poised in front of his easel. Each time he lifts his brush and looks at the unfinished painting in front of him, he is in dialogue with a horizon that, while it is his creation, now demands from him an understanding that lets him make the next stroke. His own horizon, and the horizon of the painting facing him, each must become something more, or different, than they were before. Remember how Merleau-Ponty (1964) put it: "He did not have in his mind's eye all the gestures possible, and in making his choice he did not have to eliminate all but one" (p. 45). We would be hopelessly heavy handed if we were to argue that Matisse was simply trying to select the correct brush stroke. No, he was instead deeply immersed in a negotiation between himself and the part of the painting that was already there. Merleau-Ponty again: "Matisse, set within a man's time and vision, looked at the still open whole of his work in progress and brought his brush toward the line which called for it in order that the painting might finally be that which is was in the process of becoming." That line was not predetermined, and *could not have been* predetermined; it was the outcome of reflection-in-action. Notice, too, that words are not necessarily crucial in the creation of understanding; the fusion of horizons took place for Matisse without explicit language, just as the fusions of our horizons and our patients' often do.[4]

Most importantly, notice that the event of understanding is unbidden: Gadamer tells us that it *comes to be*, it *happens*, it takes place beyond our capacity to control it. The fusion of horizons takes place when we are able to allow history, or tradition, or prejudice, to act freely within us. It simply will not work to select our course by applying a technique; if we do that, the result will not be the organic outcome of a dialogic process, as any authentic understanding must be. The decision cannot be made for us by a rule, nor can it be made by conscious, deliberate choice. It must *come about*. Gadamer would have enjoyed Winnicott's conception of play and transitional reality, I am sure of it. It is when we can play, when we can allow tradition to act freely within us—and in the case of psychotherapy, between us—that the fusion of horizons becomes possible.

Gadamer's (1960, 2004) great work is entitled *Truth and Method*, which might puzzle you, because it might seem to suggest that there is a method for discerning the truth, a conception that everything I have just said about Gadamer seems to contradict. Well, be not confused, because you are right. What Gadamer means by titling his book this way is that truth can *never* be revealed by a dependence on method. Truth is not already there, and so it cannot be revealed or uncovered. No method can create the free play of prejudice and tradition in our minds. No method can instill genuine conversation. What do we do instead? We question. We question ourselves, and we question the other, and we do it incessantly as long as the dialogue lasts. If you remove the dialogic quality from psychotherapy, that reflection-in-action, that very particular form of genuine conversation that makes up our work, you have gutted the practice. If you draw attention away from reflection-in-action and toward a conception of psychotherapeutic practice static and predictable enough to be measurable, gutting the practice of psychotherapy is liable to be the unintended effect. The continuous flux of the interpersonal field, and its nonlinear, unpredictable outcomes, simply cannot be captured in such terms.

Gutting psychotherapy is of course the last thing quantitative psychotherapy researchers want to do. These researchers are just as thoroughly committed to the future of psychotherapy as I am, and some of them have specific sympathies for psychoanalysis. Yet to the extent that they do not challenge the presumption that the results of quantitative research should be privileged in the study of psychotherapy, I think that researchers are wrong about the issues under discussion here. I cannot ignore my conviction that privileging systematic empirical research is liable to have a damaging and dampening effect—or, as Hoffman (2009) puts it, a "desiccating" effect—on our field. One of the assumptions underlying quantitative studies is that psychotherapy is a technique, a method of intervening that can be defined and described *a priori*—that is, in advance of the moments in which I would argue that it continuously comes into being as something new.

We do not need to "move beyond" our preconceptions of psychotherapy. No, we need to *consult* our preconceptions continuously, just as we do when we attend to our experience in our offices with our patients. We consult that experience not because we intend to "move beyond" our countertransference to some more basic truth that it obscures; that is a view that we left behind a generation or more ago. We attend to our experience of the patient because we understand it to be a horizon that shapes our next moment—our next intervention, silence, or expression of affect.

Most quantitative researchers agree that data do not "speak for themselves" (e.g., Safran, 2012). But a hermeneutic view goes further than that. It is not enough to say only that the data do not speak for themselves; the more significant point is that there is no objective way to *constitute* data in the first place. Data, merely by being created in a particular form, serve some purposes and not others. There is no separation between the creation of data and their interpretation; those two things are the same event (although other interpretations of the data are obviously also made later on). "Interpretation" in hermeneutic thought refers not only to assigning meanings to preexisting "evidence"; the word actually refers to the *creation of the experience*. Interpretation is constitutive; it *makes* the data. This is another route of access to the point I have been pursuing all along: when we privilege so-called objective measurements in evaluating psychotherapy, we are not just assigning meaning to preexisting data; we are taking an interpretive tack that has constitutive implications. We are saying that we agree that psychotherapy is amenable to this kind of measurement, and we are therefore taking a position about what kind of activity psychotherapy is. This is one more reason why I cannot take Fonagy's suggestion to capitulate, even if he is right that it is inevitable.

Conclusions

Given what I have said, then, what attitude makes sense for us to take toward systematic, quantitative empirical research? That seems straightforward to me, although it will be much harder to accomplish than it is to envision. In fact, the task of persuading the wider culture to accept the view I favor is an uphill battle of huge proportions. Maybe it's even quixotic. But seeing the issues as I do, I can take no other position. It's simply this: let's recognize that the hermeneutic position about the study and evaluation of psychoanalytic treatment is a valid way of thinking about these problems, and one that contradicts the objectivist agenda of systematic empirical research.

These two perspectives cannot be adjudicated against one another. We cannot decide which one is "correct," for two reasons. First, even to pose that question is to accept the objectivist agenda, because the very question implies a Cartesian acceptance that there is a single, objectively verifiable answer that exists independently of those of us asking the question. Second, both objectivism and hermeneutics account for all the relevant phenomena; they just account for them differently. In the end, the choice comes down to a preference that must be based on the outcomes that flow from the choice. I prefer the preservation of what we know about what we actually do and see in psychoanalytic treatment: the emergence of new understanding via reflection-in-action. Systematic quantitative research does not support the observation of such processes.

How, then, shall we encourage these two frames of reference to interact? It will not surprise anyone who has read this far to learn that I take Gadamer's (e.g., 1967) position here: hermeneutical reflection takes precedence over any kind of methodology. Scientific findings are partially created by preconceptions, generally less than fully visible, that influence the way the research that produces the findings is conceived, designed, and conducted. In itself, that is not a problem, because those preconceptions, as long as they are submitted to hermeneutic study, are unobjectionable instances of the same traditions that play a part in the creation of all understanding.

But those who depend heavily on systematic empirical research for their understanding of psychotherapy frequently do not acknowledge the participation of tradition in their understanding; they tend to believe that the point of doing systematic empirical research is to *subtract* the effects of bias, prejudice, and preconception, as if such a thing were possible, or even desirable. Most empirical psychotherapy researchers using quantitative measures seem to accept the objectivist tenet that the point of systematic research is to sift out, or control for, the effects of preconception, leaving data closer to some idealized "original" or "raw" state. It's good to recognize, as many researchers do, that the data collected in systematic empirical research are not bits of concrete knowledge, as if quantitative research findings were transparently understood packets of objectively defined meaning. It's good to recognize that; but it's not enough. Quantitative findings must be subjected to hermeneutic inquiry, but so must the methods used to collect them.

I have no objection to quantitative research on psychotherapy that is constructed, understood, and used according to hermeneutic values. But the findings of such research should be given no more priority than the results of case studies and other responsibly created clinical descriptions; and the findings of systematic empirical research certainly should not be used as any kind of guide to our work. Instead, as Hoffman (2009) also writes, research findings, along with case studies and theory, should be used to widen and enrich the range of clinicians' thinking.

It will also come as no surprise that I do not accept either the necessity or the desirability for evidence-based treatment. The phrase itself, "evidence-based treatment," is a brilliant piece of rhetoric. It proclaims its objectivist stance as a simple fact, leaving anyone who disagrees with it looking irresponsible to all but those who are unusually well informed about the hermeneutic alternative. I think it's probably the case, actually, that while most of those who favor evidence-based treatment exploit the rhetorical impact of the phrase routinely, they don't do it with conscious purpose. Rather, they just don't see any need for persuasion. Most of those who take that position don't really grasp the hermeneutic alternative. If they are aware of it at all, they tend to dismiss it as fuzzy, loose thinking inconsistent with a rigorous or serious attitude toward the study of psychotherapy. It simply never occurs to most of them that there exist reasonable grounds for controversy. In their minds, it just seems that it is the natural order of things for objective evidence to decide evaluative questions. Starting a discussion about the validity of hermeneutics with someone who sees things this way can be like pushing a string uphill.

I believe that case studies and theories are more valuable sources of clinical inspiration than the findings of quantitative research. Case studies, as I have already said, unfold in the same way clinical sessions do: they describe unique, emergent events; and because of that, they are well suited both to capturing and stimulating clinical thinking. Theory also offers new possibilities to clinicians; the purpose of theory, after all, is to open new routes of understanding.

But with that said, it is also true that, when sitting with a patient, I, like Hoffman (2009), have no objection at all to being inspired to a new thought, experience, or intervention, *in this individual instance*, by something that may originally have come to light in systematic empirical research. I do object, though, as Hoffman also does in his critique of the privileging of such research, to the suggestion—and we increasingly see such suggestions in the literature on evidence-based treatment—that I *should* use such findings to select what to do next, or that I should try to grasp the category of circumstances, "identified" in systematic empirical research, in which one intervention or another is the "right" or "best" or "most effective" thing to do.

We have no choice but to accept that systematic empirical psychotherapy research is winning the day, at least as far as the public is concerned. But we can still put up a fight. The preservation of psychoanalysis and psychoanalytic psychotherapy does not require us to defeat programs of quantitative research on psychotherapy; that is simply not going to happen—and it need not, and perhaps even should not. There is room for more than one way of studying our field, after all. The best outcome I can imagine would be a genuine conversation between the parties committed to both perspectives, the hermeneutic and the systematically empirical, a conversation that takes place very seldom in our discipline today. In this conversation, if we are to survive as a field, we must mount an effective case in favor of a hermeneutic understanding of what we do, and against the privileging of objectivist, quantitative research in the study and evaluation of psychotherapy and psychoanalysis.

Notes

1 The original version of this chapter was written as a discussion of a commentary by Jeremy Safran (2012) in *Psychoanalytic Dialogues* on an earlier article by Irwin Hoffman (2009). I took the opportunity to write the discussion because I felt strongly about the value of Hoffman's article. But it is also the case that I had wanted for some time to write about hermeneutics and psychotherapy research, and so the discussion of Safran's commentary that I wrote for *Psychoanalytic Dialogues* offered me the opportunity to formulate my own views on the issue. In this chapter, I have retained enough of the original references to Hoffman's work to indicate the relationship of the points made here to his article.

2 I am leaving out of consideration for the moment the fact that many of these "healthcare successes" are apparently too subtle to be easily indexed by the kinds of measures used in psychotherapy research. But that doesn't change the point I'm making here: the people we work with do "get better," and we need to acknowledge this fact in any discussion of whether psychotherapy is a medical procedure.

3 This is probably as good a spot as any for me to make the point, as I always feel I must do when discussing this subject matter, that hermeneutics is not a variety of relativism. In Richard Bernstein's (1983) memorable phrase, hermeneutics is "beyond objectivism and relativism"; or in Sass's (1988) expression, hermeneutics constitutes "a 'middle way' between objectivism and relativism" (p. 254). Bernstein's book is a good first source for those wanting to explore this perspective. What these authors and others emphasize is that so often, objectivists claim that any deviation from objectivism implies relativism, as if the choice is as simple as one position or the other. This simply is not the case. Such a simplistic choice has been presented as inevitable with depressing regularity by psychoanalytic objectivists, who just don't seem to grasp the philosophical issues (e.g., Eagle *et al.*, 2003). I present some of the relevant issues in what follows, but I simply do not have the space in this chapter to offer the entire rationale.

4 While explicitly spoken language—words—are not necessarily crucial, I would still submit that all of this goes on in a world organized and given its shape and meaning within language conceived in the broadest sense. This point is not relevant enough to the argument to take up in more detail here, but I have addressed it elsewhere (Stern, 1997, 2010a), and am in the process of doing so again in other current projects.

Chapter 10

The hard-to-engage patient
A treatment failure

Although I know that the "hard-to-engage patient" might be defined in any number of ways, I limit my consideration to those people who come for a few sessions, or maybe even a little more than that, but who just can't seem to get started. Eventually, they can't find a reason to keep showing up, and the treatment fizzles, usually in mutual frustration. More often than not, the atmosphere is not particularly uncomfortable. There are no affect explosions. The end brings discouragement, but neither analyst nor patient usually blames the other. In fact, the affect that is most frequent in these treatments is not really an affect at all, but the absence of affect. More often than not, in other words, these treatments die of boredom.

One way of defining this particular "hard-to-engage" patient emphasizes the patient's contribution, and ends up being a diagnostic formulation of some kind or other. That is, we try to characterize a group of people. We might refer to schizoid dynamics or character, the false self, borderline personality disorder, alexithymia, anhedonia, or depression. Any or all of these problems might have to do with becoming someone who is hard to engage. It is perfectly reasonable to approach the problem this way.

A second approach focuses on the countertransference—that is, the focus falls on the part played by the analyst; we define the hard-to-engage patient according to the therapist who cannot engage him. In this case, the hard-to-engage quality is created by the treatment process; the quality doesn't necessarily preexist his contact with the analyst. Perhaps with a different therapist, the hard-to-engage patient wouldn't be so hard to engage.

This approach, too, is perfectly reasonable. As far as I am concerned, it is also often quite interesting, more interesting than the diagnostic approach, since it leads to the microscopic examination of what happens between the patient and the analyst. What could the analyst have done differently?

If a transference proclivity on the part of the patient was responsible for a view of the analyst that ultimately discouraged the patient from getting involved, how should we understand the fact that the analyst did not directly address the problem? Or was the problem more directly a matter of what the analyst brought to the clinical situation? It might be very difficult for a Jewish analyst, for instance, to engage a German patient whose parents were Nazis; it can be done (see Foxe, 2004, 2006; Guralnik, 2014), but it obviously requires a great deal from both parties. The same problem might come up, with varying degrees of intensity, in any analyst–patient pair in which the members belong to groups that have had troubled power relations with one another: black and white, gay and straight, Latino and white, women and men, and so on. Unless there is some mutual capacity and willingness to discuss the troubled relations, this difficult content can clog the lines of communication, making it very difficult for either person to say anything more than social niceties. Of course, it is the analyst's responsibility to see problems such as these, to initiate an examination of them, and then to keep that examination going. The patient must be involved in such an inquiry, that goes without saying; but the analyst is the one who is responsible for beginning the inquiry and keeping it on track, even, or especially, when it is very hard.

I think of a case, for example, in which a young man came to me after having terminated a treatment in another country in which he and his highly experienced analyst stopped after six months. They just couldn't seem to get started. It was one of those situations in which it seemed that there was just nothing to say. It was boring. The analyst felt that the problem was the patient, but it turns out that that wasn't the only way of understanding the situation, and probably not the best one. After just a couple of sessions in this new treatment with me a different reason suddenly became obvious. It turns out that the young man's primary concern was what to do about being gay, which he wasn't comfortable with, and which he couldn't imagine telling his parents about. But he also could not imagine talking about this with his former analyst, whom he believed, rightly or wrongly, would not have been able to avoid being critical of him. The patient told me, once he and I began talking about all of this (and it turned out that, once he got into it, he just couldn't get enough time to talk and was *quite* engaged), that he hadn't actually realized what had been wrong with the former treatment. Maybe if he had, he said, he could have brought it up and talked about it. But neither did the analyst find a way into it, or seemingly, even imagine that the patient was avoiding something big, and avoiding it so thoroughly that he was unable or unwilling to talk about all the things that were connected to it—which didn't leave much to say.

Actually, it seems to me most likely that as soon as we take either one of the two perspectives I have introduced—the diagnostic or the countertransferential—we are also likely to end up taking the other. If we were to talk about schizoid characters, for instance, we would inevitably also have to talk about the analysts who work well with such people and the analysts who don't, and we would be interested in saying something about the difference. Or if we started out talking about a particular countertransference problem, we would also soon enough get to the subject of who the people are who set it off. In the case of my patient, for example, we do not necessarily have to start with the former analyst's countertransference. We could just as well start with the young man's belief that his analyst would be critical of his sexual orientation, which might have been a good observation on the patient's part, or might not have been. We just don't know. In either case, though, the patient is someone who could not bring up the problem, which would get us right away into trying to say something about him. Soon enough, though, even if we began this way, we would run up against the analyst's reaction to the patient.

It will come as no surprise to most readers—and to all interpersonal/relational readers—that most of the time, these two ways of defining the hard-to-engage patient—the diagnostic and the countertransferential—are each probably incomplete, because neither of them considers the whole relationship. What it would really be most productive to talk about is the interaction between the two people, conscious and unconscious. The two participants assume different roles, but are involved with one another in the same ways. From a relational perspective, this outcome is unavoidable. Once again, we come upon the interpersonal field; and, in fact, we shall find, as this chapter develops, that the matter of engagement is just another way to refer to the fate of the field in any particular encounter.

And so I want to try to address the subject of the difficult-to-engage patient in a way that folds in both the diagnostic and the countertransferential. I want to approach the issue as a problem of clinical process. I want to think about what actually happens in some of these treatments, despite the fact that engagement *doesn't* happen. This probably requires me not to think only about the nature of the relatedness in the pair that can't gain traction, but also about the *engaged* patient–analyst pair, and then to ask what the unengaged pair is missing. In any case, I am after a process description of the relevant clinical events.

The first way it occurs to me to think about the event of engagement is to imagine that it depends upon what we usually refer to as emotional connection between patient and analyst. I suppose that, in some sense, that is undeniable. But I am immediately struck by an exception. I think of an ex-patient of mine, a man I will call John, a very brilliant man who has been enormously successful in financial terms, but who is now divorced, with grown children, and who feels that his life is empty and meaningless—and always has been, with the exception of the years spent bringing up his children. And sometimes he has his doubts about even those years. My meetings with John were the most recent in a long series of treatments he had attempted, none of which had "taken." His immediate reason for consulting me was his fairly longstanding relationship with a woman who wanted to marry him, but whom he thought he did not want to marry, although he was very fond of her. His reluctance was due to the absence of a feeling of being deeply involved with her. This posed a problem, because John was someone who tried very hard to be a nice guy, and he was having difficulty figuring out how to manage this relationship and feel like a nice guy at the same time. He was also on the verge of beginning to go out with at least one other woman, against all sense of what he thought was right. But he could hardly stand the feeling he had of not being involved with his girlfriend, and he knew that he could create it with someone else, even though he also knew that it would be temporary. I knew that this was not a hopeful case.

But I felt buoyed by the fact that I took to John immediately. I felt drawn to him. He was warm, unusually intelligent, and seemed to be capable of real concern for those around him. As a matter of fact, his colleagues routinely consulted him about their problems, sometimes about work but sometimes also about their personal lives. His office door, it seemed, was always open to them, and he enjoyed being of help. For his part, John was also drawn to me, and he, too, felt hopeful that maybe this time treatment would work. Maybe this would be the treatment in which he would manage to gain some traction.

But it was not to be. Despite our initial interest in one another, and despite his very real efforts to talk to me, this man just could not come up with anything real about himself. He had a few stock phrases about his childhood, and he repeated them whenever we tried to get into that. I tried many times to open up some details about his childhood and his early life through college, but it was virtually impossible. He could only tell me the same details over and over, and my observation of this fact, despite his agreement with me, was of no help to him. All he could do was smile in an embarrassed way and shrug his shoulders.

He really was empty. He was empty of desire, mainly. He did not know what he wanted. He knew only that he *wanted to want* very badly. He took up hobbies, sometimes quite arcane and expensive ones, and because he was so unusually talented (across the board) he mastered them quickly. He then lost interest, not being particularly gripped by the substance or process of what he was doing, but only by gaining that sense of mastery. Once he could do something reasonably well, the prospect of continuing it, or developing it further, just bored him. He would resist this bored feeling for a while, knowing that he was once again in the same place, back to having nothing to do and no interests—but it didn't work. The boredom always won out, and he moved on to some other activity. He had wealthy, high-flying friends all over the world, with whom he sailed and fished and drank and cruised the oceans; but he did not miss them as soon as he left them, and he did not especially want to do more of this. But he did, because there was nothing else to do—and sometimes it came alive for him and he had a great time. More often it didn't.

You might imagine what happened. After a few months of increasing difficulty in figuring out what to say to me that really mattered to him, and of me trying whatever I could think of to help him in this, John finally allowed the continuous difficulty we had always had in scheduling our meetings to begin interrupting the treatment. After a few weeks of missed meetings it was clear enough to both of us that he just wasn't going to expend the effort to continue. We each acknowledged that it was a shame, that we enjoyed one another's company, and we discussed the possibility that he could just force himself to continue in the hope that we could identify something about what was stopping him from being involved in the process. But it was hard enough for him to find the time to come that he just couldn't arouse the motivation to force it—even though he recognized that this meant he was reproducing the same kind of experience yet again. I racked my brains to think of something that we could do to catalyze his involvement, some question I could ask, some observation I could make, something vital that I could feel in his presence and then report to him for his reaction—but to no avail. Actually, while I regretted the end immensely, I also felt sympathetic with John:

he really did want to be able to work with me, and he just couldn't. He simply had nothing more to say, despite wanting to have something to say rather badly. We parted as friends, both of us feeling that same interest in one another's company that we had identified at the outset. It was quite strange, actually.

I introduced this brief period of work with John by saying that we usually take it for granted that engagement in treatment depends on a sense of emotional connection between analyst and patient. I have no reason to revise that impression after my experience with John. But it is also true that, despite a connection between him and me, or at least what seemed to me like a nascent connection, a mutual appeal that could very easily have developed into a sense of connection, this treatment did not work. We just could not find a way to engage one another. Apparently there are instances in which the real possibility that you and the patient could be friends doesn't mean that the two of you can create the particular kind of involvement that is required between patient and analyst.

You might ask me, at this juncture, to consider the possibility that I was wrong, that perhaps John was a schizoid kind of guy whose apparent connection to me masked a deeper emptiness and absence of relatedness. What about all those "friends" on their yachts? Wouldn't they have said, like me, that John was connected to them? And yet didn't I know, from John himself, that he really didn't care if he ever saw them again? In answer, I would say that such a diagnostic query is right on the mark. But I would also say that, despite that fact, I believe that John and I did have a connection that was authentic and that therefore should be described as "budding," at the very least. The possibility that he may have begun the same kind of relationship with some of the people he socialized with, or with those of his colleagues who sought out and valued his advice, doesn't change this part of my impression of what went on between him and me.

So what were John and I missing? Well, we were certainly missing his desire, any authentic sense of what he wanted from life—from his girlfriend, from his high-flying playmates, from me. And we were missing the presence of an inner life in his mind. He just didn't seem to have one, never had. He did not have a sense of what Bromberg (1991) calls "insideness," and Slochower (1999, 2004) refers to as "interiority." And yet, despite the fact that what happened between John and me could feel dead, he was not dead inside, not at all. That is just not what I felt in his presence. He was unique in my experience in these ways.

And so, although I do think that some kind of connection is necessary for engagement, it wasn't a connection between us that we were missing. Connection is necessary for therapeutic involvement, but apparently not sufficient.

I think that what we were most missing was curiosity, by which I mean an active attitude of openness (Stern, 1997). To be curious, you have to attend closely to your experience, but without necessarily looking for anything in particular. You are instead trying to be alert to what may emerge in it. What will happen next? How will I feel, what will I notice about myself or the other person, what new ideas about our relatedness, or the patient's life, or even about my own life, may begin to rise in my mind, like an object rising under a sheet? Whatever is in my mind, whatever is noticeable about you, becomes more and more clearly identifiable as that object rises higher and higher under that sheet, which begins to fall around it, eventually defining it as something I can recognize. But I have to *allow* that to happen, and that "allowing" must be deeper than mere conscious will; it has to happen in a way that feels as if it is happening by itself—in a way, as if it were happening in someone else's mind. To be curious is to be open to what comes unbidden, to be an onlooker in one's own mind, a grateful receiver of whatever you find, even if you don't like it (to a point, of course, since there is plenty in any of our minds that we like so little that we keep ourselves from formulating it at all).

This attitude of open expectancy toward oneself is really no different from the open expectancy that the analyst feels toward the patient, at least when things are going well. In fact, the patient's curiosity and the analyst's are even more similar than this description might suggest. The patient is open to his own mind, and so is the analyst, who can't really attend to the patient per se, but only to his or her *experience* of the patient. And so when I am attending to my patient, I am attending to my own mind, trying to allow myself whatever is novel in what emerges for me.

In order for curiosity to work in treatment, it must be mutual, because my curiosity stimulates yours and yours stimulates mine. But what does this mean, when we get right down to it? Can we describe this mutual curiosity more closely?

Here is my take on it. The mind is not monolithic and static, but multiple and continuously in flux. To be curious is to be in a more or less continuous relationship with the flux of one's mind. That is the kind of living in which novelty can emerge into awareness. But how do I stay accepting of flux? By being responsive to the other. If the other is curious, her state of being, or self-state, is shifting just as restlessly as mine, changing in response to changes in context. And so, as her state of mind shifts, mine does; and as my state of mind shifts, hers does. That is the nature of the interpersonal field. Each of us is context for the other; each of us provides the means by which the other maintains his curiosity and stays internally alive. I think this kind of mutually responsive flux is well described by Knoblauch (2000) and Ringstrom (2001, 2007) as improvisation, and even earlier by Winnicott (1971) as play. It is also what Hans-Georg Gadamer (2004), a philosopher and not a psychoanalyst at all, calls the kind of "genuine conversation" that results in new understanding.

If either partner loses touch with flux and shift, there is a deadening influence exerted on the other. We can all imagine how painfully awkward it must be to improvise into a dead audience, or, how hard it would be, in playing jazz, to find yourself having to respond to riffs by other players that were nothing but copies of something you already knew. It is virtually impossible to maintain a sense of aliveness in the presence of flatness, deadness, or the absence of novelty, as my experience with John shows: liking him wasn't enough to keep me from being terribly bored.

Now keep in mind my claim, a moment ago, that the analyst is not so much curious about the patient per se, but about the kind of presence that the patient has in his (the analyst's) mind. If the analyst's curiosity is blocked, in other words, what is happening is that he or she can't maintain the continuous flux necessary for ongoing engagement with the patient. This is precisely what happens in mutual enactment, at least from the analyst's side of things (e.g., Stern, 2010a). The analyst's experience of the patient, that is, becomes static. The obstruction is ultimately the outcome of the mind in which it occurs, of course, but it is fair to say that it can be set off by either participant. We are used to thinking about the patient's contribution in this regard. But sometimes it is more realistic for the analyst to bear the greater responsibility—that is, sometimes the analyst just cannot manage to create an experience of the patient that allows a resumption of flux and change in the relatedness. Most often, of course, both parties are responsible, although in different ways. But no matter what reason is most prominent in any particular instance, the outcome amounts to the same thing—absence of engagement. Besides, it is seldom productive, in my experience, to try to sort out "who started it" (Irwin Hoffman's [1998] wry way of putting it). What we end up with, in enactment, is a state of relatedness in which each person is trapped into rigid ways of perceiving, and thus relating, to the other.

I did keep trying to stay emotionally alive to my patient John, searching my mind for ways to jumpstart some process by which he and I would find our way to animation. But we were trapped into stalemate, despite our best intentions. I have no doubt that there was wiggle room that I missed somehow, because I firmly believe that there is somebody, somewhere, who can engage virtually anyone. There are just fewer people who can manage it with certain patients, and John was one of those people. And therefore I count this aborted treatment as a failure on my part—not necessarily a failure for which I am culpable, but a failure nevertheless: an unconsciously enforced mutual incapacity for curiosity, an enactment that John and I could not find our way out of.

Now, to repeat a point I made earlier in different circumstances: within the analytic situation patient and analyst are each the primary context for the other. And so we can rephrase the point about self-states and context thusly: as each person shifts from one self-state to another, the context for the other person changes in a way that leads to a responsive shift. Ongoing interaction is a continuous, reciprocal process of shifting states of mind. As long as each person can respond freely to the other's state shifts, interaction grows, changes, and continues the process of becoming. Elsewhere I have referred to this kind of freely moving clinical process as continuous productive unfolding (Stern, 2009b, 2010a). It is interrupted only when one participant or the other comes up against a certain kind of obstructing influence.

I have already begun to talk about the nature of this kind of obstruction: that is, I mean to refer once again to enactment (see Stern, 2010a). (In the following, "you" and "me" can refer to either the patient or the analyst.) When the context or interpersonal field you create is such that the state of mind called up in me is one I cannot bear, I do not occupy that state; I shy away from it. That state is *not-me*. It represents an identity that, because of my particular history, I cannot accept being. It is a way of being and feeling that I cannot, will not tolerate. In a word, it is a state, a possibility for being, that I have dissociated. In order not to be that person, I turn to a state of mind I *can* tolerate, which is generally accompanied by the implication that *you* are the person I will not be.

We don't actually know how this perspective might illuminate my work with John, because I never got enough data. Two things we can be fairly sure of, though: (1) being alive to his inner life would have made him feel that he was someone he would find intolerable; (2) by deadening himself to this intolerable part of himself, he deadened me to him. To work with him,

I would have had to find a way through my own boredom to something alive in my moment-to-moment responsiveness to him. It is not at all clear to me that he would have thanked me if I had managed to do that, because I strongly suspect that whatever part of himself must not come into being would be deeply uncomfortable for him to have to acknowledge.

Who might that intolerable part of himself have been? Here I can do no more than speculate, although I do have some idea of directions in which speculation might be productive. Let me go back and tell you a bit more than I already have about John's life.

John was the only child of a couple who lived in a solidly middle-class suburb in the Midwest. His father worked at a mid-level white-collar job; his mother was a housewife. Life at home was stable, predictable, and, for John, as boring as it was dependable. John manifested great talent in many areas from his earliest youth. He read at the age of three, he got the best grades without trying, and he was always the best athlete in his class. His parents were proud of him, but he felt little emotional connection, either between them or between them and him. Life was emotionally flat. He remembers his parents, now dead, as unbearably boring, and from the time he started school, he spent as little time in their presence as he could. He told them nothing about his life, and they never asked. Quite literally, they didn't know him. And he didn't know them.

Over and over again I tried to develop a picture of John's parents that contained some detail. It was virtually impossible; John simply could not tell me anything that truly distinguished them, despite agreeing with me that it was highly unlikely that their images in his mind could have been as blank as they seemed to be.

The one thing John did care about throughout his childhood was hard science and mathematics, and as he got older he mastered ever more complex material of this kind, almost entirely on his own. He became an accomplished amateur practitioner of several hobbies that required highly sophisticated scientific knowledge. In the meantime, he also became the captain of his high school football and basketball teams, president of his class during various years, and eventually, president of the high school student body. He told me that all the way along, from childhood through high school, he had made good friends. In one way his social success seemed inevitable, because while I was in John's company he was nothing if not charming and warm (I do recognize that this characterization is hard to reconcile with the deadness of his inner life), and I imagined he had been the same way earlier in his life; but it also seemed to me, from what I could learn, that these "friends" from his early years tended to be either other popular boys, who were attracted to John by his status, or boys and girls who John could help, either by listening to their problems or by helping them with homework or athletics. John was generous to these people, from what I could tell, but I do not believe he was close to them.

As he entered adolescence, girls found him very attractive, and he dated from a young age; but again, although it was believable that he treated them in the way we describe as "well" (that is, he was not cruel or dismissive, and he tried to be responsive), he did not love any of them, or even feel particularly attached to them. He did not remember having had "crushes." He met his future wife a couple of years after he finished college, and he married her not so much because he cared about her, but rather because she seemed like the right kind of person for him: beautiful, highly athletic, sociable, and from the kind of upper-class background to which, by then, he had learned to aspire. They had little in common otherwise, however, and she was not notably bright, which John claims he did not mind, because they did not talk much about matters that would have demanded a great deal of intelligence. Those things (e.g., the serious literature he read more or less continuously) John continued to do and to think about alone.

When they had children (three, two sons and a daughter), John, seemingly uncharacteristically, reported feeling that they were everything to him, and he went on to devote himself to them throughout their childhoods. By the time John and I met, the children had all left home about a decade earlier. At that point, having no particular reason to continue to live together, John and his wife divorced.

At the time that John applied to college there occurred an episode that I believe was crucial to everything that came after. During high school, although John had practiced his scientific hobbies in isolation, he had carried them out with great intensity, and with an enduring interest and commitment that he was never to devote to anything again until he had children. When it came time to apply to college, John, following his interests, applied to the undergraduate schools with the best hard science programs in the country, as well as several of the best and most prestigious general programs. He was admitted to all the schools he applied to. He went to visit the one he thought he preferred over the others, a school specialized in math and science, and he spent a weekend in a dormitory with the then current students. He was surprised at their brilliance (he had thought they would be bright, but not *that* bright), and contemptuous of their social backwardness, and he convinced himself that he would be unhappy in such an environment, both because he felt he probably could not compete (he was mistaken in this, I believe—he lacked an appropriate confidence in his gifts) and because he wanted a more colorful social life. He then visited another prestigious university, one not specialized in science and math, and he saw fraternity life for the first time. He never looked back. John did well in college, but he spent much of the time drinking and partying, and he left high-level research in science and math behind forever.

John portrayed college as having been a wonderful time, and I can imagine that it was. It also seemed to me, though, to be sad that he had taken the path toward the frat life and away from what had been his passions. It had been one or the other in his mind, apparently—math and science or the high life—and he had made his choice. He was thrilled about the prospects of this new life, which was much more exciting than what he had known. And it is quite true that the social part of this new life did require, and further develop, John's very real talents in the social arena. With the combination of his intelligence and his sociability, he would have been an excellent politician. He was well prepared, in fact, for success in a wide variety of professional, academic, or business activities.

I knew that my reaction to John's choice was an expression of my own values, of course, not just what was best for him. There was no way for me to ignore that point. I had to keep in mind, too, that John himself did not share my feeling about it.

But no matter how much my values may have contributed to my perception of the situation, there was still the fact that this decision, so momentous for John, had been made quickly, easily, and without much soul searching. One might almost say it was flippant. It was made with a relief born of John's worries about whether he was as capable as he would have demanded of himself if he had followed his academic interests. For a time I thought maybe *this* would be the problem that would get the treatment into gear; but that was not to be, either.

There had been no guidance for him in his decision, of course. His parents did not even know where he applied to college, and did not participate in his choice. In the end, one could hardly say that John's brilliance was wasted—his mathematical ability was crucial to his hugely successful career in finance. That success did satisfy his desires for prestige and wealth; and it was obviously nothing to sneeze at. Furthermore, it allowed him to succeed without the sense of terrible risk he had about competing on the highest levels of academics.

But I still believe that John had very special talents, and that he cared about what he studied early in his life in a way that he did not care about his activities after that. I believe, on the basis of what he accomplished in high school (I cannot be more specific without risking John's anonymity, but the achievements were remarkable), that he had creative brilliance of real magnitude, and that, after high school, it went undeveloped. Instead of challenging himself to become what he could have been, he chose safety. John himself would agree with this assessment—but he would say that he did not regret it.

John grew up not only with a dead mother (Green, 1986), but a dead family—although I have no reason to believe that either of John's parents suffered the kinds of symptomatic depression that André Green tells us are the source of a mother's deadness. From John's report, it seems that the deadness John encountered in his family was a kind of family-wide dysphoria—a flattened mood and absence of authentic affect and animation that never descended to frank depression. Or perhaps the deadness is better captured in a word coined by Bollas (1989), the definition of which is clear as soon as it is spoken or written: normotic. I have the impression that, from the beginning of John's life, while there were episodes of affective liveliness with other people (as there were, remember, in his dealings with me, too), ongoing relationships during his childhood never really caught fire. I would say that John was alone in a disconnected world; but once again, John himself would not describe it that way. For him, it was simply the unremarkable world he lived in. It seems that, through high school, he kept something alive in the form of his excitement about science and math. When he went to college, though, he deserted these commitments, leaving him with little that was lively besides episodic, sensuous pleasure; and while alcohol and recreational sex were a lot better than nothing (and often pretty wonderful in those years, too), I believe they could not have replaced the genuine interests he had had before. One last time, though, I must repeat that this is my observation, one that John himself would not necessarily agree with. He would agree that, after some years of this kind of living, life lost meaning for him; but he would not necessarily say that there was a connection of this lost meaning to his lost interests. The birth of his children reanimated his life. But they, too, were now gone, living their own lives. John visited them, made sure they had enough material support, and eagerly awaited grandchildren. But they could not give him what they had when they were children themselves.

What would it be like for John to feel alive? What would it have taken for him to open himself to me and to the process of psychoanalysis? To my mind, John would have had to come to terms with the enormity of the choice he made when he went to college, a choice that, I believe, sealed other choices, as well. He chose not only to leave his academic interests. I think, at least partly as a result, his romantic, family, and social life, too, did not bring him the satisfaction they might have otherwise. It seems to me that for John to explore any of this would be to expose himself to all of it. There is the threat here of an awareness of self-betrayal—which John either denies (my speculation) or simply does not feel (John's understanding). It seems to me, quite simply, that John did not become what he could have been.

In addition to all of this, if John were to be genuinely curious about himself, would he also not have had to recognize the emotional deprivation he grew up with? Is it not likely that this amiable man has another side, perhaps a rageful and contemptuous dissociated self that is the other, more deeply emotional heir of those early years? It goes without saying, I think, that *that* John, the angry one, if he really does exist, is not a nice guy—and as I hope I have made clear, John needs to be a nice guy. In order for John to maintain an open, curious attitude toward himself, in other words, wouldn't he have had to accept states of being that he cannot bear? That, at least, is my speculation.

I worry that John will never arrive at what he cannot bear; and then again, I worry that he will. The enormity of what I imagine to be his hidden despair scares me. If I had to characterize my attitude about my patients' futures, I would say that I am generally optimistic. I am not as optimistic in John's case as I am used to being, or as I would like to be. I would like to believe that John will find his way to a life different than the one he has had. But I know the odds against that outcome. I know he may not.

But I also try to remember that the choices John has made are his own. They were not mine to make, not even mine to judge. I can certainly have my opinions; and given that I am a psychoanalyst, I *should* have opinions about John's life, or at least I should know what I think the important questions are. But who is to say, other than John himself, that the choices he made were not the best ones for him, given the family he grew up in and the life he had? Who can even be sure that the curiosity he and I could not muster between us would have been the best thing for him?

Chapter 11

Curiosity

Dealing with divergent ideas in the ideal psychoanalytic institute

The task of describing the ideal psychoanalytic institute is flat-out impossible. You can describe an institute that is ideal for yourself. That you can do; and perhaps that is all I am doing in this chapter, although I hope otherwise. In any case, we all know that, over the decades since the beginning in Vienna, we psychoanalysts have not exactly been relaxed about the differences between us. We might even say, if we were inclined to be entirely straightforward, that we have been unreasonably fractious. There have been personal differences, political differences, ethical differences, and theoretical differences. Any one of these sets of differences might have been enough to bring the house down. Somehow, though, they have not broken the roof, a fact that should probably impress our good luck upon us more than it does.

We have been like hermit crabs: when one house no longer suits our purpose, we desert it and inhabit another. If we follow the lead of our illustrious interpersonal psychoanalytic forebear, Clara Thompson, we leave the rusting old hulk (in this case, the New York Psychoanalytic Institute) while singing "Go Down, Moses," a hymn celebrating the liberation of the Jews from the tyranny of Pharaoh (Green, 1964, p. 362).[1] As passionate an origin as that was for what eventually became the William Alanson White Institute, it does not hearten us about the prospects of devising a single course of training for everyone.

But perhaps that view is unduly monolithic. Perhaps unanimity about the design of an institute merely requires that we not think too big. Perhaps if small groups of like-minded psychoanalysts come together, as Thompson, Horney, and the others did when they marched away from the New York Psychoanalytic Institute that day, purportedly with arms locked in comradeship (a comradeship, we are told by Green [1964], created by what they felt was the grave injustices done to some of their number), they can forge among their smaller numbers training institutes in which at least *internal* fractures are avoided. Perhaps then differences within our institutes could be negotiated peacefully, and combat could be restricted to the internecine realms of theoretical discourse. That way we would only have to fight with those from *other* institutes. It would seem to be a great advantage to keep the bloodshed between us and them.

But of course, this stratagem doesn't work any better for psychoanalytic institutes than it does for families. (It may seem to work pretty well for nations, but that impression is gained only at the cost of ignoring the frequency of politically motivated assassinations, lynchings, kidnappings, and the subversion of the justice system by political interests.) As Clara Thompson (1958) famously observed, "The psychoanalytic institute has many of the qualities—both good and bad—of a close family group" (p. 54). That is, while there are situations in which you can depend upon your fellow analysts to be there, there are other circumstances in which you are really courting trouble if you expect your colleagues to love you. (At such times you shouldn't necessarily even always rely on them to get your back.) The trick is to know when to expect what; and it is not entirely clear that it is a trick that can be learned.

Thompson was right. Institutes *are* like families: intimacy simply does not breed peace and quiet. We are hopelessly doomed if we imagine that we can avoid conflict over the nature of the ideal institute by creating training centers from small numbers of congenial and like-minded people. Soon after Thompson, Horney, and Fromm established their new psychoanalytic institution, Thompson and Fromm left it, with others, and under less than pleasant circumstances. (The story I know has to do with Horney being pretty unreasonable, but then I am not from the group that stayed with Horney, and so the story could well be apocryphal, or at least one-sided.)

The lesson seems to be that like-mindedness does not necessarily last forever, and sometimes not even through next week. That particular fracture, the one between Fromm and Horney, was the immediate impetus for Thompson, Fromm, Sullivan, Fromm-Reichman, and Janet and David Rioch to move from their old shell (remember the hermit crab) to our new one, the White Institute (not so new now), which perseveres to this day (it was a commodious shell).

And so maybe we should shift gears and paraphrase Mark Twain's well-known *bon mot* about quitting smoking: creating the ideal psychoanalytic institute is the easiest thing in the world—we've done it hundreds of times. We all know that the history of psychoanalysis is littered along its entire length with organizational disasters.

And yet the impossible task is exactly what we keep being called upon to do, because "institute" is a singular noun. In the end, an institute must have a single set of policies. There may be room for wiggle, but not for a different policy, at least not until whatever formal decision-making policy is in place has been followed. A curriculum, even though it may be composed of diverse offerings, must serve one vision and not another. There is no getting around the necessity for decisions, each one singular, that affect groups of people, not all of whom will like them.

Now, this all puts us in the same untenable position as (going meta now) everyone else in the world. We all live in groups that have some kind of governance over us—countries, states and provinces, cities, political parties, even psychoanalytic institutes. The same problem comes up for every one of them: what is the ideal? I don't know the literature on political philosophy. No doubt it is immense. We could probably bring the literature of ethics to bear, too, and maybe several other branches of knowledge. I can't even name all the disciplines relevant to ideal policy making; I am certainly not going to try. And for that same reason (ignorance), I am not going to use anything but psychoanalysis and my own wits, such as they are, in addressing the issue. Here or there I may pull an example from another field out of the air, but that is all.

Now of course, in this examination of the ideal, one must also ask what part of an institute's functioning one is talking about. We could discuss the ideal means for ensuring the widest participation in the institute's activities by its graduates. We could even discuss whether the widest participation is ideal. We could discuss how those who do participate advance in the organizational hierarchy (that is, supervisor of psychotherapy, faculty, supervising analyst, training analyst, and so on). We could talk about how to select the representatives who govern our affairs. We could discuss the ideal psychoanalytic curriculum. We could discuss the ideal psychoanalytic candidate: who should be selected, or encouraged to apply?

We can conceive an ideal for each of these aspects of psychoanalytic institutes, and for many more besides. My contribution to this multi-vocal conversation has to do with intellectual commitments and the politics that come with those things. It has been clinical and theoretical differences, after all—or rather, what we analysts have done and not done about these differences—that have been responsible for the schisms that have been such a central part of psychoanalytic history.

It obviously has not been a good solution to prepare candidates only by indoctrinating them in one way of thinking and leading them to believe that other ways are wrong (see, for example, Kernberg, 1986). That kind of education prepares them to deal neither with analysts from other institutes who have different theoretical allegiances nor with analysts from their own institutes who may come to see the field differently than they do. It would seem that we need to think hard about how institutes should deal with difference, or otherness.

I want to discuss how we should prepare candidates to deal with these differences; and that task has to do with the values an institute ought to have, since the way we prepare candidates for the differences they will encounter emerges from what we think is important. What is the ideal in this regard? How should we try to teach people who are becoming psychoanalysts to think about theory and practice?

Given that we are discussing ideals, it does not contradict expectation that my argument is idealistic. No pragmatics here. I do not discuss the ways in which we should go about creating the ideal I describe. What I have to say, for instance, does not suggest the content of a curriculum that might accomplish my goals. On the other hand, I do recommend the attitude that should be taken in courses, whatever the content. I am focusing only on the kind of intellectual atmosphere that I believe is most desirable for a psychoanalytic institute.

As I said a moment ago, it goes without saying that we do not wish to encourage people to feel a loyalty to one theory that precludes their capacity to engage others; and so my task is to describe the ideal of such an engagement. I am going to discuss two views of that engagement. Each is a way of understanding the encounter with otherness within psychoanalysis, and especially the process by which we deal with the kind of differences that arise over time.

The accretion model

If we employ the *accretion model*, we acknowledge divergent ideas as we move along in time, accommodating to them (often quite slowly, in fits and starts, with episodes of nostalgia for the old and resistance to the new), sometimes assimilating them (without undue enthusiasm, we can hope, for their absorption), integrating what we already know with what we encounter. This is the model that we all use in clinical practice most of the time. Dialectical theories, such as Irwin Hoffman's (1998) or Jessica Benjamin's (1988, 1995, 1998), are good illustrations of what it looks like to think this way.

For Benjamin, the significant dialectic exists between our recognition of the other as a separate center of subjectivity, on one hand, and our constitution of the other by the projection of our own reality, on the other. Benjamin's profound point is that these two modes of relatedness between human beings are essential for one another. Neither could exist without the other, and life is the history of their continuous interchange. Furthermore, we need both if we are to sustain certain parts of living. Note, for example, that complementarity, or projection/introjection, is hardly all bad: it is the original source of the internal world of phantasy, from which novelty in experience arises, and is the means by which that crucial part of existence is continuously replenished.

For Hoffman, whatever is in the foreground of experience gains its meaning by its relationship to what is in the background. It is all of a piece. The past is contextualized in the present, the present in the past; the inside and outside worlds are contextualized in one another; and so on. Hoffman's best-known application of the principle comes in his theory of the psychoanalytic situation: psychoanalytic ritual and personal spontaneity are each an important source of the other's meaning, each working silently in the background whenever the other is in the foreground.

The dialectical view of life is well suited to the study of how we deal with difference, and it might very well be used in the construction of an ethics. From dialectical vantage points, the other, whether the otherness is cultural or intellectual, is always already part of us, part of the background of what we are aware of being. In the most general sense, every experience we have not yet had is part of the background of being that gives familiar meaning to the experience we know. In a more specific sense, prejudicial perceptions of others—people who are unlike us in skin color, religion, culture, or sexual preference—must be understood as the background against which we create our perceptions of ourselves. Everyone by now knows these analyses: to be white is to *not be* all those things identified with being African-American, Latino, Native American, or Asian; to be straight is to *not be* all those thing identified with being gay. The list goes on.

When dialectic is allowed to work freely, difference is addressed and recognized as it arises. In the terms of hermeneutics, this process is characterized as a dialogue or conversation in which our conversational partner, whether that partner is a person or a work of art or some other cultural product, offers us something unfamiliar. We set that unfamiliar experience against what we already know, and in favorable instances we are able to see the difference, and we learn from it. In less favorable outcomes we do not note the difference, otherness disappears into the familiar, and we do not grow (Stern, 1991).

In this process, when it goes well, difference may not become comfortable, but it is made comprehensible from within the point of view of the other—and when you comprehend the other this way, disagreement remains disagreement and does not descend into schisms and wars. But dissent does remain possible: following comprehension, one can take issue.

The ideal psychoanalytic institute, from this perspective, is one whose members understand that their own ideas are meaningful partly because of the context provided by all those ideas with which they differ. Such an institute, while it might very well have a central theoretical commitment, would promote the comparative study of ideas among its candidates, encouraging them to immerse themselves in, and become knowledgeable about, many different ways of thinking. If the institute has a theoretical commitment, teaching would center around the way that that commitment gains part of its meaning from being situated in the context of ideas from which it diverges. Learning, to the extent that it has to do with different ways of thinking, would be understood as the conversation of ideas; and to allow the conversation of ideas is to be curious. The accretion model relies on the capacity to maintain an active attitude of openness.

The revolution model

But what if we are fooling ourselves? What if the situation is otherwise? What if, instead of accomplishing a reasonably comfortable and continuous negotiation with otherness, we are managing, by following the accretion model, to do nothing more than *ignore* the most radical implications of otherness? What about, in other words, the possibility that the accretion model does too good a job of preserving the past, and is thus unduly conservative? And, from a separate vantage point, what about those instances in which the old guard simply will not converse with those who propose change? Under those circumstances it is hard to see why new ideas will ever be absorbed by those in power.

What if real change, in other words, at least under some circumstances, cannot be accomplished by assimilation and accommodation, but requires throwing out the bath water *and* the baby? Could it be that certain kinds of change require revolution?

We do not have to embrace *Das Kapital* to take this view seriously—it comes to us from more sources than Marx and Lenin. Nor do we have to think of revolution in the terms of any kind of violence, including the intellectual variety. We know from nonlinear dynamic systems theory, for instance, that when a system reaches a tipping point, change is often not gradual and linear, but sudden. We also know from Thomas Kuhn's (1962) classic text, which is widely accepted at this juncture and even includes the word "revolutions" in its title, that basic change in science only takes place when the old paradigm, stretched beyond its breaking point in the vain attempt to accommodate observations inconsistent with it, finally collapses of its own weight. The implosion of the old paradigm is virtually simultaneous with the advent of the new one. Kuhn did not mean to describe all changes in intellectual life, only the huge ones that deserve to be called paradigm shifts, changes on the order of those brought about by Galileo, Darwin, and Einstein. But as long as we don't call them paradigm shifts, there is no reason not to apply his thinking to smaller conceptual changes, including those in psychoanalysis, and many writers have.

Certainly, change in psychoanalysis can be large and sudden. This is as true of changes in our theory as it is of changes in the patient and the analyst during the clinical process. The change wrought by the early interpersonal analysts, for instance, does not seem to have been the result of an orderly conversation, or of any conversation at all. In fact, the problem was, as Kuhn argues is routinely the case, that those who supported the old theory—classical analysts in our instance—simply would not take the new findings seriously, and so the resulting absence of dialogue (more than that, actually: the early interpersonalists were actively ostracized) virtually required, if the new observations were to be accommodated, that the old model collapse and a new one arise.

Of course, it is hardly the case that the interpersonal model simply supplanted the Freudian one, as Galileo's view of the solar system replaced the one that came before it. But there is no doubt that the burst of intellectual activity during the 1930s and 1940s in the work of Sullivan, Fromm, and Fromm-Reichmann has eventually resulted in a seachange in our field. Today, every psychoanalyst, even if he wishes to disagree, must at least take seriously certain principles that were the message of those first interpersonalists: "what happened matters" (in Levenson's words); the analytic situation is the interaction of two real people; relatedness is the core of clinical work and should be the heart of theory; the analyst's subjectivity matters. The fact that dialogue about these and other matters *does* take place today between analysts of different schools should not obscure the fact that these views did not originate in a dialogue between those who created them and those who opposed them.

I recently read another compelling example of the revolution model, a classic psychoanalytic example, Anton Ehrenzweig's (1967) *The Hidden Order of Art*, a book that proposes a psychoanalytic understanding of the processes by which art is both perceived and created. At one point Ehrenzweig tries to explain how he keeps himself open to fresh perception in looking at art.

> I feel that my researches can only be supported by holding onto "first impressions" in modern art such as most people are liable to forget. In this manner one is able to neutralize the effects of the secondary processes which obscure the . . . structure of creative work.
> (p. 86)

That is, most of what is most original in experience simply disappears over time into the stereotypies of familiarity. In his famous memory experiments, Bartlett (1932) referred to this effect as "conventionalisation." Ernest Schachtel (1959), who saw all of life as a struggle between the challenge to individuate, on the one hand, and our temptation to remain embedded in what is familiar, on the other, referred to "secondary autocentricity," which he described as the means by which what is novel or creative habitually disappears into comfortable conventionality. For Harry Stack Sullivan (1953), the self-system, the agent of selective attention, develops to exclude novelty and to preserve repetitive, safe experiencing. For these writers and any number of others, the aim of embracing familiarity is emotional comfort, reassurance: what we don't know can't hurt us.

Part of the reason for this retreat to comfort, says Ehrenzweig—sounding like Lacan in emphasizing that truth lies in flux and change, and self-deception in the perception of stasis—is that we are reassured by a vision of a fixed, unchanging world.

> Perception, particularly vision, secures our hold on reality. This is probably why we are so unwilling to accept that perception is unstable, its data shifting and subject to the interplay of the uncontrollable forces within our mind . . .
>
> (p. 87)

For Ehrenzweig, perception exists at various levels of differentiation. Only conscious perception has a firm and stable structure. The unconscious mode of perception is "dedifferentiated," and because of this it can grasp much larger realms of information and experience at once. These large and vague tracts of experience are the source of all creative endeavor and are the product of the primary process, which becomes, in Ehrenzweig's hands, something very different from the chaos Freud postulated, and different also, and for the same reasons, from Kris's (1952) theory of regression in the service of the ego. (Schachtel [1959] makes a similar argument in rejecting the idea that creativity has anything to do with regression.) For Ehrenzweig, the primary process is organized in a highly sophisticated way. But this organization is not the precise grasp of individual items that characterizes secondary process experiencing.

> as we penetrate into deeper levels of awareness, into the dream, reveries, subliminal imagery, and the dreamlike visions of the creative state, our perception becomes more fluid and flexible. It widens its focus to comprehend the most far-flung structures. These different levels of differentiation in our perception interact constantly, not only during the massive shifts between dreaming and waking, but also in the rapid pulse of differentiation and dedifferentiation that goes on continually undetected in our daily lives.
>
> (p. 87)

This is why Ehrenzweig wants to hold on to his first impressions of art: in them he grasps more than he will when the secondary process takes over. In his way of thinking, we need secondary process perception (and thought) for the workaday, everyday world. We need to be able to negotiate conventional reality. But we are too attached to this way of perceiving and knowing and the security it provides.

To make art that is more than the application of the ways of seeing created by the last great innovators, the artist must sink into the dedifferentiated perception of primary process, which then informs the artist's ego and secondary process. Only in this way can anyone create something that deserves to be called art. The very same process is required for any creative work, including psychoanalytic clinical practice, writing, teaching, and learning.

The world changes over time. That we all know well enough. But in psychoanalysis this fact has special import, because clinical psychoanalysts always treat the inhabitants of the world as it is *now*. Yet the ideas analysts use to do this are always from the world of *then*. Dedifferentiated perception, says Ehrenzweig, has such value because it connects the inner world of imagination with the outer world of reality in ways that are not only new, but more comprehensive than the differentiated perception of the secondary process can manage.

Because we must always be ready to treat the patients of our own time, psychoanalysts continuously need dedifferentiated perception. Perhaps we actually need it more than most other professionals and academics. Theory and clinical practice need to be changed, even replaced, as time passes. People do not remain the same. This is one way of understanding the trouble, to which I have already referred, between the very early interpersonalists and the classical analysts of that time. What I am about to say is an oversimplification, but with that caveat I will say it: the early interpersonalists were practicing in a way that reflected the people of their own time; classical analysts were dealing with people as if they inhabited a world that was quickly vanishing. The interpersonalists were reacting to a number of changes in the world around them. One of them had to do with authority: Sullivan, Fromm, and Fromm-Reichmann recognized that much of what had been the analyst's unquestioned authority over the patient needed to be reevaluated. They did not make an explicit issue of authority; they just behaved differently in the consulting room, sacrificing some of their authority without saying anything about it. It was no accident that they devised these new forms of clinical conduct just as our world was changing in the same direction. They were changing with the world; the classical analysts of their day were not (see Chapter 2).

While Ehrenzweig's thinking is unique (a fact I fear that my abbreviated presentation does not represent), it is hardly the only psychoanalytic statement of the view that creative work requires the special grasp provided by unconscious mentation. Besides Kris, one thinks immediately of Milner (1969, 1987), Bion (1977), Loewald (1978, 2000), Ogden (1994b, 1997, 2001, 2005), and, among interpersonalists, Tauber and Green (1959). I have myself (Stern, 1983, 1997) championed such a view. In considering otherness in psychoanalysis, the upshot of these views is this: we should not only assimilate and accommodate difference; we should open wide the doors, let difference in, ask it to stay for dinner.

What implications does the revolution model have for psychoanalytic training? Well, if we agree that we want to encourage dedifferentiation, we should encourage creative thought among our candidates and our graduates—something psychoanalytic institutes have not exactly been famous for doing (e.g., Kernberg, 1996).[2] Ironically enough, freedom of thought requires discipline: the discipline to attend to our own vague preconceptions, those unformulated beginnings of mentation that Ehrenzweig calls dedifferentiated perception and that I have called unformulated experience. This discipline is a kind of curiosity; it involves allowing what is dedifferentiated or unformulated to come to fruition in its own time, without rushing or forcing it. While it is percolating, we must remain attuned to it, but without succumbing to the temptation to give it premature shape (Stern, 1997). We should encourage ourselves, and teach others, to do this, to listen with our third ear (Reik, 1949), not only to our patients, but also while we read and write.

A policy like this one faces certain difficulties in the early years of training, of course, because one has to know a certain amount about psychoanalysis to be creative in thinking about it. But such encouragement in our institutes should begin as early as possible and go on throughout training, and then beyond it. The climate of a psychoanalytic training center should be one in which new ideas are welcome, even if they contradict what some older analysts treat as received wisdom. (Actually, in this ideal institute, there would be no received wisdom.)

Since new ideas in any discipline often come from exposure to material beyond the discipline's bounds, candidates and graduates would be encouraged to explore other fields (philosophy, neuroscience, anthropology, sociology) and to take seriously the insights of literature, film, and other arts. If the inner world and the outer one are allowed to commingle as freely as Ehrenzweig recommends, inspiration can come from anywhere. I firmly believe that creative, useful psychoanalytic writing would burgeon in any institute in which the desirability of interdisciplinary exploration was taken for granted.

And finally, the revolution model would lead us to believe, and to teach candidates, that all ideas, however beautiful and beloved, are temporary expressions of local truth, to be changed or replaced altogether as time passes. We must not become too attached to them—or rather, we must try to grasp and accept our attachments thoroughly enough to be able to let go of our ideas when we need to.

What to do with the two models?

I have loyalties to both accretion and revolution. So do we all, I imagine. Both models accept difference; they diverge only in the degree of their enthusiasm about it. Both are descriptions of curiosity. It will not surprise anyone that I am going to end by saying that I believe we need both these kinds of curiosity. We need to conserve what continues to help us understand, and we need to change or replace what is no longer useful. If we encourage the kind of engagement of difference within our own field that I have described, I believe that we are doing what is within our power to preserve our institutes and to nurture psychoanalysis.

But what makes it possible for us to have this degree of sensitivity to otherness in psychoanalysis? What makes it possible for us to know when to conserve and when to innovate? We cannot turn to method here. As Ehrenzweig (1967) writes, "There is no definite recipe for breaking the pernicious rule of preconceived design and for setting free the diffuse inarticulate vision of the unconscious" (pp. 49–50). We can, though, say something sensible about what the task requires. Simply put, curiosity requires intellectual commitment and rigor. But intellect is not intellectualization, and commitment is not devotion. In the psychoanalysis of my era, it has sometimes seemed to me that the recognition of these differences has suffered, as if affect were somehow contaminated by intellect, and as if we were duty-bound to come to the defense of our favored theories. The result, when these things occur, is a kind of psychoanalytic parochialism. Sometimes that narrowness has resulted in a certain anti-intellectualism in many psychoanalytic institutes.

Thought of any depth and power, though, is thoroughly imbued with feeling. Actually, real intellectual innovation is *guided* by affect (see, for example, Damasio, 1994). In the ideal institute, everyone would be a thinker—not necessarily a writer, but someone whose primary values include curiosity, the desire to stay open to what is new, to the way the world is changing, and to protect what remains valuable in the traditions we have inherited from those who have come before.

Even then, though, armed with the best intentions, we sometimes fail. I recently taught a course that was designed to accomplish exactly the kinds of goals I am proposing here. Yet I repeatedly found myself taking a position about the theoretical differences I was presenting. Worse than that, I sometimes found myself speaking as if I were trying to influence the candidates I was teaching to take the position I favored. There is obviously nothing wrong with teaching a point of view. But I *thought* I was trying *not* to; I thought I was trying to focus on the nature of the *differences* between points of view, with evaluation left for another time. If we are to remain curious, in the consulting room, on the one hand, and as candidates, teachers, and supervisors, on the other, we must keep close track of our theoretical and clinical preferences so that we can temporarily lay them aside when it serves our broader purposes. We like to think we are *committed* to the ideas we favor, because commitment suggests thoughtful choice. But so often our passionate involvement with ideas and the politics that go along with them make our commitments into something more like allegiances. We routinely find in ourselves the same unthinking devotion to our favored ideas that can make patriotism so dangerous. Curiosity is a demanding ideal.

Notes

1 I don't know whether this story is historically accurate, but Green certainly reports it as if it actually took place. I do hope it did!
2 The governance of the White Institute could be harsh, even despotic, during my first 15 years there. That changed dramatically, and for the better, 25 years ago. But despite that atmosphere, I never faced any attempt to control my theoretical and clinical writing or thinking, nor did my relative youth lead anyone to try to discourage me from publishing. When I criticized aspects of interpersonal thinking, I felt a certain disapproval from some senior analysts, but I never faced outright censure for these views. A colleague of mine who started writing at the same time I did told me that when he presented his early work to analysts from a classically oriented institute, young analysts came up to him afterward and expressed their amazement that he had been allowed to present his own thoughts at such a young age. So institutes apparently differ in this respect. These experiences took place long ago, though, in the mid-1980s. The atmosphere of the classical institute where my colleague presented may well have changed since then.

References

Argyris, C. and Schön, D. A. (1976). *Theory in Practice: Increasing Professional Effectiveness*. San Francisco: Jossey-Bass.

Aron, L. (1996). *Mutuality in Psychoanalysis: A Meeting of the Minds*. Hillsdale, NJ: The Analytic Press.

Aron, L. (2006). Analytic impasse and the third: Clinical implications of intersubjectivity theory. *International Journal of Psychoanalysis*, 87:349–68.

Atwood, G. E. and Stolorow, R. D. (1994). *Faces in a Cloud: Intersubjectivity in Personality Theory*. Revised edition. New York: Jason Aronson.

Aulagnier, P. (1975/2001). First published as *La Violence de l'Interprétation: Du pictogramme à l'énoncé*. Paris: Presses Universitaires de France, 1975. Trans. A. Sheridan as *The Violence of Interpretation: From Pictogram to Statement*. Hove: The New Library of Psychoanalysis and Phildelphia: Brunner-Routledge, 2001.

Balint, E. (1993). *Before I Was I: Psychoanalysis and the Imagination*. London: Guilford.

Balint, M. (1968). *The Basic Fault: Therapeutic Aspects of Regression*. London: Tavistock Publications.

Baranger, M. (1993). The mind of the analyst: From listening to interpretation. In: L. G. Fiorini (Ed.), *The Work of Confluence: Listening and Interpreting in the Psychoanalytic Field*. London: Karnac Books, 2008, pp. 89–105.

Baranger, M. (2005). Field theory. In: S. Lewkowicz and S. Flechner (Eds.), *Truth, Reality, and the Psychoanalyst: Latin American Contributions to Psychoanalysis*. The International Psychoanalysis Library. London: Karnac Books, pp. 49–71.

Baranger, M. and Baranger, W. (1961–62/2008). The analytic situation as a dynamic field. *International Journal of Psychoanalysis*, 89:795–826. (Original work published 1961–62 in Spanish. This is a translation of the 1969 revision of the original article.)

Baranger, M. and Baranger, W. (1964). "Insight" in the analytic situation. In: L. G. Fiorini (Ed.), *The Work of Confluence: Listening and Interpreting in the Psychoanalytic Field*. London: Karnac Books, 2009, pp. 1–15.

Baranger, M., and Baranger, W. (2009). L. G. Fiorini (Ed.), *The Work of Confluence: Listening and Working and Interpreting in the Analytic Field*. London: Karnac Books.

Baranger, M., Baranger, W. and Mom, J. M. (1983). Process and non-process in analytic work. In: L. G. Fiorini (Ed.), *The Work of Confluence: Listening and Interpreting in the Psychoanalytic Field*. London: Karnac Books, 2008, pp. 63–88.

Baranger, W. (1979). Spiral process and the dynamic field. In: L. G. Fiorini. (Ed.), *The Work of Confluence: Listening and Interpreting in the Psychoanalytic Field*. London: Karnac Books, 2009, pp. 45–61.

Bartlett, F. C. (1932). *Remembering*. Cambridge: Cambridge University Press.

Bass, A. (2001). It takes one to know one; or, Whose unconscious is it anyway? Psychoanalytic Dialogues, 11:683–702.

Bass, A. (2003). "E" enactments in psychoanalysis. Psychoanalytic Dialogues, 13: 657–75.

Bass, A. (2014). Three pleas for a measure of uncertainty, reverie, and private contemplation in the chaotic, interactive, nonlinear dynamic field of interpersonal/intersubjective relational psychoanalysis. *Psychoanalytic Dialogues*, 24: 663–75.

Benjamin, J. (1988). *The Bonds of Love: Psychoanalysis, Feminism, and the Problem of Domination*. New York: Pantheon.

Benjamin, J. (1990). Recognition and destruction: An outline of intersubjectivity. In: S. A. Mitchell and L. Aron (Eds.), *Relational Psychoanalysis: The Emergence of a Tradition*. Hillsdale, NJ: The Analytic Press, 1999, pp. 183–200.

Benjamin, J. (1995). *Like Subjects, Love Objects*. New Haven, CT: Yale University Press.

Benjamin, J. (1998). *Shadow of the Other: Intersubjectivity and Gender in Psychoanalysis*. London: Routledge.

Benjamin, J. (2004). Beyond doer and done to: An intersubjective view of thirdness. *Psychoanalytic Quarterly*, 73:5–46.

Benjamin, J. (2009). A relational psychoanalysis perspective on the necessity of acknowledging failure in order to restore the facilitating and containing features of the intersubjective selationship (the shared third). *International Journal of Psychoanalysis*, 90:441–50.

Berk, J. H. (1998). Trauma and resilience during war: A look at the children and humanitarian aid workers of Bosnia. *Psychoanalytic Review*, 85:639–58.

Bernstein, R. J. (1983). *Beyond Objectivism and Relativism*. Philadelphia: University of Pennsylvania Press.

Bion, W. R. (1961). *Experiences in Groups and Other Papers*. London: Tavistock.

Bion, W. R. (1962a). A theory of thinking. In: *Second Thoughts: Selected Papers on Psycho-Analysis*. New York: Jason Aronson, pp. 110–19, 1967.

Bion, W. R. (1962b). Learning from experience. In: *Seven Servants: Four Works by Wilfred R. Bion*. New York: Jason Aronson, pp. 1–111, 1977.

Bion, W. R. (1963). *Elements of Psycho-Analysis*. London: Heinemann.

Bion, W. R. (1977). *Seven Servants: Four Works by Wilfred R. Bion*. New York: Jason Aronson.

Birksted-Breen, D. (2003). Time and the après coup. *International Journal of Psychoanalysis*, 84:1501–15.

Bloom, H. (1973). *The Anxiety of Influence: A Theory of Poetry*. London: Oxford University Press.

Bollas, C. (1989). *The Shadow of the Object: Psychoanalysis of the Unthought Known*. New York: Columbia University Press.

Bollas, C. (2001). Freudian intersubjectivity: Commentary on paper by Julie Gerhardt and Annie Sweetnam. *Psychoanalytic Dialogues*, 11:93–106.

Bonovitz, C. (2009). Looking back, looking forward: A reexamination of Benjamin Wolstein's interlock and the emergence of intersubjectivity. *International Journal of Psychoanalysis*, 90:463–85.

Boston Change Process Study Group (Bruschweiler-Stern, N., Lyons-Ruth, K., Morgan, A. C., Nahum, J. P., Sander, L. W., and Stern, D. N.). (2008). Forms of relational meaning: Issues in the relations between the implicit and reflective-verbal domains. *Psychoanalytic Dia*logues, 18:125–48.

Boston Change Process Study Group. (2010). *Change in Psychotherapy: A Unifying Paradigm*. New York: W. W. Norton.

Botella, C. and Botella, S. (2005). *The Work of Psychic Figurability: Mental States without Representation*. Trans. A. Weller and M. Zerbib. Hove: Brunner-Routledge.

Boulanger, G. (2007). *Wounded by Reality: Understanding and Treating Adult Onset Trauma*. Mahwah, NJ: The Analytic Press.
Brenner, C. (2000). Observations on some aspects of current psychoanalytic theories. *Psychoanalytic Quarterly*, 69:597–632.
Bridgman, P. W. (1955). *Reflections of a Physicist*. New York: Philosophical Library.
Bromberg, P. M. (1991). On knowing one's patient inside out: The aesthetics of unconscious communication. *Psychoanalytic Dialogues*, 1:399–422.
Bromberg, P. M. (1998). *Standing in the Spaces: Essays on Clinical Process, Trauma, and Dissociation*. Hillsdale, NJ: The Analytic Press.
Bromberg, P. M. (2006). *Awakening the Dreamer: Clinical Journeys*. Hillsdale, NJ: The Analytic Press.
Bromberg, P. M. (2011a). *The Shadow of the Tsunami: And the Growth of the Relational Mind*. New York: Routledge.
Bromberg, P. M. (2011b). "Grown-up" words: A perspective on unconscious fantasy. In: *The Shadow of the Tsunami: And the Growth of the Relational Mind*. New York: Routledge, pp. 145–63.
Brown, L. J. (2010). Klein, Bion, and intersubjectivity: Becoming, transforming, and dreaming. *Psychoanalytic Dialogues*, 20:669–82.
Brown, L. J. (2011a). Rickman, Bion, and the clinical applications of field theory. *International Forum of Psychoanalysis*, 20:89–92.
Brown, L. J. (2011b). *Intersubjective Processes and the Unconscious: An Integration of Freudian, Kleinian, and Bionian perspectives*. Hove: Routledge.
Bruner, J. (1962). The conditions of creativity. In: *On Knowing: Essays for the Left Hand*. Expanded edition. Cambridge, MA: Belknap Press of Harvard University Press, 1979, pp. 17–30.
Bucci, W. (1997). *Psychoanalysis and Cognitive Science: A Multiple Code Theory*. New York: Guilford Press.
Busch, F. (2001). Are we losing our mind? *Journal of the American Psychoanalytic Association*, 49:739–51.
Caligor, L. (1981). Parallel and reciprocal processes in psychoanalytic supervision. *Contemporary Psychoanalysis*, 17:1–27.
Caligor, L., Bromberg, P. M. and Meltzer, J. D. (Eds.). (1983). *Clinical Perspectives on the Supervision of Psychoanalysis and Psychotherapy*. New York: Plenum Press.
Canestri, J. (2006a). Introduction. In: J. Canestri (Ed.), *Psychoanalysis: From Practice to Theory*. London: John Wiley, pp. 1–11.
Canestri, J. (2006b). Implicit understanding of clinical material beyond theory. In: J. Canestri (Ed.), *Psychoanalysis: From Practice to Theory*. London: John Wiley, pp. 13–28.
Canestri, J., Bohleber, W., Denis, P., and Fonagy, P. (2006). The map of private (implicit, preconscious) theories in clinical practice. In: J. Canestri (Ed.), *Psychoanalysis: From Practice to Theory*. London: John Wiley, pp. 29–43.
Chianese, D. (2007). *Constructions and the Analytic Field: History, Scenes, and Destiny*. London: Routledge.
Civitarese, G. (2008). *The Intimate Room: Theory and Technique of the Analytic Field*. London: Routledge.
Civitarese, G. (2012). *The Violence of Emotions: Bion and Post-Bionian Psychoanalysis*. London: Routledge.
Civitarese, G. (2014). *The Necessary Dream: New Theories and Techniques of Interpretation in Psychoanalysis*. London: Karnac.

Coburn, W. (2013). *Psychoanalytic Complexity: Clinical Attitudes for Therapeutic Change*. Hove: Routledge.
Conci, M. (2009). Bion and Sullivan: An enlightening comparison. *International Forum of Psychoanalysis*, 18(2):90–9.
Cooper, S. H. (1993). Introduction: Hermeneutics and you. *Psychoanalytic Dialogues*, 3:169–76.
Cooper, S. H. (2014). The things we carry: Finding/creating the object and the analyst's self-reflective participation. *Psychoanalytic Dialogues*, 24:621–36.
Cooper, S. H., Corbett, K. and Seligman, S. S. (2014). Clinical reflection and ritual as forms of participation and interaction: A reply to Bass and Stern. *Psychoanalytic Dialogues*, 24:684–90.
Corbett, K. (2014). The analyst's private space: Spontaneity, ritual, psychotherapeutic action, and self-care. *Psychoanalytic Dialogues*, 24:637–47.
Cushman, P. (1991). Ideology obscured: Political uses of the self in Daniel Stern's infant. *American Psychologist*, 46:206–19.
Cushman, P. (1995). *Constructing the Self, Constructing America: A Cultural History of Psychotherapy*. Reading, MA: Addison-Wesley.
Cushman, P. (2005). Between arrogance and a dead-end: Gadamer and the Heidegger/Foucault dilemma. *Contemporary Psychoanalysis*, 41:399–417.
Cushman, P. (2007). A burning world, an absent god: Midrash, hermeneutics, and relational psychoanalysis. *Contemporary Psychoanalysis*, 43:47–88.
Cyrulnik, B. (2005). *The Whispering of Ghosts: Trauma and Resilience*. Trans. S. Fairfield. New York: Other Press.
Dahl, G. (2010). The two time vectors of *Nachträglichkeit* in the development of ego organization: Significance of the concept for the symbolization of nameless traumas and anxieties. *International Journal of Psychoanalysis*, 91:727–44.
Damasio, A. R. (1994). *Descartes' Error: Emotion, Reason, and the Human Brain*. New York: G. P. Putnam's Sons.
Davies, J. M. (1996). Linking the pre-analytic with the postclassical: Integration, dissociation, and the multiplicity of unconscious processes. *Contemporary Psychoanalysis*, 32:553–76.
Davies, J. M. (1997). Dissociation, therapeutic enactment, and transference–countertransference processes: A discussion of papers on childhood sexual abuse by S. Grand and J. Sarnat. *Gender and Psychoanalysis*, 2:241–57.
Davies, J. M. (1998). Multiple perspectives on multiplicity. *Psychoanalytic Dialogues*, 8:195–206.
Davies, J. M. (1999). Getting cold feet defining "safe-enough" borders: Dissociation, multiplicity, and integration in the analyst's experience. *Psychoanalytic Quarterly*, 78:184–208.
Davies, J. M. (2001). Back to the future in psychoanalysis: Trauma, dissociation, and the nature of unconscious processes. In: M. Dimen and A. Harris (Eds.), *Storms in Her Head*. New York: Other Press, pp. 245–64.
Davies, J. M. (2003). Falling in love with love: Oedipal and post Oedipal manifestations of idealization, mourning and erotic masochism. *Psychoanalytic Dialogues*, 13:1–27.
Davies, J. M. (2004). Whose bad objects are we anyway? Repetition and our elusive love affair with evil. *Psychoanalytic Dialogues*, 14:711–32.
Davies, J. M. (2005). Transformations of desire and despair: Reflections on the termination process from a relational perspective. *Psychoanalytic Dialogues*, 15:779–805.
de León de Bernardi, B. (2000). The countertransference: A Latin American view. *International Journal of Psychoanalysis*, 81:331–51.

de León de Bernardi, B. (2008). Introduction to the paper by Madeleine and Willy Baranger: The analytic situation as a dynamic field. *International Journal of Psychoanalysis*, 89:773–84.
DiAmbrosio, P. E. (2006). Weeble wobbles: Resilience within the psychoanalytic situation. *International Journal of Psychoanalytic Self Psychology*, 1:263–84.
Druck, A. A. (2012a). Modern conflict theory: A critical review. In: A. A. Druck, C. S. Ellman, N. Freedman, and A. Thaler (Eds.), *A New Freudian Synthesis: Clinical Process in the Next Generation*. London: Karnac Books, pp. 1–24.
Druck, A. A. (2012b). Modern structural theory. In: A. A. Druck, C. S. Ellman, N. Freedman, and A. Thaler., (Eds.), *A New Freudian Synthesis: Clinical Process in the Next Generation*. London: Karnac Books., pp. 25–50.
Druck, A. A., Ellman, C. S., Freedman, N. and Thaler, A. (2012). *A New Freudian Synthesis: Clinical Process in the Next Generation*. London: Karnac Books.
Eagle, M. N., Wakefield, J. C., and Wolitzky, D. L. (2003). Interpreting Mitchell's constructivism. *Journal of the American Psychoanalytic Association*, 51:163–78.
Edelman, G. (1987). *Neural Darwinism: The Theory of Neuronal Group Selection*. New York: Basic Books.
Edelman, G. (1990). *The Remembered Present: A Biological Theory of Consciousness*. New York: Basic Books.
Ehrenberg, D. B. (1974). The intimate edge in therapeutic relatedness. *Contemporary Psychoanalysis*, 10:423–37.
Ehrenberg, D. B. (1992). *The Intimate Edge: Extending the Reach of Psychoanalytic Interaction*. New York: Norton.
Ehrenzweig, A. (1967). *The Hidden Order of Art*. Berkeley: University of California Press.
Epstein, L. J. and Feiner, A. H. (Eds.). (1979). *Countertransference: The Therapist's Contribution to the Therapeutic Situation*. New York: Jason Aronson.
Etchegoyen, H. R. (1990). *The Fundamentals of Psychoanalytic Technique*. London: Karnac Books.
Faimberg, H. (2005a). Après coup: Revisiting what has been real. In: *The Telescoping of Generations: Listening to the Narcissistic Links between Generations*. London: Routledge, pp. 108–116.
Faimberg, H. (2005b). Après-coup. *International Journal of Psychoanalysis*, 86:1–6.
Faimberg, H. (2007). A plea for a broader concept of *Nachträglichkeit*. *Psychoanalytic Quarterly*, 76:1221–40.
Fairfield, S., Layton, L. and C. Stack (Eds.). (2002). *Bringing the Plague: Toward a Postmodern Psychoanalysis*. New York: Other Press.
Feiner, A. H. (1975). Reminiscences of supervision with Erich Fromm. *Contemporary Psychoanalysis*, 11:463–64.
Ferenczi, S. and Rank, O. (1925). *The Development of Psychoanalysis*. New York: Nervous and Mental Disease Publishing Co.
Ferro, A. (1996). *In the Analyst's Consulting Room*. Trans. P. Slotkin. Hove: Brunner-Routledge, 2002.
Ferro, A. (1999). *Psychoanalysis as Therapy and Storytelling*. Trans. P. Slotkin. Hove: Routledge, 2006.
Ferro, A. (2002a). Some implications of Bion's thought: The waking dream and narrative derivatives. *International Journal of Psychoanalysis*, 83:597–607.
Ferro, A. (2002b). *Seeds of Illness, Seeds of Recovery*. Hove: Routledge, 2004.
Ferro, A. (2006a). *Mind works: Technique and Creativity in Psychoanalysis*. Trans. P. Slotkin. New York: Routledge, 2008.

Ferro, A. (2006b). Clinical implications of Bion's thought. *International Journal of Psychoanalysis*, 87:989–1003.
Ferro, A. (2007). *Avoiding Emotions, Living Emotions*. Trans. I. Harvey. Hove: Routledge, 2011.
Ferro, A. (2009). Transformations in dreaming and characters in the psychoanalytic field. *International Journal of Psychoanalysis*, 90:209–30.
Ferro, A. and Basile, R. (2004). The psychoanalyst as individual: Self-analysis and gradients of functioning. *Psychoanalytic Quarterly*, 73:659–82.
Ferro, A. and Basile, R. (Eds.). (2009a). *The Analytic Field: A Clinical Concept*. Hove: Routledge.
Ferro, A. and Basile, R. (2009b). The universe of the field and its inhabitants. In: A. Ferro and R. Basile (Eds.), *The Analytic Field. A Clinical Concept*. New York: Routledge, pp. 5–29.
Ferro, A. and Civitarese, G. (2013). Analysts in search of an author: Voltaire or Artemisia Gentileschi? Commentary on "Field Theory in Psychoanalysis, Part II: Bionian Field Theory and Contemporary Interpersonal/Relational Psychoanalysis" by Donnel B. Stern. *Psychoanalytic Dialogues*, 23:646–53.
Fiscalini, J. (2004). *Coparticipant Psychoanalysis: Toward a New Theory of Clinical Inquiry*. New York: Columbia University Press.
Fiscalini, J. (2007). The coparticipant field: Commentary on a paper by Juan Tubert-Oklander. *Psychoanalytic Dialogues*, 17:133–41.
Flax, J. (1990). *Thinking Fragments: Psychoanalysis, Feminism, and Postmodernism in the Contemporary West*. Berkeley: University of California Press.
Flax, J. (1993). *Disputed Subjects: Essays on Psychoanalysis, Politics, and Philosophy*. New York: Routledge.
Fliess, R. (1953). Countertransference and counteridentification. *Journal of the American Psychoanalytic Assocation*, 1:268–84.
Foehl, J. C. (2010). The play's the thing: The primacy of process and the persistence of pluralism in contemporary psychoanalysis. *Contemporary Psychoanalysis*, 46:48–86.
Foehl, J. C. (2013). Field theory: Commentary on paper by Donnel B. Stern. *Psychoanalytic Dialogues*, 23:502–13.
Foehl, J. (2014). A phenomenology of depth. *Psychoanalytic Dialogues*, 24:289–303.
Fogelman, E. (1998). Group belonging and mourning as factors in resilience in second generation of Holocaust survivors. *Psychoanalytic Review*, 85:537–49.
Fonagy, P. (2006). The failure of practice to inform theory and the role of implicit theory in bridging the transmission gap. In: J. Canestri (Ed.), *Psychoanalysis: From Practice to Theory*. London: John Wiley, pp. 69–86.
Fonagy, P., Gergely, G., Jurist, E., and Target, M. (2002). *Affect Regulation, Mentalization, and the Development of the Self*. New York: Other Press.
Foxe, G. (2004). But that was in another country, and besides . . . : Collision and collusion in the countertransference between German Jewish-descended analyst and German Nazi-descended patient. *Contemporary Psychoanalysis*, 40:239–52.
Foxe, G. (2006). "I will not let you go unless you bless me": Wrestling with the angel of history in the aftermath of analytic work between a German-Jewish-descended Analyst and a German-Nazi-descended patient. *Psychoanalytic Review*, 93:57–69.
Frankel, J. B. (1998a). Are interpersonal and relational psychoanalysis the same? *Contemporary Psychoanalysis*, 34:485–500.
Frankel, J. B. (1998b). Reply to Hirsch. *Contemporary Psychoanalysis*, 34:539–41.

Freedman, N. (2012). A new Freudian synthesis: Reflections and a perspective. In: A. A. Druck, C. S. Ellman, N. Freedman, and A. Thaler (Eds.), *A New Freudian Synthesis: Clinical Process in the Next Generation*. London: Karnac Books, pp. 249–64.
Freud, S. (1895). Project for a scientific psychology. *Standard Edition*, 1:281–391.
Freud, S. (1899). Screen memories. *Standard Edition*, 3:299–322.
Freud, S. (1900). The interpretation of dreams. *Standard Edition*, 4–5.
Freud, S. (1901). The psychopathology of everyday life. *Standard Edition*, 6:vii–296.
Freud, S. (1909). Analysis of a phobia in a five-year-old boy. *Standard Edition*, 10:1–150.
Freud, S. (1913). On beginning the treatment. *Standard Edition*, 12:121–44.
Freud, S. (1918). From the history of an infantile neurosis. *Standard Edition*, 17.
Freud, S. (1937). Constructions in analysis. *Standard Edition*, 22:255–70.
Freud, S. (1950 [1887–1902]). *The Origins of Psycho-Analysis: Letters to Wilhelm Fliess, Drafts and Notes*. M. Bonaparte *et al.*, ed. Trans. E. Mosbacher and J. Strachey. London: Imago, 1954; partial revised tr. in *Standard Edition*, 3.
Fromm, E. (1941). *Escape from Freedom*. New York: Rinehart and Company.
Fromm, E. (1947). *Man for Himself*. New York: Rinehart and Company.
Fromm, E. (1955). Remarks on the problem of free association. In: D. B. Stern, C. Mann, S. Kantor and G. Schlesinger (Eds.), *Pioneers of Interpersonal Psychoanalysis*. Hillsdale, NJ: The Analytic Press, 1995, pp. 123–34.
Fromm, E. (1964/1991). The causes for the patient's change in analytic treatment. *Contemporary Psychoanalysis*, 27:608–22.
Fromm, E., Suzuki, D. T. and de Martino, R. (1970). *Zen Buddhism and Psychoanalysis*. New York: Harpers.
Fromm-Reichmann, F. (1955). *Principles of Intensive Psychotherapy*. Chicago: University of Chicago Press.
Fromm-Reichmann, F. (1959). *Psychoanalysis and Psychotherapy: Selected Papers of Frieda Fromm-Reichmann*. Chicago: University of Chicago Press.
Gadamer, H.-G. (1960). *Wahrheit und Methode: Grundzüge einer Philosophische Hermeneutik*. [*Truth and Method: Fundamentals of Philosophical Hermeneutics.*] Tübingen, Germany: Mohr.
Gadamer, H.-G. (1966). The universality of the hermeneutical problem. In: D. E. Linge (Ed.), *Philosophical Hermeneutics*. Berkeley, CA: University of California Press, 1976, pp. 3–17.
Gadamer, H.-G. (1967). On the scope and function of hermeneutical reflection. In: D. E. Linge (Ed.), *Philosophical Hermeneutics*. Berkeley, CA: University of California Press, 1976, pp. 18–43.
Gadamer, H.-G. (1976). In: D. E. Linge (Ed.), *Philosophical Hermeneutics*. Berkeley, CA: University of California Press.
Gadamer, H.-G. (2004). *Truth and Method*. Revised translation, by J. Weinsheimer and D. G. Marshall, from the 2nd edition in German (first published 1965). London: Continuum.
Galatzer-Levy, R. M. (1995). Psychoanalysis and dynamical systems theory: Prediction and self similarity. *Journal of the American Psychoanalytic Association*, 43:1085–113.
Galatzer-Levy, R. M. (2002). Emergence. *Psychoanalytic Inquiry*, 22:708–27.
Galatzer-Levy, R. (2004). Chaotic possibilities: Toward a new model of development. *International Journal of Psychoanalysis*, 85:419–42.
Galatzer-Levy, R. M. (2009a). Finding your way through chaos, fractals, and other exotic mathematical objects: A guide for the perplexed. *Journal of the American Psychoanalytic Association*, 57:1227–49.

Galatzer-Levy, R. M. (2009b). Good vibrations: Analytic process as coupled oscillations. *International Journal of Psychoanalysis*, 90:983–1007.
Gerson, S. (1996). Neutrality, resistance, and self-disclosure in an intersubjective psychoanalysis. *Psychoanalytic Dialogues*, 6:623–45.
Gerson, S. (2004). The relational unconscious: A core element of intersubjectivity, thirdness, and clinical process. *Psychoanalytic Quarterly*, 73:63–98.
Gerson, S. (2009). When the third is dead: Memory, mourning, and witnessing in the aftermath of the holocaust. *International Journal of Psychoanalysis*, 90:1341–57.
Ghent, E. (1990). Masochism, submission, surrender: Masochism as a perversion of surrender. *Contemporary Psychoanalysis*, 26:108–36.
Gill, M. M. (1983). *The Analysis of Transference*, Vol. 1. New York: International Universities Press.
Gill, M. M. (1995). *Psychoanalysis in Transition*. Hillsdale, NJ: The Analytic Press.
Green, A. (1975). The analyst, symbolization, and absence in the analytic setting. *International Journal of Psychoanalysis*, 56:1–22.
Green, A. (1986). The dead mother. In: *On private madness*. London: The Hogarth Press, pp. 142–73.
Green, A. (1999). *The Work of the Negative*. Trans. A. Weller. London: Free Association Books.
Green, A. (2005). The illusion of common ground and mythical pluralism. *International Journal of Psychoanalysis*, 86:627–32.
Green, M. R. (1964). Her life. In: M. Green (Ed.), *Interpersonal Psychoanalysis: The Selected Papers of Clara M. Thompson*. New York: Basic Books, pp. 347–77.
Greenberg, J. (1995). Psychoanalytic technique and the interactive matrix. *Psychoanalytic Quarterly*, 64:1–22.
Greenberg, J. R. and Mitchell, S. A. (1983). *Object Relations in Psychoanalytic Theory*. Cambridge, MA: Harvard University Press.
Grossmark, R. (2012). The unobtrusive relational analyst. *Psychoanalytic Dialogues*, 22:629–46.
Grotstein, J. (2000). *Who is the Dreamer Who Dreams the Dream? A Study of Psychic Presences*. Hove: Routledge.
Grotstein, J. (2002). "We are such stuff as dreams are made of": Annotations on dreams and dreaming in Bion's works. In: C. Neri, M. Pines, and R. Friedman (Eds.), *Dreams in Group Psychotherapy: Theory and Technique*, London: Kingsley, pp. 110–45.
Grotstein, J. (2007). *A Beam of Intense Darkness. Wilfred Bion's Legacy to Psychoanalysis*. London: Karnac Books.
Grotstein, J. (2009). "The play's the thing in which I'll catch the conscience of the king!" Psychoanalysis as a passion play. In: A. Ferro and R. Basile (Eds.), *The Analytic Field: A Clinical Concept*. New York: Routledge, pp. 189–212.
Grünbaum, A. (1984). *The Foundations of Psychoanalysis: A Philosophical Critique*. Berkeley: University of California Press.
Grünbaum, A. (1993). *Validation in the Clinical Theory of Psychoanalysis: A Study in the Philosophy of Psychoanalysis (Psychological Issues)*. Madison, CT: International Universities Press.
Guralnik, O. (2014). The dead baby. *Psychoanalytic Dialogues*, 24:129–45.
Heimann, P. (1950). On counter-transference. *Inernational Journal of Psycho-Analysis*, 31:81–4.
Hirsch, I. (1996). Observing-participation, mutual enactment, and the new classical models. *Contemporary Psychoanalysis*, 32:359–83.

Hirsch, I. (1997). The integration of the interpersonal school into the psychoanalytic mainstream: A review essay on *A Meeting of minds: Mutuality in psychoanalysis* by Lewis Aron. *Contemporary Psychoanalysis*, 33:656–69.

Hirsch, I. (1998). Further thoughts about interpersonal and relational perspectives: Reply to Jay Frankel. *Contemporary Psychoanalysis*, 34:501–38.

Hirsch, I. (2014). *The Interpersonal Tradition: The Origins of Psychoanalytic Subjectivity*. New York: Routledge.

Hoffman, I. Z. (1983). The patient as the interpreter of the analyst's experience. In: *Ritual and Spontaneity in the Psychoanalytic Process: A Dialectical-Constructivist View*. Hillsdale, NJ: The Analytic Press, 1998.

Hoffman, I. Z. (1996). The intimate and ironic authority of the analyst's presence. In: I. Z. Hoffman (Ed.), *Ritual and Spontaneity in the Psychoanalytic Process: A Dialectical-Constructivist View*. Hillsdale, NJ: The Analytic Press, pp. 69–95.

Hoffman, I. Z. (1998). *Ritual and Spontaneity in the Psychoanalytic Process: A Dialectical-Constructivist View*. Hilldale, NJ: The Analytic Press.

Hoffman, I. Z. (2006). The myths of free association and the potentials of the analytic relationship. *International Journal of Psychoanalysis*, 87:43–61.

Hoffman, I. Z. (2009). Doublethinking our way to "scientific" legitimacy: The desiccation of human experience. *Journal of the American Psychoanalytic Association*, 57:1043–69.

Hogman, F. (1998). Resilience in ethnic experiences with massive trauma and violence. *Psychoanalytic Review*, 85:487–8.

Howell, E. (2006). *The Dissociative Mind*. New York: Routledge.

Isaacs, S. (1948). The nature and function of phantasy. *International Journal of Psychoanalysis*, 29:73–97.

Jacobs, T. (1991). *The Use of the Self: Countertransference and Communication in the Analytic Situation*. Madison, CT: International Universities Press.

Jacobs, T. (2013). *The Possible Profession*. New York: Routledge.

James, W. (1890). *Principles of Psychology*. New York: Henry Holt.

Jiménez, J. (2009). Grasping psychoanalysts' practice in its own merits. *International Journal of Psychoanalysis*, 90:231–48.

Kalayjian, A. and Shahinian, S. P. (1998). Recollections of aged Armenian survivors of the Ottoman Turkish genocide: Resilience through endurance, coping, and life accomplishments. *Psychoanalytic Review*, 85:489–504.

Keats, J. (1899). *The Complete Poetical Works and Letters of John Keats, Cambridge Edition*. Boston: Houghton, Mifflin and Company.

Kermode, F. (1967). *The Sense of an Ending: Studies in the Theory of Fiction*. New York: Oxford University Press.

Kernberg, O. (1965). Notes on countertransference. *Journal of the American Psychoanalytic Association*, 13:38–56.

Kernberg, O. F. (1986). Institutional problems of psychoanalytic education. *Journal of the American Psychoanalytic Association*, 34:799–834.

Kernberg, O. F. (1996). Thirty methods to destroy the creativity of psychoanalytic candidates. *International Journal of Psychoanalysis*, 77:1031–40.

Klein, G. (1976). *Psychoanalytic Theory: An Exploration of Essentials*. New York: International Universities Press.

Knoblauch, S. H. (2000). *The Musical Edge of Therapeutic Relatedness*. Hillsdale, NJ: The Analytic Press.

Kris, E. (1952). *Psychoanalytic Explorations in Art*. New York: International Universities Press.

Kuhn, T. S. (1962). *The Structure of Scientific Revolutions*. Chicago: University of Chicago Press.
Kwawer, J. S. (1975). A case seminar with Erich Fromm. *Contemporary Psychoanalysis*, 11:453–5.
Kwawer, J. S. (1991). Fromm on clinical psychoanalysis. *Contemporary Psychoanalysis*, 27:608–22.
Lacan, J. (1977). *Ecrits: A Selection*. Trans. Alan Sheridan. London and New York: Tavistock/Norton.
Lacan, J. (2004). The function and field of speech and language in psychoanalysis. In: *Écrits: A Selection*. Trans. B. Fink, H. Fink, and R. Grigg. New York: Norton. (Original work published 1953.)
Lakoff, G. and Johnson, M. (1999). *Philosophy in the Flesh: The Embodied Mind and its Challenge to Western Thought*. New York: Basic Books.
Lakoff, G. and Johnson, M. (2003). *Metaphors We Live By*, 2nd edition. Chicago: University of Chicago Press.
Landis, B. (1981). Fromm's approach to psychoanalytic technique. *Contemporary Psychoanalysis*, 17:537–51.
Laplanche, J. (1976). *Life and Death in Psychoanalysis*. Trans. J. Mehlman. Baltimore: Johns Hopkins University Press. (Original work published 1970.)
Laplanche, J. (1999). Notes on afterwardsness. In: J. Fletcher and L. Thurston (Eds.), *Essays on Otherness*. Trans. P. Slotkin and L. Hill. London: Routledge. (Original work published 1998.)
Laplanche, J. and Pontalis, J.-B. (1968). Fantasy and the origins of sexuality. *International Journal of Psychoanalysis*, 49, 1–18. (Originally published 1964.)
Laplanche, J. and Pontalis, J.-B. (1974). *The Language of Psycho-Analysis*. Trans. D. Nicholson-Smith. London: Hogarth/Institute of Psycho-Analysis; New York: Norton. (Originally published 1967.)
Laub, D. (1991). Truth and testimony: The process and the struggle. *American Imago*, 48: 75–91.
Laub, D. (1992a). Bearing witness or the vicissitudes of witnessing. In: S. Felman and D. Laub, (Eds.), *Testimony: Crises of Witnessing in Literature, Psychoanalysis, and History*. New York: Routledge, pp. 57–74.
Laub, D. (1992b). An event without a witness: Truth, testimony, and survival. In: S. Felman and D. Laub (Eds.), *Testimony: Crises of Witnessing in Literature, Psychoanalysis, and History*. New York: Routledge, pp. 75–92.
Laub, D. (2005). Traumatic shutdown of symbolization and narrative: A death instinct derivative? *Contemporary Psychoanalysis*, 41:307–26.
Laub, D. and Auerhahn, N. (1989). Failed empathy: A central theme in the survivor's Holocaust experience. *Psychoanalytic Psychology*, 6:377–400.
Lecours, S. and Bouchard, M. (1997). Dimensions of mentalisation: Outlining levels of psychic transformation. *International Journal of Psychoanalysis*, 78:855–75.
Leed, E. J. (1979). *No Man's Land: Combat and Identity in World War I*. Cambridge: Cambridge University Press.
Levenson, E. A. (1972). *The Fallacy of Understanding*. New York: Basic Books.
Levenson, E. A. (1979). Language and healing. *Journal of the American Academy of Psychoanalysis*, 7: 271–82.
Levenson, E. A. (1982). Follow the fox: An inquiry into the vicissitudes of psychoanalytic supervision. *Contemporary Psychoanalysis*, 18:1–15.
Levenson, E. A. (1983). *The Ambiguity of Change*. New York: Basic Books.

Levenson, E. A. (1987). The purloined self. *Journal of the American Academy of Psychoanalysis and Dynamic Psychiatry*, 15:481–90.

Levenson, E. A. (1991). In: A. H. Feiner (Ed.), *The Purloined Self: Interpersonal Perspectives in Psychoanalysis*. New York: Contemporary Psychoanalysis Books.

Levenson, E. A. (1992). Harry Stack Sullivan: From interpersonal psychiatry to interpersonal psychoanalysis. *Contemporary Psychoanalysis*, 28:450–66.

Levenson, E. A. (2001). The enigma of the unconscious. *Contemporary Psychoanalysis*, 37:239–52.

Levenson, E. A. (2008). In search of the person in the patient: An interpersonal perspective on "Roles in the psychoanalytic relationship". *Psychoanalytic Dialogues*, 18:89–94.

Levine, H. B. (in press). The field theory of Antonino Ferro: An introduction. In: H. B. Levine and G. Reed (Eds.), Responses to the Work of Antonino Ferro. *Psychoanalytic Inquiry*.

Levine, H. B., Reed, G. S., and Scarfone, D. (Eds.). (2013). *Unrepresented States and the Construction of Meaning: Clinical and Theoretical Contributions*. London: Karnac Books.

Lewin, K. (1935). *A Dynamic Theory of Personality*. New York: McGraw-Hill.

Lewin, K. (1936). *Principles of Topological Psychology*. New York: McGraw-Hill.

Lewin, K. (1951). *Field Theory in Social Science*. New York: Harper and Brothers.

Linge, D. E. (1976). Editor's introduction. In: H.-G. Gadamer (Ed.), *Philosophical Hermeneutics*. Trans. D. E. Linge. Berkeley: University of California Press, pp. xi–lviii.

Lionells, M. L., Fiscalini, J., Mann, C. and Stern, D. B. (Eds.). (1995). *The Handbook of Interpersonal Psychoanalysis*. Hillsdale, NJ: The Analytic Press.

Little, M. (1951). Counter-transference and the patient's response to it. *International Journal of Psychanalysis*, 32:32–40.

Loch, W. (1977). Some comments on the subject of psychoanalysis and truth. In: J. H. Smith (Ed.), *Thought, Consciousness, and Reality*. New Haven: Yale University Press, pp. 217–56.

Loewald, H. W. (1960). On the therapeutic action of psycho-analysis. *International Journal of Psychoanalysis*, 41:16–33.

Loewald, H. (1978). Primary process, secondary process, and language. In: *The Essential Loewald: Collected Papers and Monographs*. Hagerstown, MD: University Publishing Group, pp. 178–204.

Loewald, H. (2000). *The Essential Loewald: Papers and Monographs*. Hagerstown, MD: University Publishing Group.

Lothane, Z. (2006). Reciprocal free association: Listening with the third ear as an instrument in psychoanalysis. *Psychoanalytic Psychology*, 23:711–27.

Malcolm, J. (1981). *Psychoanalysis: The Impossible Profession*. New York: Knopf.

McLaughlin, J. T. (1981). Transference, psychic reality, and countertransference. *Psychoanalytic Quarterly*, 50:639–64.

McLaughlin, J. T. (1991). Clinical and theoretical aspects of enactment. *Journal of the American Psychoanalytic Association*, 39:595–614.

McLaughlin, J. T. (2005). *The Healer's Bent: Solitude and Dialogue in the Clinical Encounter*, ed. W. Cornell. New York: Routledge.

Merleau-Ponty, M. (1942). *The Structure of Behavior*. Trans. A. Fischer. Boston: Beacon, 1963.

Merleau-Ponty, M. (1945). *Phenomenology of Perception*. Trans. Colin Smith. New York: Routledge, 2002.

Merleau-Ponty, M. (1964). *Signs*. Evanston, IL: Northwestern University Press.

Milner, M. (1969). *The Hands of the Living God.* London: Hogarth.
Milner, M. (1987). *The Suppressed Madness of Sane Men: 44 Years of Exploring Psychoanalysis.* London: New Library of Psychoanalysis/Routledge.
Mitchell, S. A. (1988). *Relational Concepts in Psychoanalysis: An Integration.* Cambridge, MA: Harvard University Press.
Mitchell, S. A. (1993). *Hope and Dread in Psychoanalysis.* New York: Basic Books.
Mitchell, S. A. (1997). *Influence and Autonomy in Psychoanalysis.* Hillsdale, NJ: The Analytic Press.
Mitchell, S. A. (2000). *Relationality.* Hillsdale, NJ: The Analytic Press.
Mitchell, S. A. and Aron, L. (Eds.). (1999). *Relational Psychoanalysis: The Emergence of a Tradition.* Hillsdale, NJ: The Analytic Press.
Mitrani, J. (1995). Toward an understanding of unmentalized experience. *Psychoanalytic Quarterly,* 64:68–112.
Modell, A. H. (1984). *Psychoanalysis in a New Context.* New York: International Universities Press.
Modell, A. (1990). *Other Times, Other Realities.* Cambridge, MA: Harvard University Press.
Modell, A. (2003). *Imagination and the Meaningful Brain.* Cambridge, MA: MIT Press.
Modell, A. (2005). Emotional memory, metaphor, and meaning. *Psychoanalytic Inquiry,* 25:555–68.
Modell, A. (2009). Metaphor: The bridge between feelings and knowledge. *Psychoanalytic Inquiry,* 29:6–17.
Modell, A. (2011). Not even wrong. *Psychoanalytic Inquiry,* 126–33.
Mosher, P. W. and Richards, A. (2005). The history of membership and certification in the APsaA: Old demons, new debates. *Psychoanalytic Review,* 92:865–94.
Murphy, G. and Cattell, E. (1952). Sullivan's field theory. In: P. Mullahy (Ed.), *The Contributions of Harry Stack Sullivan: A Symposium on Interpersonal Theory in Psychiatry and Social Science.* New York: Hermitage House, pp. 161–79.
Nagata, D. K. and Takeshita, Y. J. (1998). Coping and resilience across generations: Japanese Americans and the World War II internment. *Psychoanalytic Review,* 85:587–613.
Nagel, T. (1986). *The View from Nowhere.* Oxford: Oxford University Press.
Ogden, T. H. (1992). The dialectically constituted/decentred subject of psychoanalysis. I. The Freudian subject. *International Journal of Psychoanalysis,* 73:517–26.
Ogden, T. H (1994a). The analytic third: Working with intersubjective facts. *International Journal of Psychoanalysis,* 75:3–19.
Ogden, T. H (1994b). *Subjects of Analysis.* Northvale, NJ: Aronson.
Ogden, T. H. (1997). *Reverie and Interpretation: Sensing Something Human.* Northvale, NJ: Jason Aronson.
Ogden, T. H. (2001). *Conversations at the Frontier of Dreaming.* Northvale, NJ: Jason Aronson.
Ogden, T. H. (2004). The analytic third: Implications for psychoanalytic theory and technique. *Psychoanalytic Quarterly,* 73:167–95.
Ogden, T. H. (2005). *This Art of Psychoanalysis: Dreaming Undreamt Dreams and Interrupted Cries.* London: New Library of Psychoanalysis (Routledge).
Ornstein, A. (1985). Survival and recovery. *Psychoanalytic Inquiry,* 5:99–130.
Ornstein, A. (1994). Trauma, memory, and psychic continuity. *Progress in Self Psychology,* 10:131–46.
Parens, H., Blum, H. P., and Akhtar, S. (Eds.). (2009). *The Unbroken Soul: Tragedy, Trauma, and Resilience.* New York: Jason Aronson.

Peltz, R. and Goldberg, P. (2013). Field conditions: Discussion of "Field theory in psychoanalysis, Part II: Bionian field theory and contemporary interpersonal/relational psychoanalysis" by Donnel B. Stern. *Psychoanalytic Dialogues*, 23:660–6.

Phillips, J. (1991). Hermeneutics in psychoanalysis: Review and reconsideration. *Psychoanalysis and Contemporary Thought*, 14:371–424.

Pizer, S. A. (1996). The distributed self: Introduction to symposium on "The multiplicity of self and analytic technique". *Contemporary Psychoanalysis*, 32:499–507.

Pizer, S. A. (1998). *Building Bridges: The Negotiation of Paradox in Psychoanalysis*. New York: Routledge.

Poland, W. S. (2000). The analyst's witnessing and otherness. *Journal of the American Psychoanalytic Association*, 48:17–34.

Poland, W. S. (2011). Self-analysis and creativity: Views from inside and outside. *Psychoanalytic Quarterly*, LXXX:987–1003.

Polanyi, M. (1958). *Personal Knowledge. Revised Edition*. New York: Harper Torchbooks, 1964.

Protter, B. (1985). Toward an emergent psychoanalytic epistemology. *Contemporary Psychoanalysis*, 21:208–27.

Protter, B. (1988). Ways of knowing in psychoanalysis. *Contemporary Psychoanalysis*, 24:498–526.

Putnam, H. (1978). *Meaning and the Moral Sciences*. Henley: Routledge and Kegan Paul.

Racker, H. (1960). *Estudios Sobre Técnica Psicoanalítica*. Buenos Aires: Paidós. Translated as *Transference and Countertransference*. London: Hogarth Press and Institute of Psycho-Analysis, 1968.

Racker, H. (1968). *Transference and countertransference*. New York: International Universities Press.

Rangell, L. (2002). The theory of psychoanalysis: Vicissitudes of its evolution. *Journal of the American Psychoanalytic Assocation*, 50:1109–37.

Rangell, L. (2006). An analysis of the course of psychoanalysis: The case for a unitary theory. *Psychoanalytic Psychology*, 23:217–38.

Rangell, L. (2008). Reconciliation: The continuing role of theory. *Journal of the American Academy of Psychoanalysis*, 36:217–33.

Reis, B. E. (1995). Time as the missing dimension in traumatic memory and dissociative subjectivity. In: J. L. Alpert (Ed.), *Sexual Abuse Recalled*. Northvale, NJ: Jason Aronson, pp. 215–33.

Reis, B. E. (1999a). Adventures of the dialectic. *Psychoanalytic Dialogues*, 9:407–14.

Reis, B. E. (1999b). Thomas Ogden's phenomenological turn. *Psychoanalytic Dialogues*, 9:371–93.

Reis, B. E. (2006). Even better than the real thing. *Contemporary Psychoanalysis*, 42:177–96.

Reis, B. E. (2009). Performative and enactive features of psychoanalytic witnessing: The transference as the scene of address. *International Journal of Psychoanalysis*, 90:1359–72.

Reis, B. E. (2010). Enactive fields: An approach to interaction in the Kleinian-Bionian Model: Commentary on paper by Lawrence J. Brown. *Psychoanalytic Dialogues*, 20:695–703.

Richards, A. (2013). The American Psychoanalytic Association's long march to inclusion. *Bulletin of the Association for Psychoanalytic Medicine*, 48:4–16.

Richardson, F. C. and Zeddies, T. J. (2004). Psychoanalysis and the good life. *Contemporary Psychoanalysis*, 40:617–57.

Richman, S. (2006). Finding one's voice: Transforming trauma into autobiographical narrative. *Contemporary Psychoanalysis*, 42:639–50.

Ringstrom, P. (2001). Cultivating the improvisational in psychoanalytic treatment. *Psychoanalytic Dialogues*, 11:727–54.

Ringstrom, P. (2007). Scenes that write themselves: Improvisational moments in relational psychoanalysis. *Psychoanalytic Dialogues*, 17:69–100.

Rousseau, C., Said, T. M., Gagné, M., and Bibeau, G. (1998). Resilience in unaccompanied minors from the North of Somalia. *Psychoanalytic Review*, 85:615–37.

Safran, J. D. (2012). Doublethinking or dialectical thinking: A critical appreciation of Hoffman's "Doublethinking" critique. *Psychoanalytic Dialogues*, 22:710–20.

Sandler, J. (1976). Countertransference and role-responsiveness. *International Review of Psychoanalysis*, 3:43–7.

Sandler, J. (1983). Reflections on some relations between psychoanalytic concepts and psychoanalytic practice. *International Journal of Psychoanalysis*, 64:35–45.

Sass, L. A. (1988). Humanism, hermeneutics, and humanistic psychoanalysis: Differing conceptions of subjectivity. *Psychoanalysis and Contemporary Thought*, 12:433–504.

Schachtel, E. (1959). *Metamorphosis: On the Conflict of Human Development and the Psychology of Creativity*. New York: Basic Books.

Schachtel, E. (1973). On attention, selective inattention, and experience: An inquiry into attention as an attitude. In: E. G. Witenberg (Ed.), *Interpersonal Explorations in Psychoanalysis*. New York: Basic Books, pp. 40–66.

Schafer, R. (1983). *The Analytic Attitude*. New York: Basic Books.

Schafer, R. (1992). *Retelling a Life: Narration and Dialogue in Psychoanalysis*. New York: Basic Books.

Schecter, D. E. (1981). Contributions of Erich Fromm. *Contemporary Psychoanalysis*, 17:468–80.

Schneider, J. A. (2003). Janus-faced resilience in the analysis of a severely traumatized patient. *Psychoanalytic Review*, 90:869–87.

Schön, D. A. (1983). *The Reflective Practitioner: How Professionals Think in Action*. New York: Basic Books.

Schön, D. A. (1987). *Educating the Reflective Practitioner: Toward a New Design for Teaching and Learning in the Professions*. San Francisco: Jossey-Bass.

Searles, H. (1955). The informational value of the supervisor's emotional experiences. *Psychiatry*, 18:135–46.

Searles, H. F. (1965). *Collected Papers on Schizophrenia and Related Subjects*. New York: International Universities Press.

Searles, H. F. (1979). *Countertransference and Related Subjects: Selected Papers*. New York: International Universities Press.

Segal, H. (1957). Notes on symbol formation. *International Journal of Psychoanalysis*, 38:391–7.

Seligman, S. (2005). Dynamic systems theories as a metaframework for psychoanalysis. *Psychoanalytic Dialogues*, 15:285–319.

Seligman, S. (2014). Paying attention and feeling puzzled: The analytic mindset as an agent of therapeutic change. *Psychoanalytic Dialogues*, 24: 648–62.

Shattuck, R. (1984). Life before language. *The New York Times Book Review*, April 1, pp. 1, 31.

Sigal, J. J. (1998). Long-term effects of the Holocaust: Empirical evidence for resilience in the first, second, and third generation. *Psychoanalytic Review*, 85:579–85.

Slochower, J. (1999). Interior experience within analytic process. *Psychoanalytic Dialogues*, 9:789–809.

Slochower, J. (2004). But what do you want?: The location of emotional experience. *Contemporary Psychoanalysis*, 40:577–602.

Spence, D. P. (1982). *Narrative Truth and Historical Truth: Meaning and Interpretation in Psychoanalysis*. New York: Norton.

Spezzano, C. (1993). A relational model of inquiry and truth: The place of psychoanalysis in the human conversation. *Psychoanalytic Dialogues*, 3:177–208.

Steele, R. S. (1979). Psychoanalysis and hermeneutics. *International Review of Psycho-Analysis*, 6:389–411.

Stern, D. B. (1983). Unformulated experience: From familiar chaos to creative disorder. *Contemporary Psychoanalysis*, 19:71–99.

Stern, D. B. (1985). Some controversies regarding constructivism and psychoanalysis. *Contemporary Psychoanalysis*, 21:201–8.

Stern, D. B. (1989). The analyst's unformulated experience of the patient. *Contemporary Psychoanalysis*, 25:1–33.

Stern, D. B. (1990). Courting surprise: Unbidden perceptions in clinical practice. *Contemporary Psychoanalysis*, 26:452–78.

Stern, D. B. (1991). A philosophy for the embedded analyst: Gadamer's hermeneutics and the social paradigm of psychoanalysis. *Contemporary Psychoanalysis*, 27:51–80.

Stern, D. B. (1992). Commentary on constructivism in clinical psychoanalysis. *Psychoanalytic Dialogues*, 2:331–63.

Stern, D. B. (1995). Cognition and language. In: M. L. Lionells, J. Fiscalini, C. Mann, and D. B. Stern (Eds.), *The Handbook of Interpersonal Psychoanalysis*. Hillsdale, NJ: The Analytic Press, pp. 79–138.

Stern, D. B. (1997). *Unformulated Experience: From Dissociation to Imagination in Psychoanalysis*. New York: Routledge.

Stern, D. B. (2002). Words and wordlessness in the psychoanalytic situation. *Journal of the American Psychoanalytic Association*, 50:221–47.

Stern, D. B. (2003). The fusion of horizons: Dissociation, enactment, and understanding. *Psychoanalytic Dialogues*, 13:843–73.

Stern, D. B. (2004). The eye sees itself: Dissociation, enactment, and the achievement of conflict. *Contemporary Psychoanalysis*, 40:197–237.

Stern, D. B. (2009a). Shall the twain meet? Metaphor, dissociation, and co-occurrence. *Psychoanalytic Inquiry*, 29:79–90.

Stern, D. B. (2009b). Partners in thought: A clinical process theory of narrative. *Psychoanalytic Quarterly*, 78:701–31.

Stern, D. B. (2010a). *Partners in Thought: Working with Unformulated Experience, Dissociation, and Enactment*. New York: Routledge.

Stern, D. B. (2010b). Unconscious fantasy versus unconscious relatedness: Comparing interpersonal/relational and Freudian approaches to clinical practice. *Contemporary Psychoanalysis*, 46:101–11.

Stern, D. B. (2012). Witnessing across time: Accessing the present from the past and the past from the present. *Psychoanalytic Quarterly*, 81:53–81.

Stern, D. B. (2013a). Field theory in psychoanalysis, Part I: Harry Stack Sullivan and Madeleine and Willy Baranger. *Psychoanalytic Dialogues,* 23:487–501.

Stern, D. B. (2013b). Field theory in psychoanalysis, Part II: Bionian field theory and contemporary interpersonal/relational psychoanalysis. *Psychoanalytic Dialogues*, 23:630–45.

Stern, D. B. (2013c). Relational freedom and therapeutic action. *Journal of the American Psychoanalytic Association*, 61:227–55.

Stern, D. N. (2004). *The Present Moment in Psychotherapy and Everyday Life*. New York: Norton.
Sullivan, H. S. (1940). *Conceptions of Modern Psychiatry*. New York: Norton, 1953.
Sullivan, H. S. (1947a). Ten years of *Psychiatry*: a statement by the editor. *Psychiatry*, 10:433–35.
Sullivan, H. S. (1947b). The study of psychiatry: Three orienting lectures. *Psychiatry*, 10:355–71.
Sullivan, H. S. (1948). The meaning of anxiety in psychiatry and in life. In: *The Fusion of Psychiatry and Social Science*. New York: Norton, 1971, pp. 229–54.
Sullivan, H. S. (1953). In: H. S. Perry and M. L. Gawel (Eds.), *The Interpersonal Theory of Psychiatry*, New York: Norton.
Sullivan, H. S. (1954). In: H. S. Perry and M. L. Gawel (Eds.), *The Psychiatric Interview*. New York: Norton, 1970.
Sullivan, H. S. (1956). Selective inattention. In: *Clinical Studies in Psychiatry*. New York: Norton, pp. 38–76.
Symington, N. (1983). The analyst's act of freedom as agent of therapeutic change. *International Review of Psycho-Analysis*, 10:283–91.
Tauber, E. S. (1954). Exploring the therapeutic use of counter-transference data. *Psychiatry*, 13:332–6.
Tauber, E. S. (1959). The sense of immediacy in Fromm's conceptions. In: S. Arieti (Ed.), *The American Handbook of Psychiatry*. New York: Basic Books, pp. 1811–15.
Tauber, E. S. and Green, M. R. (1959). *Prelogical Experience: An Inquiry into Dreams and Other Creative Processes*. Hillsdale, NJ: The Analytic Press, 2006.
Thompson, C. M. (1950). *Psychoanalysis: Evolution and Development*. New York: Hermitage.
Thompson, C. M. (1958). The emotional climate of psychoanalytic institutes. In: M. Green (Ed.), *Interpersonal Psychoanalysis: The Selected Papers of Clara M. Thompson*. New York: Basic Books, 1964, pp. 54–62.
Thompson, C. M. (1964). In: M. Green (Ed.), *Interpersonal Psychoanalysis: Selected Papers of Clara M. Thompson*. New York: Basic Books.
Tower, L. E. (1956). Countertransference. *Journal of the American Psychoanalytic Assocation*, 4:224–55.
Tubert-Oklander, J. (2007). The whole and the parts: Working in the analytic field. *Psychoanalytic Dialogues*, 17:115–32.
Tublin, S. (2011). Discipline and freedom in relational technique. *Contemporary Psychoanalysis*, 47:519–46.
Ullman, C. (2006). Bearing witness: Across the barriers in society and in the clinic. *Psychoanalytic Dialogues*, 16:181–98.
Valent, P. (1998). Resilience in child survivors of the Holocaust: Toward the concept of resilience. *Psychoanalytic Review*, 85:517–35.
Wachtel, P. L. (2003). The surface and the depths: The metaphor of depth in psychoanalysis and the ways in which it can mislead. *Contemporary Psychoanalysis*, 39:5–26.
Wachtel, P. L. (2014). Depth, perception, and action: Past, present, and future. *Psychoanalytic Dialogues*, 24:332–40.
Wilner, W. (1999). The un-consciousing of awareness in psychoanalytic therapy. *Contemporary Psychoanalysis*, 35:617–28.
Winnicott, D. W. (1949). Hate in the counter-transference. *International Journal of Psychoanalysis*, 30:69–74.
Winnicott, D. W. (1971). *Playing and Reality*. London: Tavistock.
Wolstein, B. (1959). *Countertransference*. New York: Grune and Stratton.
Wolstein, B. (1964). *Freedom to Experience*. New York: Grune and Stratton.

Index

abstraction 84–5
accretion model 223–5, 231
adult-onset trauma 146
affect 43–4, 231–2; the Barangers 79–80; Bionian field theory compared with interpersonal/relational psychoanalysis 85–6, 96–7, 107
affect categories 133–4, 151
allowing 23
alphabetization 85, 86
ambiguity, essential 8, 68–71
American Institute of Psychoanalysis 47, 59
American mainstream psychoanalysis 31, 45–58; acceptance of the interpersonal field 52–8; ostracism of interpersonal psychoanalysis 45–52, 55
American Psychoanalytic Association (APsaA) 42, 52, 53, 58, 59; exclusionary practices 50–1
analyst's authority 104–6, 180, 229
analyst's conduct 73–6, 78–9, 80, 81
analytic relationship 91–5
analytic third 89–90, 106–7
anxiety of influence 55
Argyris, C. 157
Aristotle 188
art 227–9; Matisse in the process of painting 194–5, 196, 199–200
Atwood, G.E. 176, 185
authenticity 43–4
authoritarianism 57–8, 104–5
authority 180, 229; cultural differences 104–6

Balint, E. 22
Balint, M. 22
Barangers, the (M. and W.) 26, 31–2, 64, 65, 66–7, 81; affect 79–80; analyst's conduct 73–6; enactments and bastions 76–9, 112; essential ambiguity 7–8, 68–71; field theory 67–80; unconscious phantasy 71–4, 91
Bartlett, F.C. 227
Basile, R. 66–7, 100–1
bastions/bulwarks 76–9, 112
being 34
Benjamin, J. 89–90, 224
Bernstein, R. 205
beta-elements 135
Bion, W.R. 15, 67, 71, 87, 88
Bionian field theory (BFT) 54, 64, 65; compared with interpersonal/relational psychoanalysis 14–15, 32, 83–107
bi-personal field 68, 69, 70
Birksted-Breen, D. 153
Bloom, H. 55
Board on Professional Standards (BOPS) 51
Bollas, C. 117, 218
Bone, H. 42
Botella, C. and S. 86
Boulanger, G. 146, 147
Bridgman, P. 49
Bromberg, P.M. 19, 20–1, 86, 90, 211
Brown, L.J. 60–3
Bruner, J. 23

Caligor, L. 61–2
Canestri, J. 176, 185
care, professional 189
case studies 204
casting of characters 88
Cattell, E. 38–9, 81
"cellar" clinical illustration 8–14
change 40; social 179–81; symptom relief and other changes 190–1
children, working with 20
choice of interpretation 97–103
chronos (scientific/objective time) 135–6
Civitarese, G. 16–17, 31
client vs patient terminology 189
clinical collaboration 4, 13, 34, 84–5, 105
clinical illustrations: felt sense of emergence 8–14; hard-to-engage patient 209–19; relational freedom 118–26; unconscious relatedness 158–62; witnessing 140–6
clinical process 2–3, 23, 42–3, 164; hard-to-engage patient 208–19; process research 193–4
clinical supervision 43, 61–2, 174
co-creation 84–5, 95–7
coinciding phantasies 73–4
collaboration, clinical 4, 13, 34, 84–5, 105
comfort, retreat to 227
commitment 231, 232; risks that come with commitments to theory 24–9
communication difficulties 175
complementarity 224
Conci, M. 81–2
conduct: analyst's 73–6, 78–9, 80, 81; Sullivan's concept of the field 38
confrontational radicals 25
connection, emotional 209–12
consequential uniqueness 193
constrictions 24; relaxation and relational freedom 115–16, 126–30
constructivism 69, 97, 98, 169, 171
containment 87, 98–9
contemporary Freudian approaches 32–3, 155–64
context of application 181–4
continuous productive unfolding 8–14, 214

control 193
conventionalisation 227
Cooper, S.H. 25–6
Corbett, K. 19, 20, 25
countertransference 39–40, 53, 63; the Barangers 74–6; hard-to-engage patients 206–7, 208; transference–countertransference 40, 62, 111
countertransference dreams 62
countertransference micro-neurosis 77
courting surprise 109, 115
creativity 23, 194–6; revolution model 227–30
Crowley, R. 42
culture 170; cultural differences 104–6
curiosity 23, 27, 164, 190–1; hard-to-engage patient 212–14, 219; ideal psychoanalytic institute 34, 220–32

Dahl, G. 153
"Darryl" 143–6
Davies, J. 19, 21
dead third 148–9
dedifferentiated perception 228–30
deepest nondefensive intentions 117
depth 4, 5–6; as a field concept 6–8
derealization, retrospective 146–53
descriptive process research 193–4
detailed inquiry 43, 175
diagnostic formulation of hard-to-engage patients 206, 208
dialectical thinking 95, 224–5
Dilthey, W. 197
discipline 230
dissociation 30, 111–12, 139, 146–7, 164
divergent ideas 220–32
drive 49, 53, 181–2; the Barangers' uncoupling of phantasy and 71–2
drive/structure models 5–6
Druck, A.A. 17

Edelman, G. 133
effective surprise 23
ego psychology 17, 183
Ehrenzweig, A. 227–30, 231
emergence 1–31, 115, 193; clinical illustration of the felt sense of 8–14; felt sense of 3–4, 6–14; link to the

unconscious 2, 14–18; living-knowing gap 30–1; relational freedom 118; in the third person 2–3; in the work of interpersonal and relational writers 18–24
emotional categories 133–4, 151
emotional connection 209–12
empiricism 182, 183; *see also* quantitative psychotherapy research
enactments 7–8, 34, 40, 48, 75, 111–12, 115; bastions and 76–9, 112; hard-to-engage patients 213–14; sense of groping and being pulled 184–5
engagement 27–8; hard-to-engage patients 206–19
epistemological pluralism 167
espoused theories 157
essential ambiguity 8, 68–71
Etchegoyen, H.R. 81–2
ethics 188
evaluation of technical theory 181–4
evenly hovering attention 117–18, 131–2
evidence-based treatment 203–4
excess, risks of 28–9
experience 3–4, 6–7, 76, 166–7; formulation 27–8, 109–13, 131, 185; freedom to experience 108–13; gap between living and 30–1; as interpretation in philosophical hermeneutics 171; relational freedom and novel experience 116; unformulated 15, 22, 30, 34, 86, 163–4, 230; unmentalized 15, 86
experience-near clinical content 84–5
explicit theories of technique 173–4, 174–5, 176, 177; appearance of new theories 179–81
external worlds 91–5

facilitative unconscious participation 103
Faimberg, H. 136
Fairbairn, R. 66, 179–80
fallacy of understanding 26–7, 97–103
familiarity 227
family-wide dysphoria 218
felt sense of emergence 3–4; clinical illustration 8–14; and the phenomenology of depth 6–8

Ferro, A. 16–17, 31, 32, 64, 83–4, 105, 106; the Barangers' field theory 66–7; bulwarks 112; casting of characters 88; co-creation 84, 96; internal worlds 91–5; selection of interpretations 98–103; transformation 85, 86, 87–8
field constrictions *see* constrictions
field processes 86–90
field theory 31–2, 64–82; the Barangers 67–80; comparison of Bionian field theory and contemporary interpersonal/relational psychoanalysis 14–15, 32, 83–107; Sullivan 64–7, 80
Fliess, R. 74
flux 66, 112, 113, 212–13
Foehl, J. 7, 8, 19, 26; depth 4, 6; emergence 21–2; focus on clinical process 166–7
Fonagy, P. 189–90, 194
formulation 27–8, 109–13, 131, 185
free association 23, 117–18, 131–2
Freedman, N. 18
freedom: to experience 108–13; in the interpersonal field 109–13; relational *see* relational freedom
Freud, S. 136, 153, 191
Freudian psychoanalysis 49, 53, 54; comparison with interpersonal/relational psychoanalysis 32–3, 155–64; new Freudians 17–18
Fromm, E. 31, 41–2, 45, 59, 221, 226, 229; influence on early interpersonalists 42, 43–4
Fromm-Reichman, F. 45, 59, 221, 226, 229
fusion of horizons 199–200

Gadamer, H.-G. 188, 202; hermeneutics as alternative to objectivism 196–202
genocide 148–9
genuine conversation 167, 196–7, 213
"George" 8–14
Gerson, S. 90, 137, 147, 148–9
Ghent, E. 89
Gill, M. 45, 51, 75
Goldberg, P. 14–15, 16, 29

goodness 148, 152–3
Green, A. 15
Greenberg, J.R. 5, 56, 110
groping 116, 173, 184, 196
Grossmark, R. 19, 22
group phantasies 71, 82
growth of mind or self 86–90
Grünbaum, A. 168, 178
guns, shooting 144–5

habitual patterns of relatedness 127
hard-to-engage patients 33–4, 206–19
healthcare successes 189, 190–1, 205
hermeneutics 169–71, 184, 202–4, 205, 224–5; Gadamer's hermeneutics as alternative to objectivism 196–202
Hippocrates 189
Hirsch, I. 48–9, 51, 53
historicity 170
Hoffman, I.Z. 131–2, 188, 190, 193, 203, 204, 224; ambiguity 69–70
Holocaust 141–2, 147, 148–9, 149–50, 153–4
hope, acceptance of the absence of 148–9
horizon 198–200
Horney, K. 42, 59, 220, 221

ideal psychoanalytic institute 34, 220–32; accretion model 223–5, 231; revolution model 225–31
imaginary (internal) witnessing 137–8, 139, 142, 146, 151
implicit theories of technique 167, 181; multiple 171–8; and technical rationality 177–8
improvisation 213
"in the cellar" clinical illustration 8–14
individual mind 45–6, 184
inference 28
influence, anxiety of 55
inquiry 28; detailed 43, 175
insideness/interiority 211
instrumental values 192–4
insurance, medical 187–8
intellect 231
intent 46, 117, 181, 185–6
interactive matrix 110

interdependence 179–80
interdisciplinary exploration 230
internal (imaginary) witnessing 137–8, 139, 142, 146, 151
internal worlds 47, 53; association of depth with 5–6; comparison of Bionian field theory with interpersonal/relational psychoanalysis 91–5
International Psychoanalytic Association 51
interpersonal field 1–2, 4, 31, 35–63, 131; American mainstream psychoanalysis 31, 45–58; freedom to experience 109–13; Fromm and the early interpersonal analysts 41–4; Sullivan's conception 36–41, 110
interpersonal psychoanalysis: early 41–4; ostracised by American mainstream psychoanalysis 45–52, 55
interpersonal novelty 20–1
interpersonal/relational psychoanalysis (IRP) 45, 64, 76, 179–80; acknowledgment of criticisms of 24–9; the Barangers' field theory and 69–70, 73, 75, 77–80; comparison with Bionian field theory 14–15, 32, 83–107; comparison with contemporary Freudian practice 32–3, 155–64; critical view 16–18; emergence in the literature of 18–24; Sullivan's field theory and 65–7, 80
interpersonal relations 36, 65
interpretation 116, 126; Bionian field theory 92–4; choice of interpretations 97–103; comparison of contemporary Freudian practice and interpersonal/relational practice 157–8, 163; hermeneutics and 169–71, 201–2; saturated 93; unsaturated 93, 94, 107; verbal 116
intrapsychic conservatives 24–5
introjection 74, 224
Isaacs, S. 71
Isakower, O. 61

Jacobs, T. 28
"John" 209–19
Johnson, M. 133
joint phantasy 12, 71, 72–4, 76, 91

kairos (cyclical, nonlinear time) 135–6
Keats, J. 102
Kermode, F. 135–6
Kleinian theory 54
Kohut, H. 66
Krakow ghetto 141–2
Kuhn, T. 226

Lakoff, G. 133
Laub, D. 137, 139, 141–2, 149–51
Levenson, E. 40, 42, 50, 66, 75; emergence 14, 19; fallacy of understanding 26–7, 98
Levi, P. 147
Lewin, K. 65, 67, 81, 82, 89
literal witnessing 151
living-knowing gap 30–1
Loewald, H.W. 107, 134
logical necessity 84–5
love 148

Malcolm, J. 47
Matisse, H. 194–5, 196, 199–200
McLaughlin, J. 48
medical insurance 187–8
memory: retranscription of 32, 136–7, 146, 153; trauma and witnessing 133–9; *see also* trauma, witnessing
"Menachem" 141–3, 149–50, 151–3
Merleau-Ponty, M. 67, 194–5, 199–200
Metamorphoses (Ovid) 9
metaphor 101, 102; trauma and witnessing 133–5, 137–8, 151
"Michael" 140–1, 143
mind: growth of 86–90; individual 45–6, 184
Mitchell, S.A. 5, 56, 69–70, 72, 95, 110
model technique 171–2
Modell, A. 133, 134, 135, 136
moral/political issues 46–58
mother, photograph of 141, 142
multi-person situation 70
multiple self 70–1, 139
multiple theories of technique *see* theories of technique
Murphy, G. 38–9, 81

Nachträglichkeit (retranscription of memory) 32, 136–7, 146, 153
Nagel, T. 198
narcissistic parental relationship 121
negative capability 102
new explicit theories of technique 179–81
New Freudian Synthesis: Clinical Process in the Next Generation (ed Druck *et al*) 17–18
New York Psychoanalytic Institute 42, 47, 59, 220
nonlinear dynamic systems 2, 129–30, 226
normotic illness 218

object relations theory 56, 63
objectivism 169, 171, 202–4, 205; hermeneutics as alternative to 196–202; *see also* quantitative psychotherapy research
Oedipus conflict 49, 53
oneiric paradigm 91–2
openness 23, 24, 115, 164, 190–1, 212–13, 225; *see also* curiosity
out-of-session contact 122–3
Ovid, *Metamorphoses* 9

paradigm shifts 226
parallel process 61–2
parent–child relationships 180
participant observation 39
partner in thought 138
patient vs client terminology 189
patterns of relatedness 127
Peltz, R. 14–15, 16, 29
perception 228–30
perfection 159
perspective 7
phantasy 78–9; the Barangers 71–4, 91; coinciding phantasies 73–4; comparing contemporary Freudian and interpersonal/relational approaches 32–3, 155–64; group phantasies 71, 82; joint 12, 71, 72–4, 76, 91
phenomenology of depth 6–8
philosophical issues 168–71
photograph of mother 141–2
physicianly attitude 189

Pichon-Rivière, E. 82
pictograms 87
Pizer, S. 34
plasticity 135
play 20, 200
Poland, W. 137, 138
political/moral issues 46–58
positivism 49, 168
practical knowledge 188
pragmatism 169
preconception 197, 198, 203
prediction 193
prejudice 197, 198, 224
presence of absence 148–9, 150
primary process perception 228–9
process research 193–4
profundity 5
projection/introjection 224
projective identification 26, 74, 96
prospective derealization 147
psychic equivalence 20
psychoanalytic situation 224
psychotherapy research *see* quantitative psychotherapy research
public image of psychoanalysis 56–8
pulling (or being pulled) 173, 184–5
Putnam, H. 188

quantitative psychotherapy research 33, 187–205; Gadamer's hermeneutics as alternative 196–202; inability to measure creative work 194–6; problem of privileging 191–4; symptom relief and other changes 190–1

Racker, H. 77
Rangell, L. 166
rationality, technical 168, 177–8, 185, 193
reality 169
recognition, shock of 11
"redskin" idea 100–1, 102, 103, 104
reflection-in-action 194–6, 200
Reis, B.E. 137
relational freedom 13, 31, 32, 98, 113–30; clinical illustration of expansion of 118–26; constriction, relaxation and 115–16, 126–30

relational matrix 72, 95, 110
relational psychoanalysis 51–2, 56; *see also* interpersonal/relational psychoanalysis (IRP)
relativism 205
relaxation of constrictions 115–16, 126–30
repression 162, 163–4
research *see* quantitative psychotherapy research
resilience 153–4
responsiveness 96
retranscription of memory (*Nachträglichkeit*) 32, 136–7, 146, 153
retrospective derealization 146–53
returning combat veteran 143–6
reverie 87
revolution model 225–31
Richards, A. 50–1
Richman, S. 137
Rioch, D. 221
Rioch, J. 42, 221
risk of commitment to theory 24–9
role-responsiveness 26

safety 127
Sandler, J. 26, 165, 176
Sarraute, N. 185
saturated interpretation 93
Schachtel, E. 42, 227
Schafer, R. 57
Schleiermacher, F. 197
Schön, D.A. 157, 185, 195
"second look" 78
secondary autocentricity 227
secondary process perception 228–9
selective inattention 127–8
self, growth of 86–90
self-analysis 138
self psychology 179–80, 183
self-states 10–11, 112, 139, 214; essential ambiguity 70–1
Seligman, S. 25
sexual abuse 10–14
shift 212–13, 214
shock of recognition 11
silence 22; thoughtful 173
Singer, E. 42

Slochower, J. 211
social change 179–81
social phenomena 5–6
soldier, ex- 143–6
Spiegel, R. 42
splitting 70
squiggle game 84
Stern, D.B. 1, 22–4, 27–8, 115, 137, 138, 169
Stolorow, R.D. 176, 185
structural theory 17
structure/drive models 5–6
Sullivan, H.S. 6, 31, 45, 60, 81, 179–80, 226; ambiguity 70; American mainstream psychoanalysis and 49–50, 52; authority 229; comparison with the Barangers 31–2; detailed inquiry 43, 175; field theory 64–7, 80; influence on early interpersonal psychoanalysts 42–3, 44; interpersonal field 36–41, 110; retreat to comfort 227; selective inattention 127; South American view of 81–2; White Institute 42, 59, 221
supervision 43, 174; triadic dimensions 61–2
surprise: courting 109, 115; effective 23
surrender 89–90
symbolic, the 163
symbolization 85, 86; and field processes 86–90
symptom relief 190–1

Tauber, E. 40, 42, 62
technical rationality 168, 185, 193; implicit theories and 177–8
theories of technique 33, 165–86; explicit 173–4, 174–5, 176, 177, 179–81; implicit 167, 171–8, 181; philosophical issues 168–71; values and the evaluation of 181–4
theories-in-use 157, 185; *see also* implicit theories of technique
theory 156–7, 204; espoused theories 157; risks that come with commitments to 24–9
therapeutic action 32, 81; freedom to experience and 109–13; as the growth of mind or self 86–90; relational freedom and 113–30
therapeutic "internalization" of otherness 20–1
third: analytic 89–90, 106–7; dead 148–9
Thompson, C. 42, 45, 50, 59, 220, 221
thoughtful silence 173
time: forms of 135–6; witnessing across *see* witnessing
tradition 197–200, 203
training institutes 34, 220–32
transference 49, 53, 69, 134
transference–countertransference 40, 62, 111
transformation 26, 40, 85, 86–90
trauma 120; retrospective derealization 146–53; witnessing and 32, 133–9; *see also* witnessing
triadic dimensions of supervision 61–2
tropisms 196
troubled power relations 207
Tublin, S. 185–6

Ullman, C. 137
unbidden experience 3, 108–13
unconscious 53, 60, 97; the Barangers and 68; link to emergence 2, 14–18
unconscious phantasy *see* phantasy
unconscious regularity 72
unconscious relatedness 32–3, 155–64
unconscious symbolized meanings 162
understanding 158, 196–200; fallacy of 26–7, 97–103
unformulated experience 15, 22, 30, 34, 86, 163–4, 230
universally applicable principles 178
unmentalized experience 15, 86
unobtrusive analyst 22
unsaturated interpretations 93, 94, 107

values 167–8, 169, 177; and the evaluation of technical theory 181–4
verbal interpretation 116
verbal-reflective knowing 173
Video Archive for Holocaust Testimonies 149
Vietnam veteran 143–6

vitality 43–4
vulnerability 160–1

Wachtel, P.L. 5–6
waiting 22, 27
waking dream thoughts 87, 101–2
White Institute 24, 43, 47, 220, 221, 232; formation 42, 59; relationship with the American Psychoanalytic Association 50–1, 52, 59

"William" 118–26, 128–30
Wilner, W. 19
Winnicott, D.W. 15, 66, 179–80
Wire, The 140–1, 143
witnessing 10–11, 28, 32, 125, 133–54; clinical illustrations 140–6; internal (imaginary) 137–8, 139, 142, 146, 151; literal 151; retrospective derealization 146–53; trauma and 32, 133–9
Wolstein, B. 40, 42, 50, 75